10 TEACHERS' VIEWPOINTS ON SUZUKI® PIANO

Edited by Gilles Comeau, Ph.D.

Contributors

Fay Swadley Adams

Beverly T. Fest

Dr. Doris Leland Harrel

Doris Koppelman

Christopher Liccardo

Mary Craig Powell

Barbara Schneiderman

Marilyn Taggart

Sarah O. Williams

Michiko Yurko

CFORP

Cover layout   :   Marie-José Hotte
Word processing operator :   Lise Lauriault
Proofreader   :   Rosemary Covert
Printer   :   Centre franco-ontarien de ressources pédagogiques

© CFORP, 1998
  290 Dupuis Street, Vanier, Ontario K1L 1A2
  Orders: Telephone: (613) 747-1553
              Fax: (613) 747-0866

ISBN 2-89442-552-X
Copyright — second semester 1998
National Library of Canada

TABLE OF CONTENTS

1. PHILOSOPHY 5
   Mother-Tongue Approach... 5
   Environment is Crucial 6
   Importance of the Early Years.. 6
   Music for all Children 7
   The Suzuki Triangle.. 7
   Nurtured by Love 8
   Primary Concern for Children's Personal Growth.............. 8
   Better People and a Better World 9

2. GOALS AND BASIC ELEMENTS 11

3. PARTICIPANTS 15
   The Suzuki Triangle.. 15
   The Teacher... 16
       Characteristics differentiating a Suzuki teacher 16
       Criteria for evaluating a successful Suzuki teacher 18
   The Student 21
       Accepting a new student... 21
       Ages for beginning a new student 24
       Music education through various group lessons 25
       Adult students and the Suzuki® Method 25
   The Parent 27
       Committed parental involvement 27
       Parental responsibility at the lesson 28
       Parental responsibility at home 28
       Parents' musical training 30

4. PERFORMANCE SKILLS 33
   Listening 33
       Importance of listening... 33
       Daily listening time for beginners 35
       Nature of listening for beginners................................ 37
       Daily listening time and nature of listening for advanced students 38
   Repertoire 40
       Strength of the Suzuki repertoire 40
       Omission and sequence of pieces in early books........... 41
       Omission and sequence of pieces in later books 43
       Concerns about the Suzuki repertoire 45
       Supplementary repertoire 46
       Lists of supplementary material.................................. 47
   Review.. 53
       Importance of review 53
       Review and weekly lesson... 55
       Review assignment 56

    Reading 58
        Introducing reading 58
        Teaching pre-reading and reading skills 61
        Recommended reading materials 63
        Learning to read the Suzuki repertoire 66
        Sight-reading 67
    Musicianship 68
        Transposition, keyboard harmony, improvisation, composition 69
        Ear training and sight-singing 71
        Music history 72
        Theory 74
    Musicality and Good Performance 75

5. TECHNICAL SKILLS 83
    Adams 83
    Fest 85
    Liccardo 86
    Koppelman 88
    Harrel 90
    Powell 92
    Schneiderman 95
    Taggart 100
    Williams 103
    Yurko 103

6. LESSON PLANNING 109
    First Lessons 109
    Lesson Plans 117
    Assigning a New Piece 125
    Home Assignments 128
    Practicing Habits 132
    Group Lessons 135

7. CONCLUSION 139

BIOGRAPHICAL NOTES 145

APPENDIX 1 157

APPENDIX 2 158

APPENDIX 3 159

APPENDIX 4 160

APPENDIX 5 161

APPENDIX 6 162

PHILOSOPHY

Shinichi Suzuki, the founder of the Suzuki® Method, has explicitly stated his beliefs about music learning in his books and articles. Those writings are still the main source of information for Suzuki teachers who want to fully understand the principles of this method.

The authors of this book were asked to summarize their understanding of the Suzuki philosophy by outlining and explaining what they consider to be its principles.

There was a strong consensus in their answers as to what constitutes the basis of the Suzuki philosophy. Eight elements were regularly mentioned as being central to this method:

✔ Mother-tongue approach

✔ Environment is crucial

✔ Importance of the early years

✔ Music for all children

✔ Suzuki triangle: teacher/child/parent

✔ Nurtured by love

✔ Primary concern for children's personal growth

✔ Developing better people and contributing to a better world

Many of the respondents mentioned that to be a Suzuki teacher, you absolutely must endorse all the principles of this philosophy.

Mother-Tongue Approach

The mother-tongue approach is seen as the most natural way to learn music, similar to the way one learns a language. Based on the principle that all children learn to speak their mother-tongue by being constantly surrounded by it, even before birth, the Suzuki® Method makes the assumption that music learning follows the same natural process.

• *Children have absorbed and internalized their native language in a completely natural process. Those spoken sounds have been constantly in their environment since before birth. By surrounding children with the sounds of music even before birth, the Suzuki® Method enables them to learn the language of music in the same way they have learned their native tongue. (Harrel)*

Much attention is given to the importance of providing a proper environment where music will be absorbed and internalized even before actual teaching begins.

• *By continuous exposure to music that begins sometimes even before birth, the gift of music will be given in the most natural way, with a gradual acquisition of vocabulary and skills until the child is capable of understanding and participating in the music of the past, present and future, and therefore, also capable of directly experiencing the commonality of all the other human beings who have spoken, and will speak, this same language. (Taggart)*

According to some respondents, this approach, which was based on Dr. Suzuki's intuitions, has now strong scientific support.

• *The beginnings of musical learning are similar to those of learning one's language. Scientific evidence shows that the human organism is uniquely organized with regard to learning language and music. This learning is achieved largely by absorption and interaction with stimuli from all aspects of the environment rather than through didactic teaching. (Koppelman)*

As one respondent explained, Suzuki's great contribution was to apply his understanding of the language-learning process to music learning. This has become the cornerstone of his method.

- *Suzuki has adopted as a model the mother-tongue system of language learning, an excellent prototype of the learning process. He has explored its remarkable success, defined its attributes and applied them to music study. (Schneiderman)*

The concrete application of this learning process will be studied throughout this book.

Environment is Crucial

The Suzuki® Method often refers to the importance of the environment as a major factor contributing to the development of the child. In this method particularly, the environment is considered to be crucial since the mother-tongue approach can only work if the proper musical environment is provided by making music listening part of everyday life. According to some respondents, this position has been supported by scientific research.

- *Edwin Gordon has found ways to measure musical intelligence at a very early age. His important finding is that a child's inborn musical intelligence actually grows in proportion to the extent that music is present in his everyday environment. We know that the children of famous musicians often display the same excellent qualities of their parents. They have lived and developed in an environment rich in musical sounds. (Harrel)*

The family has an essential role in providing a good and enriching musical environment, as well as a loving and nurturing one.

- *Talent is the result of one's environment, not heredity. Consequently, home and family play a major role in the development of any ability. If a child hears music in the home and is supported and encouraged by a parent through practice and lessons, no child can fail to learn. (Fest)*

- *We begin with a child's total environment, early immersion in music as a natural part of family life and the parents' warm encouragement, assistance and expectation of success. (Schneiderman)*

Importance of the Early Years

The attention given to the environment brings out the importance of the early years. Based on scientific findings supporting the aural sensitivity of the young child, some respondents explained the value of an early start and the logic of combining it with a listening approach.

- *It is believed that the ability of a child to learn aurally is strongest from birth to age seven. (Powell)*

- *Human beings are at the peak of their aural sensitivity in their earliest years. They develop visual acuity later. So it makes sense to follow a listening approach during the early years. This makes it possible and advisable to begin lessons at an early age. This early start also stimulates brain development and functioning. (Koppelman)*

- *Although the Suzuki approach is used successfully with many age levels, it is especially appropriate to the very young child (3½ years and up) who is in the process of perfecting the spoken language.*

  A fine treatise by pediatrician Dr. Mary Lou Sheil, Eye Before Ear or Ear Before Eye, states that a baby's ears are "ready to listen, remember and reproduce musical sequences" usually at 3 years of age. Motor development is usually sufficient to begin playing at 3½ years. The eye is not ready to see and process musical symbols into playing until age 7. Therefore the Suzuki® Method is ideally suited to the very young child. (Harrel)

Music for all Children

At the center of the Suzuki® Method, there is the strong belief that every child can learn to play an instrument.

- *The Suzuki philosophy embraces the belief that all children have great abilities (or talents) and that each child, given the opportunity through good teachers, can develop their individual potential in amazing ways. (Williams)*

- *All children possess the ability to develop a high level of musical ability. (Yurko)*

This does not mean that every child has the same facility, but that each one can learn when the proper environment is provided.

- *With few exceptions, all children successfully learn their native tongue. Basically, no one fails. All children can learn the language of music as well, without fear of failing. That is not to say that all children are born with identical capacities. Each child is unique in the relative strength of various abilities. The development of those abilities is directly dependent on the quality of his environment. (Harrel)*

This position has been apparently confirmed by scientific studies:

- *While Dr. Suzuki's findings appear to be largely experiential and the result of keen observation, the research of respected university professors supports his theories. Howard Gardner in* Frames of Mind *identifies music as one of several intelligences native to all of us. (Harrel)*

This is why, in the Suzuki® Method, students are not selected based on "talent". Every child is considered a potential student.

- *Children are not screened to determine whether or not it is recommended that they study music. While the rate at which children adapt (some call this talent) varies, all children have ability and should be encouraged to develop at their own rate. (Fest)*

Some respondents even suggested that every child should have the right to learn music.

- *Each child deserves the gift of being able to express himself with the one language common to all mankind— music. (Taggart)*

- *The potential for expressing oneself through music is part of being human. It is the birthright of all people in all societies and ethnic groups at all periods of history. (Koppelman)*

The Suzuki Triangle

Another element central to the Suzuki® Method is the teacher-student-parent triangle. Respondents maintained strongly that all three people are absolutely necessary in the application of this method. In other words, the Suzuki® Method can only work when each side of the triangle works effectively with the other two.

- *The triangle consists of three components necessary for the learning of music. The first component is a child who is eager to learn music. The second is a competent teacher who is present once a week to guide the student through his or her musical journey. The third component is a parent who carries on the instruction and nurturing from lesson to lesson. Each component is an integral part of the learning triangle, and each one has the responsibility to work cohesively with the other two. (Adams)*

- *My understanding of the teacher-student-parent triangle is that it requires all three of us to make the Suzuki system work. The parent and teacher are at the bottom of the triangle, representing the two involved in the instruction. The child is at the top, representing the product of the other two. It is one of the key components of our philosophy. (Powell)*

- *I believe very strongly in a strict interpretation of the Suzuki teacher-parent-child triangle: all three are absolutely necessary to a successful outcome. I can't imagine starting a student now without the parents' help and support at home, and I would sorely miss the deep involvement and friendships that develop with the students' families as a result of the triangle. (Taggart)*

The role of each member of this triangle, as well as the way it concretely works, will be discussed in another section.

Nurtured by Love

At the heart of this method's philosophy is the love of children.

- *"Where love is deep, much will be accomplished." These famous words of Shinichi Suzuki reveal much about the depth of the man and his philosophy. It is a powerful and beautiful philosophy which emerged from his strong love for children and his desire to maintain the inherent love, joy, and trust in them. (Powell)*

This philosophy strongly stresses the importance of providing a loving and nurturing environment for every child.

- *The Suzuki philosophy teaches us that all human beings have value, each is unique and yet a part of a larger whole. All deserve to be nurtured well in infancy and childhood, and to grow up into loving, responsible adults with their abilities developed to the fullest by their experiences. (Taggart)*

It is only under these conditions that the best learning can happen.

- *The foundation of this nurturing approach is an understanding that all human beings need to believe in their ability in order to learn; that teachers can cultivate such confidence through appropriate language, tone and manner combined with a carefully designed methodology. (Schneiderman)*

- *All children can develop high levels of ability if they are raised in a loving, nurturing environment. When children are respected, praised and encouraged their abilities blossom and they become happy and healthy individuals. As Suzuki teachers, we witness this phenomenon on a regular basis. The child who is loved, cared for, encouraged and given attention develops his or her "talents" to the fullest. The child who is scolded and neglected develops slowly. These were Dr. Suzuki's original observations and they are just as true today. (Liccardo)*

Primary Concern for Children's Personal Growth

The emphasis of the Suzuki® Method on the love for children translates itself into a concern for the personal growth of the child. This method wants to be more than a music learning system; it has a strong commitment to educate the whole child.

For some respondents, this means that the child always comes first, music second.

- *Suzuki teachers teach first for the love of the child. (Harrel)*

- *The Suzuki teacher's interest lies first in the child and then in the development of that child's potential. (Liccardo)*

Others mentioned how important the development of a child's self-esteem is.

- *The Suzuki® Method includes the development of self-esteem. (Adams)*

- *A child's self-esteem is always in the foreground of a Suzuki teacher's thinking. (Schneiderman)*

Some respondents explained that the study of music leads to character development.

- *Shinichi Suzuki believes fervently in the potential nobility of all children and seeks to develop character through the study of music. (Schneiderman)*

- *One basic principal of the Suzuki® Method is that music leads to character development. (Powell)*

According to most respondents, the Suzuki philosophy is aimed at educating the whole person through music learning.

- *The Suzuki philosophy fosters the development of the whole child through the learning of music. (Adams)*

- *Suzuki teachers have a positive approach, considering the needs of the whole child. (Koppelman)*

- *The teacher must love people and especially children, and be dedicated to the ideals of nurturing and educating the whole person through music education. (Williams)*

Better People and a Better World

Two respondents explained that by educating the child through the study of music, a Suzuki teacher helps to develop better human beings and in so doing, contributes to a better world.

- *Developing sensitivity to people as well as music, and interacting in a positive way with the people in our lives will put us on a path towards a better world. (Koppelman)*

- *Adults sometimes reflect on their life experiences and can pinpoint the seminal influence of certain teachers. Often these teachers have been an example of qualities such as honesty, integrity, love of humanity and specifically love of children, love of teaching, enthusiasm for their teaching specialty, patience, and persistence. Being associated with such a teacher has a life-long effect on a child. The child models himself on the fine example.*

  Children often study with music teachers for many years. The teachers become what sociologists identify as "significant others." If they exhibit the best human qualities in the way they interact with a child, the child will reflect those attributes as an adult. Children who grow in an environment of love and nurturing will reflect that environment and become nurturing, loving adults.

  Dr. Suzuki says, "The heart that feels music will feel people." Irwin Freundlich, my teacher at the Juilliard School of Music, told me one had to be a fine person to be a fine musician. So we have the opportunity to share the message of music with children in order for them to reach their full potential as fine human beings. (Harrel)

GOALS AND BASIC ELEMENTS

When asked what constitutes the main goals of the Suzuki® Method, authors focus their answers around two poles: developing the whole child through the learning of music, and developing the musical ability and love of music in each child. The following statement is an excellent summary of the position:

- *The main goal of a teacher should be to help the child reach his highest potential as a person and as a musician. (Harrel)*

The chart that follows indicates goals proposed by the respondents.

Development of the child as a person	
Adams	Develop the whole child through the learning of music.
Harrel	Help each child to reach his or her highest potential as a person.
Powell	Reach the child through the music: with the piano as the medium, teachers seek to give the child high self-esteem, confidence, ego satisfaction, discipline, the joy of music, and the opportunity to develop into a noble human being.
Schneiderman	Nurture self-esteem, character development and "a beautiful heart".
Williams	Help every child to gain skill, self-esteem, or other life-nurturing advantages (this includes the physically, emotionally or psychologically disabled child).
Development of the child's musical ability and love of music	
Fest	Develop musical independence, self-motivation and the love of music in each student.
Harrel	Help each child to reach his or her highest potential as a musician.
Koppelman	Have every student playing musically, learning easily and enjoying the learning process and the music.
Powell	Help the student reach a fine level of playing.
Schneiderman	Instill a love of music and guide students to develop their abilities to the fullest extent.
Williams	Develop musical excellence and learn the joy of music making.

For one respondent, the main goal of a Suzuki teacher should be that of any teacher of any subject:

- *To help the student grow in knowledge, skill and wisdom to become a better human being. (Taggart)*

But the music teacher is in a very special situation:

- *A teacher of music is fortunate in that the subject matter demands the involvement of the student in so many aspects of the human experience: a worldwide common language of the blending of pitches and rhythm that elicits emotional response; the physical challenges of producing music whatever the instrument; the intellectual processes that must be employed to study, learn and recreate in performance the musical thoughts of the studied composers; and the creative processes used to make the music alive and interesting, perhaps even to compose or improvise oneself. (Taggart)*

In piano teaching, the Suzuki goals are attained through the use of certain strategies. Many of these strategies are borrowed from Suzuki violin teaching. The authors of this book were asked to outline the principal elements of this piano method. Their answers give us an idea of what constitutes for each one of them the particularities of the Suzuki® Method or, in other words, what characterizes the actual practice of teaching the "Suzuki way."

Several elements were mentioned by most of the respondents. They include the following:

- ✔ Learning by ear or Listen/Play/Read
- ✔ Recordings: listening to a specific repertoire
- ✔ Parental involvement in the lesson/home practice/listening
- ✔ Review
- ✔ Learning through mastery: step-by-step development
- ✔ Early beginning
- ✔ Group lessons (as well as individual lessons)

Other elements were not mentioned as frequently but were felt by several respondents to be important to the method. These are:

- ✔ Common repertoire
- ✔ Positive non-judgmental approach
- ✔ One-point teaching or one-point focus
- ✔ Early establishment of a fine tone quality
- ✔ Providing frequent performance opportunities
- ✔ Systematic sequential approach
- ✔ Importance of repetition
- ✔ Teaching reading
- ✔ Coordinated use of body from the beginning
- ✔ Inclusion of theoretical, historical and analytical information
- ✔ Listening approach through demonstration/imitation
- ✔ Preparation technique called "stop/prepare"
- ✔ Studying great composers very early on
- ✔ Orientation sessions for parents and students before beginning lessons
- ✔ Beginning steps (bow, rest position, ready position)
- ✔ The *Twinkles*: a laboratory of basic technique
- ✔ Learning good practicing habits
- ✔ Graduations as goals/landmarks
- ✔ Appropriate seating/footstools
- ✔ Observation of lessons before child begins instruction
- ✔ Chamber music experience
- ✔ Workshops

Even though the Suzuki® Method provides many specific guidelines on how piano teaching should be done, one respondent pointed out that there is still a lot of flexibility left for each individual teacher. The Suzuki® Method does allow for different personal teaching styles.

- *While many elements are fundamental to the framework of the Suzuki® Method, there is freedom within that framework. First, there is no specific Suzuki technique. Teachers can develop individual approaches to technique which are natural and effective for their students. Second and similarly, there is no dogma as to how far one needs to teach playing right hand only before adding the left, or the value of playing more advanced repertoire hands separately. Third, many teachers have some type of group activity in their programs, although that is not essential for piano. Some teachers have performance classes, others have group theory lessons with little or no playing. Others offer improvisation or composition classes. These are not essential to the Suzuki® Method, but can serve to enhance the students' playing and to stimulate new ways to think about music. Fourth, there is no prescribed material for learning to read music or to supplement the Suzuki repertoire. Teachers are free to select materials for teaching music reading. Also the teacher determines when it is appropriate and beneficial to include music outside the prescribed Suzuki repertoire. (Fest)*

PARTICIPANTS

The Suzuki Triangle

The Suzuki® Method depends on the involvement of three people: the teacher, the parent and the child. This unit is referred to as the Suzuki triangle. Each participant is involved in pursuing the same goal: learning music in a loving environment. The responsibilities of each person must be well understood and the interaction between them must be well worked out.

- *The triangle is a blend of three people trying to make music education work for the student. This takes much more expertise than meets the eye and demands more skill than is perhaps thought. Professionalism and knowledge is required of the teacher in many areas beyond the musical arena. There has to be enough tension to create a challenge for both the parent and the student, but the teacher must know the right amount of tension in order for it all to work well. This statement is true musically but it also applies to the psychology of working with people. There has to be good communication, trust, dedication, love, and commitment for the interaction of the triangle to create an atmosphere of positive learning in a progressive way. Each person in the triangle is important and each must be respected. The teacher must be the leader in this educational process. No one way is the answer but a unique blend of all ingredients must be mixed together to fit each specific student's needs. (Williams)*

- *It is imperative that the teacher and parent work together to help create a learning environment that is enjoyable, nurturing and satisfying to the child. This requires that the teacher and parent keep an open dialogue and that they both commit their time and energy towards the common goal of developing the potential within the child. The child is the benefactor of this commitment and love, and flourishes because of it. It affects not only his development as a musician, but more importantly his development as a caring, feeling human being. (Liccardo)*

- *The strength of the triangle is dependent on the extent to which the parent and the teacher truly believe that every child can learn the language of music and are willing to accept that the child they work with is OK just the way he is. If problems occur, one cannot basically alter the child, so one looks at the possibility of altering the environment in the lesson or at home. When the parent and teacher are committed to providing the emotional and physical environment that makes it possible for the child to learn naturally, the triangle is strong. (Harrel)*

- *This is an opportunity for all members of the triangle to learn human relations skills: respect for others, cooperation, solving problems in a positive manner. Each member has an important role and area of expertise. The teacher knows best how to teach music with this method. The parent knows best what is happening at home. The child knows best how she or he feels. Parent and child have a marvelous opportunity to build a strong relationship and understand each other. Those of us, like myself, who were Suzuki parents, are very grateful for that opportunity. If all these relationships succeed, we can change the world. (Koppelman)*

- *In the teacher-student-parent triangle, if one side is missing, you do not have the Suzuki® Method. Each side of the triangle must be in an effective relationship with the other two sides. The teacher encourages, guides, supports, and advises the parent in working with the child. At the same time the teacher develops a relationship of mutual love and respect with the child. The student relates to the teacher during the weekly lessons and must see the parent as home-teacher for the practice sessions. The parent must be supportive of the teacher and programs within the studio and also direct and encourage the child at home. If everyone is doing his or her job effectively, the Suzuki® Method does not fail. (Fest)*

- *The triad has been described as the most challenging social situation; its dynamics need to be clearly understood and approached with care—a significant topic for orientation before beginning lessons.*

  The roles of parent, teacher and student intersect as they work cooperatively toward the same goals: that the student build self-esteem and confidence, love music and develop his or her ability to the fullest. We relate in pairs as we work: in the lesson (teacher and student, with parent as observer), at the home lesson where the parent is teaching the child, and in communications between the teacher and parent. The teacher proceeds with sensitivity for the parents' intimate knowledge of their child and respect for this primary relationship. The parent similarly values the teacher's knowledge of music and the process of study. We learn from each other.

The parent is aware that the teacher is the main authority during lessons, that the student will be learning to relate to the teacher on his or her own, building an independent relationship which will evolve later during the weaning process. It can be intimidating for a child to be in the middle, addressed by two large authority figures at once. The student is taught by the parent to respect the teacher in lessons and by the teacher to respect the parent in home lessons. Parents also read Your Child's Self-Esteem *(Briggs) during orientation to understand the need to respect their children as well. Theirs is the most challenging job—instructing their child sensitively and effectively in a detailed course of study—because the parent/child bond is so complex.*

Teachers make suggestions and provide guidance and instruction for home practice. They may evaluate the sessions periodically by requesting that tapes of home sessions be made. Telephone calls and occasional conferences can provide expanded opportunities for private reflection. When occasions have arisen for me to visit a student's home and become familiar with their piano and practice setting, this too has been helpful. (Schneiderman)

The Teacher

Characteristics differentiating a Suzuki teacher

Respondents were ask to identify what differentiates a Suzuki teacher from a non-Suzuki teacher (often referred to as a traditional teacher). The first element suggested was the Suzuki teacher's strong commitment to develop a full human being—producing a musician is never the only goal. It was stressed that Suzuki teachers should make sure that music learning is happening in a nurturing and supportive environment that contributes to the child's self-esteem and love of music.

- *What should differentiate a Suzuki teacher from other teachers of music is a clear understanding that the goal is not just to produce musically adept students who do amazing things at a relatively young age, although this often happens. The goal is to have this happen within and because of a nurturing, supportive environment, an environment in which hard work and stimulation of all the senses becomes the reward. The development process as one works on being able to achieve at a high level becomes more important than the eventual attainment of the ability itself. (Taggart)*

- *The Suzuki teacher endorses a philosophy which is based on love for the child and which embraces the belief that all children have the potential to learn. (Powell)*

- *The Suzuki teacher is not only a trained musician and teacher, but also one who has been educated thoroughly in Suzuki philosophy and literature. A Suzuki teacher should love children, love to teach children, and be skilled in nurturing the abilities of the very young. (Adams)*

- *The teacher must love people and especially children, and be dedicated not only to the Suzuki philosophy but to the ideals of nurturing and educating the whole person through music education.*

  It is all much more than just another teaching job if taken seriously. Suzuki teaching must embody real love for children and youth and be dedicated to the best in music education. (Williams)

- *The Suzuki teacher's interest lies first in the child and then in the development of that child's potential. Suzuki teachers receive specific training to deal with the needs and abilities of the young child. Besides learning how to teach a child the required repertoire, the Suzuki teacher also learns how to motivate the child through praise and encouragement. (Liccardo)*

- *Certainly, some traditional teachers share our basic humane and nurturing style, but Suzuki teachers are steeped in this loving philosophy. They are trained in a thorough, systematic, step-by-step pedagogy derived from this philosophy, and particularly organized to promote not only a love and understanding of music but Suzuki's deeper goals. A child's self-esteem is always in the foreground of our thinking. As we teach skills, we confirm the person and validate the inner life, the individuality of each student. All future musical and personal growth is enabled to bloom from this early cultivation. (Schneiderman)*

Secondly, Suzuki teachers strongly believe in every child's ability to learn music. Talent or inherited abilities are not issues in selecting students.

- *To be involved in the development of any child is an honor, challenge, and an affair of the heart. The philosophy we have adopted is that all children can learn the language of music in the same natural way they learn their native tongue. Therefore, we work with any child whose parents will provide a nurturing musical environment. (Harrel)*

- *A Suzuki teacher may differ from a non-Suzuki teacher in believing that musical talent can be developed rather than only inherited. (Yurko)*

- *Suzuki teachers recognize and respect the uniqueness and wonderful possibilities of all children. They do not test to determine which children have talent and only teach those. They work on the assumption that all can develop ability under the right circumstances and work to bring about those most propitious conditions. They expect all students to play well. (Koppelman)*

- *The Suzuki teacher can teach the rewards of music education for the average student as the student learns to carry this gift of the arts throughout their life experiences to use and enjoy, as well as to lead a young person to a possible music career. (Williams)*

Thirdly, when starting a new student, Suzuki teachers adopt a very different approach than what has traditionally been done. Suzuki teachers are strongly committed to the fact that playing by ear must come first; only later will reading be introduced. This gives a totally different perspective to the lessons of beginning students.

- *Just as a normal child learns to speak his native language fluently long before he can read the printed page, so a child can learn to play an instrument using this mother-tongue approach to learning. Through the ear, children can learn the complexities of language; through listening they can also learn the language of music—melody, harmony, rhythm and beautiful tone. This fundamental first-step belief differentiates a Suzuki teacher from a traditional teacher. (Williams)*

- *In over-simplified terms, the beginning Suzuki® Methodology might be expressed as Listen-Play-Read. Traditional methodology is often the opposite: Read-Play-Listen. (Harrel)*

- *Suzuki teachers teach the young student to play "by ear." Many traditional teachers have been fearful of this approach in the past, but the Suzuki teacher understands that this is the most natural way for a young child to learn. (Liccardo)*

Fourthly, this method has developed certain teaching strategies that characterize the approach of a Suzuki teacher. "Learning through mastery", or step-by-step development, is one of them. A Suzuki teacher is expected to break down every new acquisition into as many small steps as possible. The student is asked to conquer each step before moving on to the next one, ensuring mastery of each new skill.

- *Learning through mastery means that each small step must be learned securely before moving on to the next skill. The Suzuki teacher uses the "one-point focus" to break down each step to its simplest level in order to ensure success with each student. Children develop mastery through discipline and repetition, another essential ingredient for natural progress. (Liccardo)*

- *As students learn, they are carefully led through many small steps, mastering each one before proceeding onward. (Taggart)*

- *From the basic beginning steps onward, we learn to work with quality and attention to detail—mastering each skill, polishing it and building all successive stages in the learning process upon this solid base and the satisfaction of a job well done. The student's confidence, expectation of success and positive attitude grow alongside the skills themselves, each reinforcing the other. (Schneiderman)*

Closely connected to step-by-step development is the one-point teaching or one-point focus. Suzuki teachers try to focus their teaching on one element at a time. Even though many things could be improved, practice results are better if children are asked to pay all their attention to correcting only one specific thing at a time.

- *An important part of the Suzuki® Methodology is one-point teaching. Teachers are admonished to see many things in a child's playing, but to work on only one important idea or skill at a time. When that skill or idea has been internalized, another is added. The Suzuki teacher becomes adept at breaking teaching points into units small enough to ensure success and self-esteem for every child. (Harrel)*

- *One-point lesson: until repertoire grows in size and complexity, we emphasize the most basic point of improvement on all material in the lesson, remembering ready position or shoulder ease or floating arms, for example. Even at more advanced levels, students learn best when concentrating on one new feature at a time. (Schneiderman)*

One respondent set out what she considers to be the five principal factors that characterize a Suzuki teacher.

- *There are several factors which differentiate the Suzuki teacher from the non-Suzuki teacher. First, we involve the parent in the lesson, the home practice and the listening. Second, we have a strong emphasis on learning through listening; this involves not only listening to tapes and CDs, but teaching through a listening approach which requires demonstration at the keyboard. Third, the beginning is uniquely different: we emphasize posture, aural development, beautiful tone and the basics of good technique and musicality before reading skills are taught. Fourth, we teach the literature of the great composers from Book 2 through the remaining books, thus exposing the child to the great classics from very early stages of development. Fifth, we have a strong emphasis on review of all the repertoire studied. While some traditional teachers might incorporate a few of these points in their teaching, for the most part, these factors are distinctly different from traditional approaches. (Powell)*

Criteria for evaluating a successful Suzuki teacher

Respondents were ask how to define the success of a good Suzuki teacher. According to them, this judgment can be based on two main criteria: the students' playing ability and the positive attitude of the students towards music and music learning. Both criteria are essential to the Suzuki® Method.

- *In judging a teacher's success, I look at the quality of the students' playing and also at the attitude of the students. (Fest)*

- *If I were to judge another teacher's success there would be two main areas I would consider: (1) the psychological—the students' attitudes toward music and playing the piano and (2) the actual playing skills—the musical diction of the teacher's students. I think it is important to clearly separate and evaluate each area, because it often happens that a teacher can be very strong in one of these areas and weak in the other, which of course lowers the overall success of his or her students. (Taggart)*

To evaluate themselves, the Suzuki teachers should always take into account their success in both of these two categories.

- *Teachers can judge themselves both by their students' knowledge and the degree of enjoyment they exhibit in their approach to the keyboard in lessons and performances. (Adams)*

- *Teachers could evaluate themselves by the quality of their students' progress with the additional indicators that they are enjoying their work and that they too are always growing and learning. (Schneiderman)*

Another respondent expressed a similar idea in explaining that teachers must have high standards and the teaching must be done in a positive manner:

- *Teachers must maintain high standards in their teaching to help the student reach a fine level of playing. Thus, if I hear a student who is playing musically, with good physical freedom and technical skills, and developing soundly in all aspects of pianism, my feeling is that their teacher is probably successful. If she or he has been able to teach these skills through a positive, encouraging and loving manner, thus reaching the child through the music, then I know she or he is successful! These points are definitely the criteria by which I judge myself as a teacher. (Powell)*

The charts below present the characteristics reported by the respondents as the essential elements of a fine Suzuki piano teacher. These have been grouped into the two areas mentioned above: students' quality of playing and students' positive attitude.

Students' quality of playing and musical knowledge	
Adams	Exhibit knowledge of basic keyboard and musicianship skills
Fest	Play with a beautiful sound Play fluently and expressively
Harrel	Demonstrate in performance an understanding of the music message
Liccardo	Play musically and sensitively Learn to read music and have a good basic knowledge of music theory
Schneiderman	Play with lovely tone, natural technique, sensitive interpretation Are developing all necessary skills at an appropriate rate
Yurko	High level of playing

To be true to the Suzuki® Method, this high-quality playing must be developed in all students, not just the selected gifted ones:

- *I believe the particular contribution of the Suzuki® Method is the ability to develop musical playing in all students. Success with selected, already able and motivated students would not be of the highest importance in my evaluation of a fine Suzuki piano teacher. (Koppelman)*

Students' positive attitude	
Adams	Enjoy the challenge of playing an instrument well
Fest	Take pleasure and pride in their playing Are excited about music
Harrel	Are happy and confident Demonstrate in performance a love of music
Liccardo	Enjoy playing Learn to read music and have a good basic knowledge of music theory Have developed good practice habits and are eventually able to work independently
Schneiderman	Are happy with their musical experiences
Yurko	Are enjoying their studies (both students and families)

One respondent tried to summarize in one sentence the ideal Suzuki teacher.

- *The ideal Suzuki teacher is a well-trained pianist, has taken intensive SAA teacher training, is committed to the Suzuki philosophy, and most of all, loves children and takes to heart Dr. Suzuki's injunction to teach first for the love of the child. (Harrel)*

The same respondent also stressed the need for teachers to continuously be in training to keep improving their skills.

- *Teachers constantly upgrade their skills and explore new ways of making the method even more effective. Many teachers, after completing Book 7, repeat courses on the early books several times because they recognize that the skills needed in advanced repertoire are prepared in the early books.*

  Rhythm is the life blood of music. It is my opinion that all Suzuki teachers should be provided with some Eurythmics as part of their teacher training. Children who experience the rhythm of Book I pieces in their bodies can then exhibit the inside-out concept of learning when they transfer that rhythmic vitality to their playing. (Harrel)

One respondent expressed some concerns about what she identifies as the actual situation of Suzuki teachers in America.

- *The Suzuki approach tends to attract teachers who have a great love of—and interest in—working with children, and generally Suzuki students have a very warm and loving relationship with their teachers. When the relationship and communication with the parents is also good, a teacher will be successful in the psychological area. How do we know if this aspect is not good? Families will not stay with the program. Any teacher with a high drop-out rate using the Suzuki approach has definite problems in the psychological aspect, and should immediately seek help from a more experienced and demonstrably successful teacher. The problem here is not* **what** *is being taught but* **how** *it is being taught, and solutions will involve a great deal of work on the teacher's personality traits and modes of communication.*

  Over the past 20 years, I have both attended and conducted numerous institutes, training workshops, etc. in Suzuki piano. Most of the time what I see and hear is a high degree of psychological success—the students and parents love what they are doing with both piano and music—but in musical diction, only an average-to-poor level of playing skills when the students are considered as a large group representative of Suzuki piano. Unfortunately, the outside world of piano professionals looks mainly at the second aspect to judge the success of Suzuki piano. Of course, there are quite a few exceptional Suzuki piano teachers whose students play with excellent musical diction, but the teaching methods and personalities which produce these results can't just be purchased like computer software, or absorbed in a one-week institute.

  We all know really good playing when we hear it; the composer's intentions and the player's communication and technical skills combine to produce something we must listen to. What is behind this result is years of passionate attention to detail, first on the part of the teacher, with the parents' help, and then as the student catches the excitement, on his or her part also.

  But what are the details? In what order should they be presented as worthy of attention? How much can the teacher ask for, and how does this change as the student matures? The less successful teacher is one who has not examined these issues enough on his or her own, who has not looked hard enough to find a mentor who can help, who accepts sloppy work as "good enough for now" and goes on in the repertoire anyway....

  What criteria can teachers use to judge themselves in the second area? Are you passionate about details of touch, fingering, rhythm, phrasing? Are you relentless about making sure the student understands how it must sound, how to practice it and how many repetitions are needed? Will you spend an entire lesson on just one thing until it is correct, even though your lesson plan is out the window as a result? Do you try many ways of saying the same thing until finally you find the right image for this particular problem for this special student? Do you try ideas you have seen other teachers use with success? Are you constantly looking for a better way, an easier way, to teach this or that concept? Do you have a sense of humor about all this hard work and convey that to the student, at the same time you demand the impossible? If these qualities are inherent in your teaching, it is highly likely you are successful in teaching musical diction also.

  Assuming that the teacher plays well personally and knows how to solve most technical problems (a big assumption that is regrettably often not true in the U.S., where anyone who can play a little may call themselves a piano teacher), any lack of success over time with a class of students indicates a need for serious self-examination in both areas discussed—and then action to rectify the situation.

  As Suzuki teaches us, it is never too late to change, to grow, to improve, to learn new things. (Taggart)

The Student

Accepting a new student

With our respondents, children are all treated equally in their request to be taken on as a new student.

- *All children are treated equally in our school with regard to ability and their placement on the wait list. (Williams)*

There are no auditions to evaluate a child's musical talent:

- *I do not audition students. I believe that every child can learn and I do my best to discover a way to reach each person, to foster personal growth and musical sensitivity to their fullest potential. (Schneiderman)*

- *Children are not selected. Our philosophy is that every child can learn the language of music if provided with a nurturing and musical environment. (Harrel)*

- *Suzuki teachers don't screen children for talent. Instead they think, here is another wonderful child whose growth I am going to be privileged to share for many years. (Taggart)*

For some teachers though, there is an interview to evaluate the child's maturity and readiness.

- *I interview the child to see if he or she is socially ready for lessons. If a child will not respond to me, will not play games with me, will not sit by me at the piano, I suggest that the parent continue to bring the child to observe until the child is ready for lessons. (Fest)*

- *The student must be attitudinally ready to learn, cooperative and respectful. Other elements such as self-esteem, eagerness to play an instrument, communication and length of attention span all play a part. Any number of individual problems can quite often dissipate with a positive and nurturing blend of parent-teacher honesty, skill and understanding. (Williams)*

For some respondents, acceptance is often based on a first-call basis.

- *Generally I interview students and parents on a first-call basis after they have observed some lessons. (Fest)*

- *When I first began teaching, I took students as they were assigned to me in the program in which I was teaching. I also taught just about any student whose parents contacted me by phone. Even through this random process, I developed many fine students. (Liccardo)*

- *I will teach whomever I have room for in my schedule, if the parents are interested after we have conferred and I have explained the method. (Koppelman)*

For many others, the acceptance of a new student is based on parental commitment. It is only after a teacher has seen that the parents are willing to make a satisfactory commitment that a new student is accepted.

- *Parents, not children, are chosen. (Harrel)*

- *In my program, new students are chosen based on the length of their observation period and the parents' willingness and ability to assume their roles as a Suzuki parents. (Yurko)*

- *Children only come to our wait list after their parents go through a rather intensive orientation program. (Williams)*

- *I ask parents to read several books, observe at least ten hours, confer with me twice and take a few private lessons before the child starts. (Schneiderman)*

- *I choose new students based on the signals of commitment and persistence from the family. At first, I give the parents a choice of observation times and request that they read a ream of material about the Suzuki approach. I tell them quite frankly that who I choose to admit to my class will be primarily based on how many times they come to observe and their own and the child's reaction to the observations over at least several months.... If the response of the parent to the initial required observations and parent sessions is lukewarm or skeptical, the prognosis for success is not good. Unless this situation improves considerably after more exposure to the Suzuki® Method, I would advise not accepting this family into the program. (Taggart)*

Respondents strongly felt the need for the parents to understand, before their child starts piano lessons, the very demanding task that learning to play an instrument represents.

- *I communicate to the family what a wonderful but often arduous, time-consuming, schedule-wrecking, lifestyle-changing thing they are embarking on. Do they really want to do this? Is their commitment strong enough? As a teacher, do I sense any hidden agendas, too high an expectation or demand or too little sense of the discipline involved? (Taggart)*

Most respondents require some form of orientation program for parents (and sometimes for the child) before starting lessons. This program often involves an interview, one or more formal or informal meetings and observation of lessons.

Orientation programs	Adams	Fest	Harrel	Koppel-man	Liccardo	Powell	Schnei-derman	Taggart	Williams	Yurko
Parents' informal meeting/interview (designed to meet parents, discuss Suzuki philosophy and parental commitment)	•	•		•	•	•	•	•	•	•
Formal presentation of Suzuki philosophy and methodology			•		•		•		•	•
Parents' observation of private lessons and group class	•		•			•	•			•
Child's observation of private lessons and group class			•				•	•	•	•
Preparatory piano classes for parents	•		•				•			
Material to read on Suzuki philosophy	•		•		•		•	•		•
Advance listening to repertoire by the child	•		•				•	•		•

After reviewing material to read, parents are invited to come to an informational meeting.

- *Our intensive orientation program consists of attending an informational meeting discussing the Suzuki philosophy and methodology, observing two private lessons and one group class lesson so that they can see the parent/teacher/child interaction. At this point they can pay a registration fee and the child's name goes on the wait list if they feel that our approach is compatible with what they want for their child. If there is a wait between this point and placement, we invite the children and parents to attend our recitals and do as much observing as is possible. We also encourage the child to become enrolled in our early childhood programs if the parent chooses—it is not mandatory. After the child is placed and before the first lesson, we insist that the parent come to a workshop where we briefly go over the Suzuki philosophy and methodology once again, help them with practice-skill techniques for home, have other piano students play for them and let the newly placed parents ask questions of these students and their parents (this has proven to be most valuable) and end up the session talking about the purchase and care of the piano. This process results in very little turnover in student enrollment because parents know what to expect. (Williams)*

- *After a call comes requesting I take a new student, a letter is sent to the parents stating they must observe a minimum of two private lessons and one group lesson before they are officially placed on my waiting list. This observation helps the parents understand the commitment required of them to become Suzuki parents. I encourage them to come for more visits than required and I take note of how many times they visit my studio in* deciding which students to admit. When I am ready to accept a new student, I have an interview with these parents, asking questions such as: why are they interested in studying, does the child show an interest in music, and do the parents like music? I also tell them that the students in my studio build up to an hour a day of practice by the end of Book I and ask if they are willing to make this kind of commitment to practice. Based on what I have learned through this process, I then make my decision. *(Powell)*

- Prospective parents are invited to an introductory meeting. There I will present a capsule history of the Suzuki® Method, an explanation of the mother-tongue approach, and detail the role of the parent. I promise to train the parents as a group in weekly sessions over a month's time. In addition, they will bring their child to observe lessons. If the parents can commit to this level of involvement and the child has built up a desire through observation of lessons, we begin lessons at the beginning of the next month.

  Several years ago at the Suzuki Teacher's Conference in Chicago, Gretchen Smith sent a presentation of her parent orientation. I am indebted to her because I have used it as a model ever since, and adapted it to my situation. Some features include :

  1) Required reading and discussion of books about the method, such as "Nurtured by Love" by Dr. Suzuki

  2) Explanation of the parents' role and how to accomplish it

  3) How I teach Book I

  4) Hands-on experience with Twinkles and a few songs

  5) My thoughts on technique

  6) How to help their children to play by ear (parents must do some of this themselves in the orientation or they won't believe it's possible)

  7) How to create an ensemble relationship in the practice session. It seems this skill is more easily achieved by parents with no musical background

  This orientation takes a month's time. The parents meet for one and one-half hours, once a week, and pay the same tuition as if their child were taking lessons. *(Harrel)*

- Prospective students on a waiting list and their parents are invited to orientation sessions to acquaint them with the Suzuki® Method. These sessions include an explanation of the following: Suzuki philosophy and methodology, parent's responsibility in the learning triad, the mother-tongue approach, and program policies. I also include a short recital by my students, and questions and answers for me and the parents of my students who are present at the recital. These families are also asked to observe two lessons of students who are studying Book I.

  After this orientation session, families who feel they can make the necessary commitment to study Suzuki piano begin lessons. The parents attend the first month of lessons alone. During this month the parents are given reading and listening assignments and begin playing the pieces from Book I. These first lessons give the parents confidence in the method and in themselves. It is also a time to get to know the parents and for the parents to get to know me.

  This orientation process has made a big difference in the commitment of the families. They begin their lessons ready to nurture and work! *(Adams)*

- Parent orientation includes education in the Suzuki philosophy and methodology; observation of lessons, where they see the triad of teacher, student and parent in action; reading; advance listening; informal, helpful conversations with other parents; parent-teacher discussions that introduce the child's personality and interests to the teacher as well as preparing the parent (parents need to understand the roles and responsibilities of each of us and how the method works, since it is so different from traditional methods they may have known); several piano lessons where I particularly aim to demonstrate how one learns a song by ear to be certain the parent will understand how to work with the child. Usually parents are very excited to discover that they themselves can play by ear and they eagerly go home to practice.

  Student orientation includes advance listening; visits to become familiar with the studio setting and to experience the format and idea of piano lessons; meeting the teacher and other students; attending monthly workshops to hear children playing music and enjoying learning in a "one-room-schoolhouse" situation.

  This preparation of parents and children before starting is essential both for procedural information and inspiration. When they have a lively experience of children making music, they can imagine the same possibility for themselves. *(Schneiderman)*

Ages for beginning a new student

Suzuki teachers take students at a very young age.

- *Suzuki teachers develop the special skills and knowledge necessary to be able to teach children in the 3 to 5 year age range. (Koppelman)*

The chart below indicates with a dot the preferred ages for beginning a student. (Many of these teachers refuse to take a student over the ideal age.) We have also shown with an X the youngest age at which a teacher will occasionally start a student.

Age	2½	3	3½	4	5	6	7
Adams		•	•	•	•		
Fest	X	•	•	•			
Harrel			•	•	•		
Koppelman		•	•	•	•		
Liccardo		X		•	•		
Powell		X		•	•		
Schneiderman		X	•	•	•		
Taggart	X	X	•	•	•		
Williams				•	•	•	•
Yurko	X		•	•			

- *I have started students as young as 2½ years old. These were siblings of children in my program, and the children had been listening in utero. However, starting children still in diapers is rare. I prefer to start children ages 3 to 4. (Fest)*

- *The youngest student I have ever officially started was 3½, but I have had several observing siblings whose mothers worked with them at home whenever they showed interest, starting around 2½ or 3. Then I would give them a few minutes of a lesson of their very own at the end of the older child's lesson. (Taggart)*

- *Generally, boys are ready to begin at age 4 or 5. Girls usually mature earlier, and are ready to start at three or four years of age. (Adams)*

- *Age 3 is the youngest I accept a new student; I usually limit this to girls since young boys are generally behind the girls in motor development at that age. I prefer age 4 or 5 for accepting most beginners, however. Since the Suzuki® Method is intended for very young beginners, I rarely accept a child older than 5 years of age; it has been wonderful having so many years to develop them as pianists and musicians. (Powell)*

- *We only take beginning students between the ages of 4 and 7 because of the ear-training approach to learning (mother-tongue) and the social age grouping of students in group classes. (Williams)*

- *In my opinion the optimum age for beginning is 3½ to 6 years of age. At that early age, children are totally absorbed in the business of learning. They are little learning machines who learn anything and everything.*

  Their ears are acute and their motor development is usually adequate to begin lessons. I have observed that my students who started in that age range had a different physical attitude to the piano than older beginners. The young ones had no fear or reluctance to take on my 7-foot Steinway. That bonding and ownership of the instrument never changed as they grew older. The older students tended to be more timid and often remained a little more detached from the instrument. (Harrel)

Music education through various group lessons

Since Suzuki students start piano lessons at a very young age, many respondents acknowledge the value of group music classes (Dalcroze, Orff, Kodály, Kindermusik) for their students either preliminary to or along with piano lessons.

- *We have a very large and fully integrated program of early childhood classes and highly recommend that students be enrolled in these classes before coming to private instrumental instruction. It already is proven that the children from these classes are more ready for private instruction. However, it is not mandatory to their enrollment in the Suzuki program. (Williams)*

- *I frequently do suggest Kindermusik classes for children prior to starting formal lessons. These are particularly valuable for children with little music exposure or a lack of social readiness for more structured lessons. (Fest)*

- *Kindermusik is strongly recommended as an introduction to piano. Two teachers in our Suzuki program are registered Kindermusik teachers, and we urge all of our young students to begin their musical experience with them. (Adams)*

- *Many Suzuki teachers have been trained in Kindermusik as well, and find it advantageous to start Kindermusik when children are still essentially babies. They gradually move the children into piano lessons at perhaps 4 to 5 years of age. This plan provides a stimulating musical environment almost from birth. (Harrel)*

- *For many children under 4, I do recommend some kind of group experience before starting lessons at the piano. For those 4 and older, I think they should have both the group experience and the lesson at the piano. I think children at this age should study at the instrument because they are perfectly capable of learning in this way and should have the benefit of an early start. (Liccardo)*

- *Group classes are fine as an adjunct but not a necessary preliminary for most children. A child with poor body control, high activity level and/or inability to be attentive would do better in a movement class before starting lessons. For most children, piano lessons can develop a high and subtle level of listening sensitivity, coordination, focus, learning how to study, poise, and self-confidence to a greater degree than in group lessons. (Koppelman)*

- *The best environment for music would include group lessons, time and the child's energy permitting. What piano lessons lack is singing, rhythm instrument experiences, and dance or movement. (Taggart)*

- *Suzuki piano lessons give a child focused attention on learning a musical instrument; however, other musically enriching activities are also valuable. (Yurko)*

- *Eurythmics, Kindermusik, music and movement are all wonderful and my advice would be to take one of these along with piano lessons, if possible. (Powell)*

- *I think such group classes as Dalcroze Eurhythmics are excellent musical introductions and I would encourage any student to combine such experiences with their piano lessons. I believe in the value of moving to music at any and all levels of music study and have found that dance improvisation has significant benefits for performers. "We feel a profound internalization of the music, a merging with it that leads to more sensitive interpretation. We experience a rare kind of emotional catharsis and an enhanced sense of physical ease with ourselves, our instruments, other people, audiences. And we grow more in touch with our own artistic impulses." (*Confident Music Performance; The Art of Preparing*, p.115). (Schneiderman)*

Adult students and the Suzuki® Method

Can the Suzuki® Method be used with adult beginners? Most respondents do not teach adults, but nevertheless they offered their thoughts on the appropriateness of the Suzuki® Method with adult beginners. Some teachers do not recommend this method for adults, others propose a modified version.

- *I would only use the Suzuki® Method with an adult if it were specifically requested or if it had a practical purpose, such as helping a Suzuki parent get better acquainted with the repertoire. I believe that the Suzuki® Method is most successful if it is taught during the language-acquiring years of ages 3 to 7. I don't see it as very beneficial for an adult who has limited time to listen and practice and in my opinion needs the knowledge, such as music reading, to work independently. (Liccardo)*

- *I do not use the Suzuki® Method with adult beginners. I am not saying that it doesn't work. I am simply saying that with a limited amount of time to teach, I would rather work with children. Also, the Suzuki® Method was originally designed to be used with preschool children. The method follows a preschool learning style, and the repertoire is pleasant for young children. For that reason, I choose not to start children who are over age 7. (Fest)*

- *The best I could offer adult beginners is a modified Suzuki approach, for they would be unlikely to have helping parents and, consequently, I would have to teach them to read music right away. With the use of the modified approach, however, I believe Suzuki instruction would be excellent for them so they could benefit from the listening, technique, tone, etc. that our method offers. (Powell)*

- *I have not used the Suzuki® Method with adults, except for the visually handicapped. I do not teach adult beginning students. However, I do know teachers who find Suzuki a viable alternative to the traditional method in working with adults. (Adams)*

A few respondents have experimented the Suzuki® Method with adults and apparently had great success.

- *I have many experiences with adult beginners who benefit from learning this way, since the methodology is organized and listening to music improves their rhythmic accuracy. (Yurko)*

- *I adapt some of the Suzuki ideas with adult beginners such as taping pieces and lessons for home listening, and I find the clarity of the beginning steps (rest, float up and ready position) excellent vehicles for teaching preparedness—a moment of composure and a graceful approach to the instrument before practice or performance. I have always recommended reviewing for students of all ages. Rather than use the Suzuki pieces, I like to find selections and presentation appropriate for each adult, except when working with some parents of my students or other adults who request the Suzuki repertoire. (Schneiderman)*

- *Absolutely, yes! The adult ear and musical senses have probably lain unused and unstimulated since early childhood. Without the stimulus of the listening and being forced to rely solely on senses other than the eye and the intellect, the adult beginner has very little chance of developing either the ear, memory or physical ability to play with fluency or true enjoyment.*

  Two adult students in particular have made it very clear to me what a difference the listening and no-reading-allowed policy at first have made to them in terms of ability and perception. These students—one was 45 years old, the other 77 when we started at Book 1—had both played the piano already for at least ten years. Neither played well at all; in fact, it was dreadful. They knew it but couldn't seem to do anything about it. The 45-year old's ear was so bad, she would even get lost in Mary Had a Little Lamb.

  They both persevered, listened everywhere, constantly, practiced prodigiously (the 77 year old did 4 hours a day for a while) and because they knew what playing was like before, they communicated to me the difference, how amazed they were at what they could hear now, that their fingers could "sense" where to go, that the music made sense, that they could hear their own mistakes rather than have to have them fixed by the teacher—a thousand things that many of us could do since childhood, without realizing what gifts they were.

  To work with both of these sensitive, articulate adults as they were musically transformed by Dr. Suzuki's simple directive to learn by listening first has brought me a deeper understanding of just how powerful and underutilized are the hidden abilities of the ear and memory for most people. Imagine a world in which every human being had this kind of ability developed as a young child, rather than discovering what they've missed at 45 or 77? Or never knowing at all? (Taggart)

The Parent

Committed parental involvement

In the Suzuki® Method, parents take part in their child's musical education. This is seen as the most natural way to learn music.

- *Parents have been actively involved in their child's language learning through modeling, repetition, encouragement, and endless patience. They are also an indispensable partner in the Suzuki® Method. They provide a home with the musical, emotional, and physical environment in which their child can develop his talent in a natural way. They guide the practice sessions at home. (Harrel)*

The involvement of a supportive parent is seen as a key element without which the Suzuki® Method can not function.

- *Without committed parental involvement, one handicaps the student and dooms the child to discouragement and failure.... Parents have a crucial role in the success of the Suzuki® Method. (Fest)*

- *The wholehearted parental participation is an absolute requirement in my studio. (Taggart)*

- *Suzuki parents serve an equally important role to the students and teachers. Without the parents' exclusive attention and guidance, the Suzuki® Method cannot be successful. (Adams)*

- *Especially with young children, enlightened parental help is needed. This requires teacher assistance with parental education. (Koppelman)*

- *Both parents must have a strong commitment to helping their child and the willingness to be creative and tenacious. They must have the desire, the time, and a daily commitment to organize and guide their child to make progress in the study of piano. (Yurko)*

- *The parent(s) must intentionally rather than casually make this life style choice since it will involve the whole family if the method is to succeed. (Williams)*

The parents' responsibilities are numerous and their effort is required in at least three main areas:

✔ attending all lessons, group classes and recitals

✔ supervising daily practice

✔ assuring that the listening to the recordings is done regularly

- *The participating parent is the one who takes responsibility for playing the tapes, attending all lessons, as well as scheduling and guiding the child in the practice session at home. (Harrel)*

- *The parents must attend all classes and lessons in order to fully understand what the child is learning. The parents must be willing to commit their time on a daily basis, to encourage and motivate their children and to supervise and organize the practice sessions. The parent must also make sure that the child listens daily. (Liccardo)*

- *Parents are expected to attend every lesson and use the lesson as a model for working with their child at home. They are responsible for taking notes in the lessons; some of them also tape or video the lessons. At home, their role is to see that the daily listening is done, as well as supervise the practice. These roles are made clear to my parents at the onset of their child's study. (Powell)*

- *From Book 1 to Book 4 generally, or around 12 or 13 years old, I expect the parents to attend every lesson, every workshop, every recital; to practice with the student every day; to devise, with my help, as many charts and games and rules as it takes to get the job done; to ensure that the listening tapes are played every day in a multitude of places (parent turns them on, not the child); to keep the music and supplies in order, in good condition* and in one place (i.e., a special music bag), to order new and supplementary music, tapes or CDs in time when we need them; to expose the child to concerts and good music in the home—and perhaps learn to love classical music themselves if they don't already. (Taggart)

Parental responsibility at the lesson

- The parent must plan to come to all lessons, both private and group, take good notes and/or record the lesson by audio- or videotape. (Williams)

- The parent needs to be a careful observer and listener during the lesson, taping it and taking detailed notes in outline form to guide the home lesson. (Schneiderman)

- I require the parent to be present at every lesson. At the lesson they sit next to the piano and take notes on what is being taught. I ask that they sit quietly with no interruptions or sound effects (sighs, laughter, groans, etc.). (Fest)

- In the lesson, parents are expected to pay full attention so they will understand the main point being taught. I ask them to take good notes so that I can use their notes for a quick review at the next lesson.

  Also, each parent brings a cassette tape and uses my recorder to tape the lesson. At the end of the lesson I speak to the child directly on the tape, summarizing the main point of the lesson and the practice techniques we worked out together, as well as a word of encouragement and appreciation of their efforts in the every-day practice. I ask them to play this "prologue" each day before practicing. Children typically love and admire their teacher. They find it easy to accept a practice regimen detailed verbally by their teacher. This procedure happily takes some pressure off the child-parent relationship. The tape provides an accurate resource in case any controversy begins to develop as to what actually took place in the lesson. The parent can gracefully say, "You may very well be right (children often are). Let's check the tape so we both can be sure we are practicing correctly for the whole week." (Harrel)

Parental responsibility at home

The parent becomes the coach or the home teacher.

- Parents act as home teachers by continuing at home the study and nurturing started at the lesson. Parents must be able to mix encouragement with correction, fun with work, and draw attention to the child's successes rather than merely the failures. (Adams)

- At home the parent uses the lesson notes to take on the role of home teacher or coach. Parents need to be physically and emotionally with the student in the practice sessions. It is the parent's responsibility (not the child's) to establish daily practice routines. The parent teaches new pieces at home after receiving an introduction and some guidance at the lesson. (Fest)

- Happy, constructive practice sessions are vital for initiating and continuing a positive growth cycle. Parents help students learn their pieces at home, guiding them only as much as is necessary—not by rote methods but only by ear, using sound itself and words like "hear, listen, ear" rather than sight or other directives. (Schneiderman)

- Another kind of listening which is extremely helpful is, of course, to tape the weekly lesson, either audio alone, or even better, videotape. Then for several days after the lesson, the student and parent actively use this tape at practice time—first listening to a particular step, turning off the tape and practicing that, then turning the tape back on, hearing what to do next, turning it off, practicing, etc. This approach is very helpful in establishing an orderly succession in which each practice step builds to the next, because it slows down both the student and parent who want so often to skip ahead to dessert before preparing, serving and eating the rest of the meal.

  A bonus to this also is that the studio teacher's voice is clearly heard giving specific directions for practice, so the inevitable arguments about "who said to do what" between parent and child are greatly reduced and eliminated. (Taggart)

One respondent pointed out the importance for parents to establish consistency in the practice routine.

- *Consistency is a great friend to parents—consistency produces routine which promotes security, expectation of events such as practice sessions, and a sense of well-being for a child.*

  A practice session which occurs at the same time every day is ideal because the consistency establishes an expectation that it will happen.

  Once children are old enough to be involved with many different activities, consistency can still be achieved by establishing a set hour for practicing on each day of the week. (Harrel)

The parent is also responsible for the listening.

- *It is also the parent's responsibility to see that listening to the Suzuki recordings takes place. Again, this is not a responsibility delegated to the student. A most important role of the parent is that of encouraging the efforts of the student. (Fest)*

- *Parents who wish to be facilitators will be consistent about playing the tape, for that promotes the ability to play by ear and develops the musical IQ of the child. (Harrel)*

Many respondents specified that the parents' principal role is to provide the proper environment that will help their child in the study of music.

- *The parent is very important in providing a home environment most conducive to learning. That includes a positive attitude, interest, support, encouragement, providing the best possible equipment, cooperation, quiet, company at practice time if desired, assistance in remembering teacher's assignment, etc. (Koppelman)*

- *The primary parent as teacher at home must be committed to consistent habits of nurturing, positive reinforcement, step-by-step, daily follow-through in practice at the piano as directed by the teacher, and be committed to daily listening to the piano tape.*

  The parent must provide a positive learning environment, good equipment such as a well-tuned and maintained acoustical instrument, a Suzuki piano tape, a tape recorder, foot and seat boosters, music books and any other necessary needs. (Williams)

- *The musical environment includes an adequate and well-tuned instrument, constant exposure to the Suzuki piano recordings, symphonies, operas, folk songs, etc.*

  The emotional environment includes a participating parent who accepts and loves his child as he is and who becomes a facilitator, i.e., one who prepares the way for natural learning to take place. This accepting quality is essential for an ensemble relationship in the practice session.

  For the physical environment, the parent provides special seating at the piano for the small child and a sturdy, adjustable footrest to give the child a firm physical foundation. The piano is situated out of the line of family traffic, away from the TV, away from a window view of dogs jumping and children playing outside. In short, this is a serene place where the child and parent can focus on music and practice. (Harrel)

If one parent is designated as the home teacher or coach and attends all lessons and activities, the other parent also has an important supportive role.

- *If a family has two parents at home, both are expected to attend the introductory parents' meeting. The spouse of the participating parent must be made aware of the extent of the commitment on the part of the other parent. Then he or she can show appreciation for that effort and help in every way possible. Together they will create a nurturing musical environment in their home. The spouse shows support by asking for home performances, being genuinely impressed by the child's efforts and achievements, attending all public performances, and perhaps popping in occasionally at a lesson or group class. (Harrel)*

One respondent described the family type that is most successful in helping their child.

- *I find that the families that do best are neither coercive nor permissive. They have a sense of order and discipline along with much love, encouragement and often humor. If the child is expected to be responsible in other aspects of life, the discipline of music study will naturally fall into place in the family schedule. (Schneiderman)*

One respondent expressed her sympathy and her support for the very demanding task of being a Suzuki parent:

- *In at least the first two years of study, a large part of the Suzuki teacher's job is to help the parents learn to organize. How to get enough listening and practicing into their families' lives is a monumental task for many parents. The teacher has to keep reminding them and suggesting ways to do it, far beyond the point that most reasonable people might expect—always with a smile and the clear expectation that the parents do want to do better—after all, this is for their children's benefit. My experience has been that most parents do eventually come to realize that listening and regular practice are their responsibilities. With these two things, the Suzuki approach works. Without them everybody struggles: parent, student and teacher. (Taggart)*

And she added:

- *This is a lot of work to expect from parents, and along with these expectations I try to be very supportive of and sympathetic to the parents as they learn to organize themselves to accomplish all this. It certainly doesn't happen overnight! They also often need gentle and respectful guidance on how to work with their children in this new, demanding field of study, so it is very helpful to be as specific as possible about every aspect of what to practice and exactly how to do it. (Taggart)*

Parents' musical training

Parents are not required to have a musical background to register their child in a Suzuki class.

- *There is no previous background required of my Suzuki parents. However, I do inquire about their musical background in the beginning. I keep a notebook with a page for each of my students; I record their response in it immediately (no music instruction, played the trumpet, sang in the choir, etc.) to keep me mindful of how much help I need to give them. (Powell)*

A parent's attitude is seen as more important than their musical background.

- *Attitude is more important than musical knowledge. No amount of knowledge will compensate for a negative attitude. (Fest)*

Parents with a music background can be an advantage, but not always.

- *Parents who already play the piano do have an advantage, but I have also learned that the parent who has had former training at the piano sometimes can be more difficult to work with than the novice, because they already have habits and some ideas formed which can be hard to change. (Williams)*

- *The teacher should never assume a parent will understand what needs to be done, even if the parent reads music and can play the piano or another instrument. The Suzuki way of learning and practicing for details from the very first lesson is so different from the way the musical parent studied as a child that sometimes the parents' remembered musical experiences can even get in the way. (Taggart)*

Parents with no musical background are expected to learn certain skills, though, to be able to help their child.

- *A parent with little or no background must be willing to learn along with the child, and I must be prepared to spend some extra time with that parent. (Powell)*

Those skills can vary a great deal from one teacher to another. First, there are the skills related to music reading.

One respondent feels it is not essential that parents learn to read music.

- *Parents do not need to be able to read music to practice with their children. Despite my assurance on this issue, a few parents feel inadequate. We must address that need by giving them a crash course in decoding the pitch symbols on the page. (Harrel)*

But for others, learning to read music is a natural consequence of the work with students.

- *It is helpful in some cases if they can read music, but it is not a requirement in my program. I have weekly theory classes using* Music Mind Games *so parents learn right along with their children. Reading music is quite straightforward, so all my parents learn to read. (Yurko)*

- *For parents with no experience reading music, I explain to them the layout of the keyboard. I write note names and fingerings in the music for them. I ask to hear them play frequently. Also, I have found it helpful to loan parents any basic traditional reading series. With the slow, repetitive, cookbook approach to reading music, the parents can learn many basics on their own. (Fest)*

- *As far as decoding notation is concerned, it is very helpful if parents work on note reading in advance of the child, but I present this training to my students in very small increments, Suzuki-style, so a parent can easily digest the information as the child learns. Even those who can already read find this careful step-by-step approach is easily understandable and presents reading in a new, clearer light for them. (Schneiderman)*

Second, there are the skills related to piano playing.

Some respondents do not feel it is essential for parents to learn how to play the piano.

- *Parents do not need to know how to play the piano. I can teach them in a few minutes to read music well enough to follow and check fingerings, which I do ask them to do. They listen to the tapes too and learn to recognize if their child is playing correctly. At lessons, I demonstrate how their child should practice. They are asked to follow this model at home. I refer them to other successful parents if they need ideas about motivation. (Koppelman)*

- *They may not be able to actually read the music and play the piano themselves, but they learn how to watch and guide their child. To achieve this I help them with little bits of information in the lessons until the understanding is solid. (Yurko)*

Other respondents teach each parent how to play the piano. The ability they are required to develop can range from basic piano skills (the *Twinkles*) to more advanced playing (Book 1 and 2).

- *I do not require any playing from my parents except on the* Twinkles. *However, I do encourage them to be able to play each hand alone at least in Book 1. I take time to teach them the tonic, dominant, and sub-dominant chords in C while the child is playing their* Twinkles, *knowing this means they can accompany the child on their* Twinkles *at home as well as most of the left hand accompaniments in Book 1. (Powell)*

- *The parent must be dedicated to the study of the instrument themselves, so that at least through Suzuki Piano Book 1 they are able to play and help the child as instructed by the teacher.*

  I expect the parent to learn to play the piano in the same manner I teach the child so that they can experience the necessary steps in this process. The parent must always be quite a bit ahead of the student so that they can set an example for the student in a proficient way. (Williams)

- *Parents are encouraged to learn along with the children; this is especially necessary for parents who have had no previous musical training. For several weeks I teach lessons to parents only, to insure correct guidance for the* Variations *and Book 1 pieces. I ask parents to play at lessons and to demonstrate assigned pieces for the students. I also use parents as duet partners with the children, which helps to coordinate playing hands together. (Adams)*

- *I ask the parents to learn all of Book 1 and at least some of Book 2, trying to keep slightly ahead of the children at least for Book 1. Experience is the best teacher, and to listen and learn as the children do (with peeks at the music to make sure the fingering is correct) is the best way for the parents to learn to teach their children. It also makes them very aware of just how difficult it is to really play the piano and get all these fingers in the right place at the right time with a nice sound.*

The parents always play their homework for me during part of the lesson for a goodly part of Book 1, and sometimes after that also. The children usually love to see their parents have a lesson, and I often ask them to share practicing at home by switching roles, with each of them in turn being the teacher for repetition games. (Taggart)

Some teachers described in more detail what they expect from the parents as well as the kind of training they provide for them.

- *Beside being able to play hands separately in at least all of Book 1, I expect them to listen to the CD or tape of each book, learn basic reading skills, and gradually develop an ability to listen so they can discern between good and bad musical sounds. I teach them, one step at a time, whatever it is necessary to know in order for them to teach each piece to the child at home. The training is done during the child's lessons, and the majority of it is done in combination with working with the child. (Powell)*

- *No previous musical knowledge is required from the parents, but much will be learned along with the child and throughout the process. Listening at home, of course, will educate the parent as well as the child in the language of music. I ask parents to take a few private lessons before the child starts. I teach them the beginning steps and emphasize their value and importance. We also work on listening skills, on the specific techniques of the Twinkle Variations and learn exactly what it means to learn a song by ear to avoid rote teaching or any focus other than on sound. I encourage the parent to continue learning at least the Book 1 songs by ear. This enables them to better help their child, provides a stimulating model for the child who hears them practice and, through their personal enjoyment of the live reality and joy of music-making, enhances the process for everyone. Some parents become very motivated and continue to study as individual adults. (Schneiderman)*

- *The parents should acquire some basic playing skills on a Book 1 level. I use part of the weekly lesson to work with them at the piano. The parent should also be able to sing in tune. If they have a problem matching pitch I also practice this with them at the lesson. Most adults can usually improve this skill. The parent also needs to acquire basic note-reading and rhythm-reading skills. These skills can be learned in the group classes, at the private lesson (crash course) and by keeping up with their child as they learn these skills. I also train the parent to hear musical nuances, such as phrasing, balance, tone quality, understanding of a steady beat, tempo and mood of a given piece. These skills continue to grow and develop over the years as they are pointed out to the parent and constantly demonstrated to them at the lesson. I am often amazed at what fine musicians, as listeners, the parents become over the years. (Liccardo)*

PERFORMANCE SKILLS

Listening

Importance of listening

In the beginning stages of the Suzuki® Method, students learn piano by ear. Paralleling the way children learn their mother tongue by being surrounded by it, young students are intensively exposed to the repertoire they are going to play through daily listening to recordings or CDs. It is by relying on the ear and not by rote learning that they master each new piece.

- *The child absorbs the language of music whole, and deeply within, by maximal listening to fine music and particularly to the music a child will study; this parallels a baby's immersion both in the general sound of the mother tongue and certain frequently heard words and phrases. Students learn initially by ear and thus develop an aural orientation to music as opposed to a visual one. The intensive listening continues, for both information and motivation, even after students are reading. (Schneiderman)*

- *The most basic element of this method is listening. Children learn by repeated listening to the music they are about to study just as babies listen to the sounds of language heard about them on a daily basis. (Liccardo)*

- *Students should be exposed to fine, carefully chosen music at a very young age, and become familiar with this selected repertoire through many, many listening repetitions.*

  They will absorb a musical vocabulary in the same way one absorbs and learns a native language: by repetition of basic words with a gradual addition of new and more complex ones. (Taggart)

- *The essential elements of the methodology are drawn directly from the successful natural method by which children have learned their native tongue.*

Spoken Language	Language of Music
1. Intensive listening from before birth Internalization of the sounds of spoken communication	1. Intensive listening to recordings as early as possible Internatization of the sounds of musical language
2. Imitation Babbling Single syllables Complete words Phrases Sentences	2. "Sounding out" on the keyboard, or playing by ear the songs which have been internalized
3. Vocabulary-Grammar Building of large vocabulary Stringing words together into meaningful units	3. Repertoire Continual growth of performing repertoire. Folk-song material from Book I of Suzuki Piano School
4. Reading	4. Reading

(Harrel)

Listening to tapes and CDs of the Suzuki repertoire is thus at the very center of this method.

- *Listening is the heart of the Suzuki® Method. To attempt to teach this method while leaving out listening to the recordings ensures failure.... If listening is deleted, you do not have the Suzuki® Method. (Fest)*

- *Listening to the tapes is of prime importance—the fuel for a positive learning cycle to become established. In fact, learning by ear is impossible without it. (Schneiderman)*

The importance of listening is stressed from the very beginning and some teachers require that listening start even before lessons begin.

- *I stress listening a great deal and require at least several months of listening and observation before starting any new students. (Taggart)*

- *The importance of listening to the tapes is stressed from the very beginning with the parents. Once the parents have requested lessons with me, a letter is sent to them which includes a request to purchase the tape and to begin having the child listen daily to it. (Powell)*

After this initial time, teachers continually emphasize the importance of listening.

- *I try to constantly remind the parents that listening to the tapes is the most essential element for their child if they are to make progress. I think that making the language analogy is the most effective way of getting this point across. A child cannot learn to speak a language if that child never hears it spoken. In the beginning of Suzuki study, a child's only point of reference is hearing the tape. (Liccardo)*

- *One needs to evaluate continually whether listening is sufficient and check with parent and student on their particular home system. (Schneiderman)*

- *At the beginning, dedication to listening is very good. As time goes on it does vary, and I find I need to constantly check, remind and strongly urge (or demand) that the listening take place consistently. (Williams)*

- *Listening can never be emphasized enough! This information is attached to parents' schedule at the beginning of every year:*

  Is your child listening every day without fail? Does he or she listen for at least an hour? The tape should be on while other quiet activity is pursued, such as getting dressed, getting ready for bed, etc. In Japan, two hours a day of listening is a required minimum. Does he or she hear the current pieces at least four or five times in succession? Do you also add the entire side of the record or tape to the listening when you can? Do you use a high-quality tape and have a fairly good tape recorder? Does the listening include the other books both behind and ahead with frequency? Do you use endless tapes for the current piece or pieces? Do you tape your child's lesson and use this tape to help guide the home practice? Do you ask your teacher to tape hands separately for you? Does your child tape himself and then listen to his playing compared to the listening tape? If you answered yes to every question, your child should be making excellent progress. If there were very many no answers, can you try to do better? (Taggart)

Our respondents say it becomes very obvious when not enough listening is taking place.

- *A teacher will recognize inadequate listening when the musical details are not in the student's ear, especially if rhythms are wrong or repeats are not taken. (Schneiderman)*

- *It is obvious from the ease (or lack of ease) with which the student can discover new material at the lesson whether or not enough listening is taking place. (Taggart)*

Some respondents explained the reasons for relying so much on listening.

- *Listening to the tapes is a must! It is the basis for the beginning of ear training and makes the Suzuki® Method truly a mother-tongue method rather than a rote method where the child copies the parent or teacher. The child must be taught how to explore and develop the ear as the vehicle which carries the child into music education. (Williams)*

- *Before people can understand music, they need to have considerable background of having heard it. A musical vocabulary is needed from which to choose one's own interpretation. Children need to listen enough to hear in their heads what they want to play before they do so. But they learn to do this from looking at the score. This is a skill we expect to teach our students as they get more advanced. (Koppelman)*

- *With the advent of CDs and classical music radio stations, we have the opportunity to enrich the lives of the entire family with all styles of music. As mentioned earlier, the musical IQ of children actually grows in proportion to the amount and quality of music present in their environment. This phenomenon continues until approximately age 9. (Harrel)*

Daily listening time for beginners

Suzuki teachers require that their beginning students listen to their tapes or CDs daily.

- *Students are required to listen every day, so listening becomes part of the daily activity. Ideally, recorded Suzuki literature should be played continuously in the students' homes. (Adams)*

- *In the beginning, we are hoping for total immersion in music to be certain children internalize it deeply as a source of information, motivation and inspiration—that they develop an aural orientation. Maximal listening launches the learning process with security. (Schneiderman)*

Some teachers explained that the amount of listening time needed can vary for every child.

- *Children differ greatly in the length of time it takes them to remember what they hear. They should listen enough to make this process easy. If I see that a student can't find the notes of a song easily, I then recommend a more specific amount of listening time. (Koppelman)*

- *All children are different. Some require much more listening than others. (Fest)*

But usually each teacher recommends a minimum time of listening from their students (and their parents), stressing the more listening the better.

Daily minimum time required	1hr	2 hrs	3hrs	4-5hrs
Adams	•			
Fest				•
Harrel				•
Liccardo	•			
Powell	•			
Schneiderman			•	
Taggart		•		
Williams			•	
Yurko		•		

- *I ask for a minimum of one hour of listening daily and preferably more. I used to ask more of the parents but I found it overwhelmed them, and they consequently did almost no listening. I am certain that some listen the length requested and that others do not. (Powell)*

- *I usually ask the parent to put the piece to be learned or sometimes several pieces on an endless cassette and to play that for at least one hour each day. I feel this is a reasonable assignment on a daily basis. However, I also point out that the more they listen, the easier it will be to learn the new piece and also to retain it as other pieces are added because the child will know it so intimately. On a realistic basis, the average child probably listens several times a week for a total of several hours. (Liccardo)*

- *I stress listening to the Suzuki tapes or CDs a great deal. I request that they be played daily for a minimum of two hours. The majority of my students achieve and even surpass this.* (Yurko)

- *I prefer not to offer a specific quantity of time but rather to recommend as much as possible and the more the better! If pressed, I will say at least three hours.* (Schneiderman)

- *At the beginning, even before lessons formally begin, I (and our school) ask for 3 hours of listening a day.* (Williams)

- *For beginning students, I ask the parents to have the child listen to Book 1 for 4 to 5 hours per day. Realistically, most beginning students listen 2 to 4 hours per day.* (Fest)

- *For the parents of pre-school children, I recommend that they play the tape as much as their children listened to learn their native tongue as babies. Of course, they concede that their children listened all the time.* (Harrel)

Suzuki teachers usually tell their students and parents which pieces to listen to.

- *I encourage the listening to the entire tape for their working pieces, review, and preview. I also encourage listening to the tapes which I have made to help with their working pieces. My tapes include each piece played several times hands separately and hands together.* (Adams)

- *For specific listening, I ask that the bulk of the listening be done on the piece the child is currently learning plus the next few; the endless cassettes make it easy to accomplish this. The student is also asked to listen daily to the entire book he or she is studying, as well as the next book and the previously studied book (to help maintain the review).* (Powell)

- *For beginning students, I ask the parent to have the child listen to Book 1. As they progress, I ask the parents to begin including recordings of the later books.* (Fest)

- *Halfway through Book 1, the parent should add listening for Book 2.* (Harrel)

- *It is very important that the child is always listening ahead in the repertoire to prepare them for the new piece. I usually have my students listening several pieces ahead. Besides listening repeatedly to the endless cassette, I also ask that they sometimes listen to the entire Suzuki tape. To help maintain repertoire, I ask that they do review listening. This means that they should listen to all of the pieces they have already learned.* (Liccardo)

- *For many reasons, I ask students to listen to the whole book. If their listening is to be focused on certain pieces, I have found that the teacher must have a plan in mind in managing regular listening.* (Williams)

- *Students' listening includes the current and the next book, a repeating tape of several pieces and other fine classical music. I also encourage listening to any of the advanced Suzuki repertoire.* (Schneiderman)

- *They listen to their current book the most, then listen ahead and from previous books. Since it's easy to program a CD player to play one song, many parents find learning is easier after a child listens repeatedly to one song. For example, if children hear the CD once, they will hear the study piece four times (if using Mrs. Kataoka's CD). If the repeat mode is selected, they will hear a piece such as* Lightly Row *60 times in just 30 minutes. Compare this to playing the tape once a day for one week and the numbers are 28 times vs. 420 times. It's easy to see which approach gives an advantage to a child who is learning* Lightly Row. (Yurko)

In the beginning levels, most teachers use the various recordings of the Suzuki repertoire available on the market. Some teachers, though, prefer to make their own tapes.

- *I prefer to record the tapes personally. Recording should include each piece played hands separately, then hands together, several times. Along with listening to the purchased tape, this allows listening to individual working pieces in addition to the entire Suzuki book.* (Adams)

Choice of recordings	Kataoka	Aide	Lloyd-Watts	Own tapes	Various recordings
Adams			•	As a supplement	
Harrel	Book 1 and parts of Book 2		Books 3-7	Bach minuets	
Koppelman	Book 1-3	Shorter works in Book 4-7			Outstanding pianists for major works in Books 4-7
Liccardo		•		•	
Powell			•		
Schneiderman	•	•	•	•	
Taggart	Book 1-2	Book 3-4			Book 5 on
Yurko	•				

Some teachers have suggestions on how to help with listening.

- *I have used charts, rewards for recorded amounts of listening time and other motivational ideas as well. (Williams)*

- *It is also helpful, especially in the beginning of piano study, to have the parents keep a listening chart, similar to a practice chart, to help establish the daily habit of listening. I have found from my experience that the amount of listening time can always be improved. (Liccardo)*

- *I have listening contests for my studio and for our entire Suzuki piano program. Trophies are given to the winners. Trophies are inexpensive and have proven to be great incentives for the students. (Adams)*

For Suzuki teachers, the task of making sure that listening occurs daily is the entire responsibility of the parent.

- *Listening is so central to the Suzuki® Method that the responsibility for such an important element must be assigned to the person ultimately responsible for the child's education—the parent. (Harrel)*

- *I feel it is totally the parents' responsibility to play the tapes until the child goes off to college. (Yurko)*

- *I require that the tape be played at least two hours every day, and that the parents accept this responsibility themselves. They are not to ask or require the children to initiate or remember to play the tape. No parental nagging about listening! (Taggart)*

Nature of the listening for beginners

The respondents suggested ways that listening should take place with beginning students.

- *I recommend that they make copies of the tape or disc they have bought and keep one in the bedroom (for night listening), one in the car (for traveling listening) and one in the kitchen or family room for the mealtimes, etc., so they can turn it on wherever they are at the moment. (Taggart)*

- *I ask my parents to make multiple copies of the tape or CD for home and for the car. The music becomes background music, playing continuously in their environment. This continous music also discourages the watching of too much TV! (Adams)*

- *Listening can be done while the child is playing, riding in the car, etc. To make listening more fun, I ask students to listen to certain parts of a piece so that they can answer questions at the next lesson. (Williams)*

- *Quiet, background music while the child is engaged in other activities. (Fest)*

- *One suggestion that helps is to play the music very softly. This way it can be background music during meals, play, homework and in the car. I request that my families have a CD or tape player in the child's room, the kitchen and in the car and that they use them. Many parents put on the music before their child wakes up so the music is playing at the beginning of the day. They also play it as they get ready for bed and as they fall asleep. Quite a few students listen all night. I request that the volume be low. (Yurko)*

- *I assure them that small children thrive on repetition, even though the rest of the family may not. If the sound is barely audible, the small child will internalize the sounds and the rest of the family will barely notice. No mention should be made that the Suzuki music is being played. It is simply part of the environment. The children's freedom of action and movement should never be restricted by listening to the tape. They are just absorbing the sound present in their milieu. (Harrel)*

- *It is important to emphasize the nature of the listening, that it be a natural part of the home environment—quiet, maximal and associated with pleasure. I recommend activities in the early stages like dancing, singing, marching, making up words, playing percussion instruments and clapping to the tape to introduce the music joyfully to the ears, imagination and whole muscular system. (Schneiderman)*

Daily listening time and nature of listening for advanced students

The time of listening in the upper levels may change or stay the same.

- *Usually the amount of time necessary declines as they go along. (Koppelman)*

- *Generally, as the student advances in the repertoire, the ear becomes more developed and sophisticated, so that several hours of listening each day is not really necessary. (Fest)*

- *Daily listening is very important in Books 1 and 2. As the student gets to the latter part of Book 2 and on to Books 3 and 4, I don't stress the listening as much because they are also learning the pieces by reading. Also, the ear has progressed to the point that they do not need to listen to the same piece for an hour a day in order to know it. (Liccardo)*

- *Although my students listen a lot, most likely they listen the most when they are in Book 1. Children who follow a dedicated listening program when they are younger need less listening and practicing time to accomplish amazing results when they are older. (Yurko)*

- *The same amount of listening time is requested in all books. (Powell)*

- *As a student advances, the amount of listening time will remain fairly constant, because new stimulating music is always being added as previous books are learned. However, there is much variety here too, as some students' tastes mature and they independently delight in listening to classical music while others' schedules become crowded with academic and other activities. In some households, students are enriched when their families regularly enjoy listening to record collections or radio. It is very important to be flexible with adolescents—to find that balance which honors their uniqueness and maintains their interest in music while keeping our standards high. (Schneiderman)*

- *It is not so much that I require more listening as the students move on in the books, as it is that the parents become more involved and convinced that the listening is vital, so the listening time usually increases (with occasional slumps which show up and are noted at the lessons). (Taggart)*

The nature of the listening in advanced levels changes.

- *The type of listening changes as they progress. It starts from absorption listening to learn what music is about, and grows continually more discriminating and sensitive. At a more advanced level it involves comparing different performances to assess possibilities. (Koppelman)*

- *The listening in Books 3, 4 and on is more for understanding the style, mood, tempo, phrasing and dynamic nuances of the piece. (Liccardo)*

- *The type of listening changes at the advanced level, however. We do more active listening (following the score while listening) instead of passive listening (music in the background). (Powell)*

- *Older children are expected to listen more specifically to their Suzuki recordings. Advanced students may be asked to compare several different recordings of the same work and answer such questions as :*

  Is the underlying spirit, or character, or message the same? If different, how are they different?

  Do you feel moved by the music? Where? Why? Did the artist do anything with dynamics, timing, or touches that affected you?

  How did the artist approach the recapitulation? Did it seem like an important event? If so, how did the artist make it significant? (Harrel)

In the upper levels, students are still requested to listen to the Suzuki repertoire, but teachers tend to use various interpretations instead of, or with, the Suzuki tape series.

- *In upper level books, I also have the same pieces on other recordings so that the students can hear other ways of interpretation and begin to claim some of their own ideas. I encourage as much listening as possible. (Williams)*

- *When they reach a more advanced level, I have them listen to other artists perform their works as well as listening to the Suzuki tape. (Liccardo)*

- *Listening to different artists play Suzuki repertoire or supplementary material will add to the total listening time. (Schneiderman)*

- *We listen to a greater variety of interpretations of the pieces being studied. (Powell)*

- *In addition to the Suzuki tapes, the parents and I are always searching for, and finding more and more, the same repertoire recorded by other pianists.*

  As students advance, I feel it is very important for them to hear more than one stylistic and musical approach to the pieces they are playing. Noticing the differences and making comparisons and then choosing how they themselves will play a certain passage is a vital part of their musical growth. (Taggart)

- *As they reach the advanced book levels, recordings by the finest artists should serve as their model. Especially notable performances of the Mozart sonatas in the Suzuki repertoire are available by Mitsuko Uchida, and Alicia de la Rocha. Richard Goode has recorded the complete Beethoven sonatas. (Harrel)*

Suzuki teachers do not limit listening to the Suzuki repertoire. They also promote a wide selection of recordings.

- *Listening includes music outside the repertoire that the family is interested in or the teacher may suggest. The teacher will prescribe whatever she or he thinks the student needs. (Koppelman)*

- *I also stress listening to music outside the Suzuki repertoire. One way I have effectively encouraged this is by having a studio "Composer of the Month." With each new composer, I distribute biographical information and recommended recordings. I encourage the families to add one or two recordings to their musical library each month and to listen especially to music by the "Composer of the Month." For some families this could be a financial hardship, in which case they can borrow recordings from the public library. (Fest)*

Repertoire

Strength of the Suzuki repertoire

The Suzuki® Method provides a set of repertoire pieces that are used, especially in the early books, by all teachers.

- *Our Suzuki Piano School Books 1 to 7 represent a core curriculum of fine music undertaken by all students. The content is derived primarily from the Baroque and Classical periods. The works from these periods are particularly accessible for small hands. Teachers are free to supplement the core material with pieces from the Romantic, Impressionistic and Contemporary style periods, as well as additional technical training. (Harrel)*

The teachers spoke very highly of the standard repertoire of the Suzuki® Method.

- *The repertoire is excellent—one of the best collections of music available. (Adams)*

- *Basically, the Suzuki material is tasteful and of very high quality. (Schneiderman)*

- *The Suzuki repertoire is very strong in its beginning repertoire. (Koppelman)*

- *The greatest thing about the pieces in the repertoire is that the children love the music and can hardly wait to get to the next piece. (Williams)*

Many respondents explained why this repertoire, especially in the early books, has so much value.

- *The Suzuki repertoire is an excellent sequence of music with pieces leading into each other in a sound pedagogical way. (Yurko)*

- *Book 1 is very well chosen and well organized. The pieces are pleasant and have pedagogical value. (Fest)*

- *In general, I feel the first three books of the repertoire provide a challenging and thoughtful collection of pianistic problems. The logical progression of skills required, acquired and then used again in subsequent pieces establishes an excellent background for more advanced playing. The almost immediate demand for complex left-hand parts and two-handed playing is far more advanced than any traditional reading method dares to be, or should try to be—given that the traditional student is trying to accomplish two enormous tasks simultaneously: how to read music and how to play the piano. (Taggart)*

- *I have great respect for the Suzuki repertoire. First, it is a beautiful collection of music. Second, it is the only method of music I know that uses almost exclusively classical literature. (Book 1, the folk-song book, is the only book that does not.) Thus it exposes the students and their parents to the world of classical literature that many would never know otherwise. Third, the literature is designed for small hands and short legs to play, thus giving children an opportunity to develop fine technique and musicianship at a young age. (Powell)*

- *I feel that the first three books of the Suzuki repertoire are particularly outstanding. Although the playing level is far more difficult than a traditional piano method, there is a wonderful logic to the way the repertoire progresses. I think it makes excellent sense to start with traditional folk music, move into smaller classical forms and then into the sonatina literature. From a pianistic and musical point of view this progression works very well. It is also to the credit of this method that from the very beginning, the student gets to play quality literature, beautiful and familiar tunes with real accompaniments in the first half of Book 1 to miniature musical gems that foster the development of musical sensitivity and expression in the second half of the book. Book 2 takes them directly into classical literature and further develops their musical sensibilities and the Book 3 sonatinas prepare them for sonata literature. From the technical point of view, we start with a series of pieces in five-finger positions (Book 1), then expand and contract the hand (Book 2), and then have a sonatina book (Book 3) which develops scales and passage work. The final benefit of these first three books is that we often end up with a seven- or eight year-old who plays the piano very well, has an excellent ear, a well-developed musical sense and a wealth of good literature already under his or her belt. (Liccardo)*

- *If I compare the Suzuki repertoire at the beginning levels to other method books, it stands out as far superior, musically speaking. That is possible because of the child's capacity to learn by ear at the outset. In a traditional method, children do not encounter many interesting rhythms until they are able to read them. The Suzuki musical experience is much richer at the outset.*

  Many pianists, myself included, have not understood the structure of the repertoire. Book 1 contains folk material. We call Book 2 our Baroque book because the emphasis is on Bach minuets. Book 3 focuses on Viennese Classical sonatinas. The later books have a variety of styles. I think there is a positive value in being immersed in a style period for a while. It's similar to absorbing a foreign language by being immersed in those sounds.

  Each book has certain works which are seminal to the development of technique or style. They are often followed with much easier pieces which are psychologically rewarding. Once students have climbed the mountain, they have a chance to relax and enjoy the view. The newly acquired skills make the next pieces easier and feed self-esteem. (Harrel)

One teacher explained why she thinks a common prescribed repertoire is good.

- *It gave me much guidance as a young teacher to have a repertoire to follow. Since Suzuki students are found in all parts of the world now, this common repertoire is invaluable at workshops, institutes or conferences. Within moments, student and teacher are able to bond and work together in a lesson because of the common philosophy and repertoire. (Yurko)*

Omission and sequence of pieces in early books

Teachers tend generally to teach all pieces in Books 1, 2 and 3, with a substitution for the Mozart *Sonatina* at the end of Book 3.

- *I teach every piece in Books 1, 2, and 3. (Adam)*

- *I teach every piece in Books 1 and 2. In Book 3, I replace the last piece (the Mozart Sonatina) with either the Kuhlau Sonatina, Op. 20, No. 1 (first movement) or the second and third movements of the Clementi Sonatina, Op. 36, No.3. (Powell)*

- *I teach all of the pieces in the first three books except an occasional substitution for the Mozart Sonatina in Book 3. For that piece I sometimes teach the second and third movements from the Clementi Sonatina Op. 36 No.3 or possibly a completely different sonatina. (Liccardo)*

Most respondents teach the repertoire of the three first books in order (except for the *Twinkles*, the last two Bach pieces in Book 2 and again the Mozart Sonatina at the end of Book 3, which is omitted by almost everyone).

- *Book 1: I use every piece in Book 1 but I spread the Twinkle Variations out over the first six months or so. The Twinkles (except the last variation) deal mainly with motion that leaves the keyboard. I feel there is too much emphasis on this and not enough emphasis on the walking-on-the-keys, being-supported-by-the-piano aspect, unless Mary, Lightly Row, Cuckoo, etc. are brought in sooner than following the book order would allow.*

  Book 2: I use every piece in order except the last two (Bach Musette and G-minor Minuet)—learning these is up to the student. The Beethoven Sonatina is such a crowning achievement to the book that these last two are a bit of an anticlimax.

  Book 3: I use everything except the Trio arrangement. This arrangement of the Mozart Trio in G, K. 564, should be omitted because it is very unpianistic and un-Mozartean in its difficulty, and it contains numerous errors in harmony compared to the original. (Taggart)

- *I teach everything in Book 1 pretty much in order. Book 2 also is well chosen. I omit the last 2 pieces, which were actually transferred from Book 3 some years ago. Ending with the Beethoven Sonatina is more satisfactory. (Koppelman)*

- *Pieces are introduced as published, except that I teach* Mary, London, *and* French Children's Song *in that order.* (Adams)

- *I follow the order of the repertoire as it is written in Books 1, 2, and 3. I do omit the Mozart Sonatina at the end of Book 3. I do not have the children play hands together on any of the unison pieces in Book 1 and I use* Mary Had a Little Lamb *as the first piece I put hands together. I teach all the pieces in the books with few exceptions.* (Williams)

- *While I would not teach the* Twinkles *in the order in which they are presented in Book 1, I generally teach the other pieces in Book 2 and all the other books in order. I do skip the Mozart Sonatina at the end of Book 3 because it is an awkward arrangement of a delightful piece not written for keyboard.* (Harrel)

- *My students learn the pieces in the repertoire in sequence except I use the order of the books as they were originally printed in the early 1970's.*

  Book 2: This book ends with the Beethoven Sonatina. This is a fitting way to end the book since it is the first two-movement work they study.

  Book 3: The Bach Musette and Minuet are learned between the first Clementi Sonatina and the Kuhlau Sonatina. This gives a welcome break between two rather lengthy pieces. Since the Mozart Sonatina is a transcription, we don't study it. (Yurko)

- *I teach all the Book 2 repertoire in the order printed, with the exception of the last two pieces. The Musette and Minuet were originally in Book 3, following the first Clementi Sonatina. There was never a pedagogical reason for moving these pieces to Book 2; it was simply for convenience in publishing the books. Book 2 is long enough and certainly offers enough Bach. Book 3 has no pieces by Bach, so I feel very comfortable teaching Musette and Minuet as they were originally placed in Book 3. In Book 3, I do not teach the Mozart Sonatina, and I do not know of anyone who does. If I feel a student needs more experience before advancing to Book 4, I assign the second and third movements of the Clementi Sonatina Op. 36 No. 3.* (Fest)

One respondent said she is flexible about the order of the pieces.

- *I am flexible about the order of pieces in Book 1, especially at the outset. For example, I have discovered that Mary is a good first song for some children because balance is most comfortable starting on the third finger. It is also a beloved tune and contains mostly step-wise motion. We gradually introduce the Twinkles and soon get into a pattern of using the given order with occasional exceptions. I like to honor students' preferences when they delight in particular pieces.*

  In Book 1, it is so important to establish the basics that I prefer to teach every piece and concentrate on building a productive process, technical skills, centering, posture, practice habits, pleasure in learning, tone quality, etc. This takes time and I like to use all the material at level 1. I will respond to a student's occasional desire to avoid a particular piece from Book 2 onward (indeed I respect this budding development of personal taste and see it as a positive sign!) but I generally teach all of Book 1. We sometimes supplement with a lively modern piece individualized to a child's personality and ability, perhaps for a recital. (Schneiderman)

Some respondents gave a detailed account of their teaching strategies with Book 1 repertoire. They go from explaining how the left hand is introduced to the presentation of a month-by-month calendar.

- *I generally follow the order of the book, teaching melodies up to Aunt Rhody (R.H.) and Twinkles, Lightly Row and Honeybee (L.H.) before going back to Cuckoo to learn the L.H. accompaniment. I start catching up with the left-hand parts but generally keep the right hand one or two melodies ahead.* (Liccardo)

- *I am pleased with the sequence my students follow in learning the Suzuki books. First they learn the RH and LH of Twinkles separately. Then they continue with the RH, learning most or all of the melodies of Book 1. The LH also learns the same melodies, usually through Aunt Rhody, playing them at the position of C below middle C. This approach enables each hand to develop independence, a sound technique and tone. Once this is accomplished they learn Cuckoo with both hands. Mary is the second piece to be learned with both hands, followed by the remainder of the pieces from Lightly Row in order. As they approach the end of the book they enjoy figuring out the accompaniments for Honeybee and the Twinkles from listening, since neither is printed in the score.* (Yurko)

- *When teaching Book 1, I work with only the right hand through* Little Playmates *approximately. At that point I continue teaching right hand alone in the subsequent pieces while starting the left hand at the beginning of the book. Usually I teach the chordal left hand in* Mary Had a Little Lamb *prior to learning the left hand of* Cuckoo. *I do not have the children play the* Twinkles *hands together. I do have them do* Lightly Row *and* The Honeybee *in unison as their first experience playing hands together. (Fest)*

- *Order—Book 1:*

    1 to 2 Months—Preparatory things:

    > *Walking 123454321;* Twinkle Variation D *first.*
    > *Stroking, lifting off—*Twinkle Variation A *on single notes.*
    > *Honeybee—walking each hand separately;* Mary Had a Little Lamb—*RH only;* Cuckoo—*RH only*

    3 to 4 Months:

    > Twinkle Variation A
    > *Collect RH melodies for* Lightly Row, French Children's Song, London Bridge, Chant arabe
    > *Add LH chords to* Mary

    4 to 5 Months:

    > *Add more* Twinkle Variations
    > *Add LH to* Chant arabe
    > *Choose* Cuckoo *or* Lightly Row *for two-hand work.*

    5 to 6 Months:

    > *RH continues learning new melodies and keeping old ones.*
    > *Work on LH skill for either Bottom Middle Top (5 3 1 or Cuckoo-type) pieces, or Bottom Top Middle Top (5 1 3 1 or Lightly Row-type) pieces, and changing from a I to V by demand of the ear. Parent and teacher play RH, student plays LH.*
    > *Depending on students' choices, then we do groups of pieces hands together.*
    > *BTMT:* Lightly Row, London Bridge, Go Tell Aunt Rhody, French Children's Song, Au clair de la lune, Long Long Ago, *etc.*
    > *BMT:* Cuckoo, Allegretto 1, Musette

    7 to 12 Months:

    > *Consolidate and polish both BTMT and BMT pieces*

    > *Go on to the oddballs—*Allegretto 2, Christmas-Day Secrets, Good-bye to Winter.

    12 Months on:

    > *Prepare for a concert of all the pieces in Book 1. (Taggart)*

Omission and sequence of pieces in later books

All of our respondents make more changes to the sequence and the choice of pieces in the later books. Most teachers skip Mozart Minuet VIII in Book 4. They all have their own individual preferences as to what should be deleted or replaced in Books 5, 6, and 7 and in which order it should be taught. All feel that supplementary material is essential at this level.

- *In Book 4, I skip the Mozart Minuet VIII, usually without a replacement. In Book 6, I replace the Bach* Little Prelude *with a Bach Two-Part Invention (usually No. 8). In Book 6, I always teach the Mozart Sonata, K. 545 before the Sonata, K. 330. It is in Books 6 and 7 that I allow myself to skip around and/or replace pieces when needed. If, for example, I have a student who is preparing a program requiring certain literature, I often will either skip to the needed piece or supplement a different one. (Powell)*

- *I skip Mozart Minuet VIII in Book 4 because of all the octaves. (Harrel)*

- *Book 4: Minuets III and VIII by Mozart are omitted because there are so many minuets in a row and few students can reach the octaves in Minuet VIII.*

  Book 5: I teach all the pieces in this book except the Bach Invention. The book ends with First Loss.

  Book 6: This book begins with the Little Prelude

  Book 7: This begins with the Mozart K. 331. (Yurko)

- *In Book 4, the Beethoven Sonata and Bach Partita are wonderful choices. The Rondo and first Mozart Minuet can be used to teach Mozart style. In addition to these, I go outside the Suzuki repertoire.*

  In Book 5, the Haydn Sonata and Bach Invention are good. I also teach more inventions at this point and other material from here on that I think is suitable for the particular child. I use the other pieces in Book 5 as reading practice.

  I usually don't teach Mozart K. 330 or K. 331 (except the last movement) to young children. Beyond this point, I use whatever I think the student needs. (Koppelman)

- *In Book 4, I do not teach the Mozart Minuet VIII. Most children cannot comfortably play octaves. Also this piece has been preceded by three other works of Mozart. Again, I supplement heavily, particularly with music from the Romantic period and the twentieth century.*

  I teach all the repertoire in Book 5. However, I do not teach all the pieces in Books 6 and 7. I select repertoire appropriate for each student, using several of the pieces from these books. (I never teach the Paderewski Minuet; I hate it.) At this level, students are able to play music from the standard repertoire; it's not necessary to follow the prescribed repertoire of the advanced level books. (Fest)

- *I do like to teach several of the Mozart minuets and the Bach Musette in Book 4; however, I have found that only the outstanding students are really able to handle the Opus 49 Beethoven Sonata and the Bach Partita movements. If I do continue with these pieces in the order they are presented, I do not see the need to teach the Beethoven F Major Sonatina in Book 5 for instance. For many students, I think it makes sense to teach the F Major Sonatina before the Sonata and even to teach another Kuhlau or Clementi Sonatina or movements from several sonatinas before embarking on the Opus 49 Sonata. I think it is also appropriate to teach some more substantial romantic literature at this point.*

  I feel that the Haydn C Major Sonata is a rather weak work. I usually substitute another Haydn sonata such as the E Major No. 13, the G Major No. 27, the E minor No. 34 (at a later point), or the D Major No. 37, and there are many other early works that are appropriate. It also makes sense to teach the Bach Invention No. 1 and possibly several others before tackling the Partita movements. The Mozart Sonatas K. 330 and 331 are both great works. However, I do not always teach them to each student, as at this level I like the freedom to choose another Mozart sonata that might better suit the individual student. I also do not like my more advanced students always studying the same literature. I would not teach both K. 330 and 331 to the same student unless they have been exposed to several other sonatas by different composers. I think it is important for them to be exposed to as many different styles and works as possible. At the upper levels the teacher must not feel confined to the same literature for every student. (Liccardo)

- *In Book 4, I use everything except the third Mozart Minuet—in order to make this piece playable for small hands you have to revise the octaves so much that the music suffers. Also, sometimes the student is not emotionally ready for the Partita (Minuets and Gigue) so we skip these temporarily and go on to the shorter Burgmüller and Beethoven F-Major Sonatina in Book 5, the Für Elise, then return to the Bach. I expect very mature and musically polished work on the Bach, and am willing to wait for the appropriate serious dedication on the student's part, rather than accept "just the notes", fast performances one so often hears of these great masterpieces.*

  A further note: the Partita is laid out in such a visually crowded way in the Suzuki edition that I require the students to purchase either the Henle or Alfred edition. The newer Book 5 is also a visual disaster and until something is done about this, I recommend finding these pieces in other editions even though it means extra trouble and expense for all concerned. How can we expect the students to enjoy reading and to learn to use the score more independently and willingly when they have to look at pages such as these?

There are too many Mozart sonatas and the one Haydn sonata included is one of the least inspired of the multitude he wrote. There is no Chopin, only rudimentary Schumann and the Paderewski Minuet is such an insignificant piece to represent that style. The jump from Beethoven's Op. 49 to Op. 31, No. 2 is ridiculous, and to require Mozart's Coronation Concerto without a taste, for example, of K. 414, 488 or 271 is also a choice I find unacceptable.

I do wish we could rework the repertoire from mid-Book 4 onwards officially, but until that time I will just continue to do what I have been doing. Once the student is in mid-Book 4 and reading well, we choose a balanced and varied diet of pieces from all periods, still listening to as much of the working repertoire as is accessible on recordings. (Taggart)

Concerns about the Suzuki repertoire

Over the years, the Suzuki repertoire has been criticized for its choice and sequence of pieces (too many pieces of similar style, big leaps in difficulty from one piece to another) and for its lack of Romantic and Contemporary selections.

- *I would suggest several changes in the early repertoire:* French Children's Song *should be later in Book 1, the use of the ¾ time signature should be delayed and there should be fewer minuets in succession with more contemporary pieces included. (Adams)*

- *I agree with those who complain about the extensive number of minuets in Book 2; that book can become tedious before finished. (Powell)*

This same respondent explained why the big jumps in the sequence of the pieces do not bother her.

- *Others feel that some of the repertoire, especially in Book 4, has big leaps in difficulty that are too extreme. My understanding is that these pieces are intentionally planted throughout the literature to elevate the student to a new plateau of playing. I, personally, have enjoyed the challenge and results of these pieces. (Powell)*

One respondent explained that the difficulty in dealing with the Suzuki repertoire can be overcome.

- *I believe the strengths of the repertoire in Books 1 to 5 outweigh the weaknesses, because it is progressive, builds on the orderly fashion of skill acquisition and allows review of older pieces to be the foundation of concrete techniques and musicality. The challenge, I have learned, is more with the teacher knowing how to effectively use the material in a productive and beneficial way. I have learned this takes time and dedication to the researching process in improving individual teaching skills rather than being a fault of the repertoire. (Williams)*

The problem of the lack of Romantic and Contemporary pieces in the standard Suzuki repertoire is a concern shared by almost everyone, although for some the problem is not as acute in the early books. One respondent explained in detail why starting with Baroque and Classical repertoire seems to be a very sound approach.

- *Before becoming a Suzuki teacher I taught extensively for 12 years, using the best contemporary methods I could find. Comparing that experience with almost 20 years now of Suzuki repertoire beginnings, I have to say that there is something inherently right, both technically and musically, about beginning with the early flowerings of piano music and working through the increasing complexity demanded by Romantic, Impressionistic, etc., as opposed to starting with contemporary single-line sound and playing and then working both forward and backward (historically speaking) in the repertoire. Each composer in the historic timeline of style development had studied and absorbed the music of his predecessors, and this knowledge of what came before is in every note they subsequently composed.*

  I have come to feel that if you have studied Bach, Mozart, Beethoven, etc., you can then play Chopin, Brahms, Debussy, Bartok, Shostakovich, Ginastera, Xenakis, Crumb, jazz, rock.... But if you start with Bartok, Shostakovich and mostly contemporary teaching pieces for years, it is then almost impossible to play Brahms, Schumann or Ravel, or Bach, Mozart and Beethoven for that matter, with any technical fluency or musical understanding of style.

  The strong points, then, of the first three books reside both in the technical demands and the preponderance of Classic and Baroque repertoire. (Taggart)

Some reasons were given to explain the difficulty of dealing with Romantic repertoire.

- *Only limited Romantic music can be found for the small child who can't pedal and/or has a limited reach. (Koppelman)*

- *Everyone notices that the Suzuki repertoire has very little music from the Romantic period, and no contemporary music. The Japanese children begin so early and are so industrious that they are often finished with the Suzuki repertoire by the time they reach age 6 or 7. That precludes using much Romantic music because of hand size and inability to reach the pedal comfortably. (Harrel)*

Another teacher explained that the absence of Contemporary repertoire can be overcome.

- *The lack of contemporary sound...can easily be remedied when the Suzuki student learns to read music, or even before that. Since so many contemporary teaching pieces readily lend themselves to rote/ear learning, these may and should be included in the students' repertoire whenever the teacher feels the time is right to do so. Also, when the ears and fingers have become comfortable with music and the piano, the students should be encouraged to improvise and make up their own pieces and explore contemporary sound. (Taggart)*

But these teachers, as well as many others, expressed their concerns regarding the lack of variety in the repertoire and strongly emphasized the need to use supplementary material.

- *The Suzuki repertoire focusses on the Classical period and is weak on all the other periods, which need to be supplemented. It also neglects to teach pedaling skills in any organized way. This also needs to be added. (Koppelman)*

- *I feel the repertoire has significant weaknesses. These include a lack of Romantic repertoire, a significant dearth of pieces which require pedaling and development of a singing tone in the right hand (dolce, cantabile), a lack of character and imagery/programmatic pieces, and a lack of pieces with a more vertical chordal makeup to prepare for the bigger Romantic works and the complexity of reading these pieces. (Taggart)*

- *The fact that there is very little Romantic literature and no Contemporary literature can become a concern as the students advance. Finding Romantic repertoire to suit young students is challenging due to its often-required big reaches, big chords, use of pedal and general virtuosity. On the other hand, contemporary literature is easy to find. Through the use of supplementary material, the absence of these materials in the Suzuki literature ceases to be a problem. (Powell)*

Supplementary repertoire

As one respondent explained, the necessity for using supplementary material to go along with the Suzuki repertoire is now generally recognized.

- *The concept of using supplementary material was included at the Chicago SAA conference in 1992, when I and other teacher trainers were asked to lead discussion groups. The issue by then was not "whether" but "what, when and how" and it became apparent that it was increasingly accepted usage. I believe there are many valid reasons for this practice. These include the stimulation, pleasure, knowledge and experience that flow from exposure to the widest range of our vast musical heritage; the satisfaction of students' personal needs; the reinforcement of particular skills; the delight, motivation and inspiration of unique repertoire ("This is **my** piece."); the development of personal taste through the selection process; awareness of a particular composer's breadth of output and evolution; the refreshment of variety for both student and teacher; the growth of the teacher through the search for new literature; and the broadened perspective resulting from exposure to a variety of styles. (Schneiderman)*

Supplementary material is also used for special events.

- *We enjoy learning Christmas music around the holidays and any popular pieces the children find on their own. Occasionally there are competition pieces we learn for participating in local events. (Yurko)*

- *We usually begin to introduce supplementary material in Book 2 but also sometimes in Book 1 for motivation or special events—for example, if I determine that a student would benefit from studying for Certificate of Merit exams or a theme festival. Some students respond very positively to preparing for and participating in musical happenings in the community. (Schneiderman)*

Students of Barbara Schneiderman after a Regional Bach Festival.

For most teachers, the supplementary material is used to broaden the students' repertoire with new styles and new periods.

- *I do recommend supplementing the Suzuki repertoire with music of contemporary composers like Bartok, Kabalevsky, Gretchaninoff, etc., perhaps in Book 2 and above. As soon as the pedal can be reached, students should experience the sonorous capabilities of the piano through easy pieces in Romantic or Impressionistic styles. Jazz pieces are certainly appropriate as well. (Harrel)*

Lists of supplementary material

One respondent referred us to her publication dealing with supplementary material.

- *Fest, Beverly. Suzuki Pianists' List of Supplementary Materials. Secaucus, NJ: Summy-Birchard, 1991. (Fest)*

Other respondents provided us with a list of the composers and types or names of pieces.

- *In Book 2, we sometimes choose a non-Suzuki Anna Magdalena Bach Notebook piece for the Bach festival. The Certificate of Merit syllabus of the California Music Teacher's Association provides a wide variety of ideas, as does Beverly Fest's bibliography. I particularly like, and find that students enjoy, Khachaturian's Adventures of Ivan and Kabalevsky's Op. 39 and 27. Some anthologies I value (and later use for sight-reading) are Denis Agay's editions. Composers Lynn Freeman Olson, Waxman, Rocherolle and Rollin are also favorites—colorful, appealing material.*

  The Suzuki repertoire is strongest in material from the Baroque and Classical periods, but we sometimes include such composers as Galuppi, Scarlatti and C.P.E. Bach. From Book 3 onward, we expand more into the Romantic, Impressionistic and Modern repertoire with several Chopin preludes, gradually moving into the mazurkas, waltzes and other treasures of the standard repertoire by Chopin, Mendelssohn, Schubert, Brahms, Debussy, Ravel, Bartok, Prokofiev, Gershwin and more. Duets also add variety. (Schneiderman)

- In the Book 3 level I teach quite a few of the Burgmüller Op. 100 pieces to give better preparation for the Chopin works to follow. Also, I like the Kabalevsky piece Op. 39 and sometimes use other sonatinas such as Clementi Op. 36, No. 5 (second and third movements), Op. 36, No. 6 (both movements), Kuhlau Op. 20, No. 1 and Op. 55, No. 2 and No. 3. I also sometimes use books or sheet music by such composers as Olson, Vandall, Hartsell, Alexander, Rollin and others.

  I very often teach several short Schumann pieces along with the Tchaikovsky at the Book 4 level and then some smaller Chopin works.

  From Book 4 on, I sometimes supplement with other volumes such as the Alfred Applause books or the Harris Celebration series as well as individual volumes and pieces like Solfeggio by C.P.E. Bach, pieces by Lichner like On the Meadow, lyric pieces by Grieg, as well as his Nocturne, Schumann's Scenes from Childhood, Bartok's Mikrokosmos and Rumanian Dances, waltzes, nocturnes and preludes by Chopin, various sonatas by Scarlatti, Haydn, Mozart and Beethoven, Two-Part Inventions and French Suites by Bach, etc. (Liccardo)

- In teaching the piano repertoire, I feel it is essential to use supplementary materials along with the Suzuki volumes. I begin in Book 2 with simple twentieth century works to help broaden the students' knowledge of sounds, harmony, and reading. Examples are as follows:

Kabalevsky:	Children's Pieces, Op. 27
	24 Pieces for Children, Op. 39
Bartok:	10 Easy Pieces, Sz. 39
	For Children, Sz. 42
	First Term at the Piano
	Mikrokosmos, Vols. 1-3
L.F. Olson, ed.:	First Steps in Keyboard Literature
Bigler and Lloyd-Watts, eds.:	Everybody's Perfect Masterpieces Vols. 1 to 4
Frances Clark, ed.:	Contemporary Piano Literature Vols. 1 to 2. (Adams)

- All the students study at least:

  J. S. Bach—Little Preludes, preludes & fugues from the Well-Tempered Clavier, Inventions—two or more.
  Scarlatti—sonatas—two to four
  Haydn—any sonata other than the Book 5 C Major.
  Beethoven—Variations on Nel cor più; Rondo, Op. 51; Sonatas, either Op. 2 No. 1,
  Op. 7, Op. 14, then later ones.
  Chopin—mazurkas, waltzes, nocturnes—at least one each.
  Debussy—miscellaneous preludes, arabesques, Pour Le Piano Suite, Rêverie, Children's Corner.
  Schumann—Scenes from Childhood and other selections.
  Brahms—one of the Intermezzi, etc.
  Contemporary (twentieth century)—Muczynski, Tcherepnin, Kabalevsky,
  Bartok, etc.

  Here are my favorite Scarlatti Collections:

  Scarlatti—Selected Sonatas (Alfred No. 108, Maurice Hinson, ed.)
  This contains the Pastorale, D minor K. 9, L. 413 in a much clearer format.
  Also, I use A Major K. 322, L. 483; C Major K. 420, L. S2; C Major K. 159, L. 104; G Major K. 146, L. 349; A Major K. 113, L. 345; G Major K. 14, L. 387 and on occasion the very difficult "changing finger" Sonata in D Major K. 96 L. 465.

  A new edition with companion CD by Vladimir Horowitz, 17 sonatas, all wonderful.
  Classic Edition D. Scarlatti Edition Peters/Sony music 1995
  First Encounters: E Major K. 531, L. 430; A Major K. 322, L. 483; G Major K. 146, L. 349; E Major K. 162, L. 121.
  Medium Difficulty: F Major K. 525, L. 188; F Minor K. 466, L. 118; F Minor K. 481, L. 187.
  Very Tricky: D Major K. 491, L. 164; D Major K. 33, L. 424; D Major K. 96, L. 465.

  In the last few years, I have been using the Applause Books I and II collections a great deal, because of the wide variety of periods and companion recordings. The student and I look at the table of contents and I mark the ones

I wish them to learn, then they listen and choose their favorites from the list. These collections, with a few deletions and additions (where's Chopin?) would make a wonderful Book 5/6 in place of what we now have, which is inadequate and unbalanced.

A final word—wouldn't it be wonderfully appropriate to place Mozart's Twinkle Variations (Ah! Vous dirais-je Maman) in Book 6 or 7 instead of K. 330, 331? Most of my students study these variations with great delight, a kind of closing of the circle. (Taggart)

• I do use supplementary repertoire, especially in the upper-level books. I am commited to developing a well-balanced diet of literature for my advanced students, thus requiring the addition of Romantic and Contemporary literature. In the early books, my students usually learn one supplementary piece annually, which is required for them to participate in a junior music festival. Otherwise, my only other reason for supplementing in the early books is to slow down the progress in the Suzuki books of the exceptionally quick student who needs time to assimilate and polish the Suzuki literature before continuing, but who also needs something fresh to learn in the meantime.

Here is a list of some of my favorite supplementary material. Much of it has been selected for small hands.

I. Romantic repertoire–(excellent for developing pedal skills and lyrical playing)

　1. Chopin

　　a) Waltzes—Book 5 and beyond

　　　1) Op. 69, No. 2 (B minor)—fairly easy
　　　2) Waltz in E Minor (no opus)—brilliant
　　　3) Op. 64, No. 1 (Minute)—a favorite
　　　4) Op. 64, No. 2 (C# minor)—contains wonderful variety

　　b) Nocturnes—Book 5 and beyond

　　　1) Op. 7, No. 2 (E♭)—a favorite

　　　2) Op. 72, No. 1 (E minor)—requires 2 against 3

　　　3) Nocturne in C# (Posthumous)—can be found in the Henle edition and in Paderewski Minor Works XVIII

　　　4) Fantaisie-Impromptu, Op.66—needs a strong Book 6 (or beyond) student. Requires 3 against 4.

　2. Mendelssohn

　　a) Songs Without Words—Book 5 and beyond
　　　1) Venetian Gondola Song, Op. 19, No. 6. (G minor)—the easiest one
　　　2) Venetian Gondola Song, Op. 30, No. 6 (F# minor)—gorgeous! Not difficult
　　　3) May Breezes, Op. 62, No. 1 (G Major)—slow, expressive, beautiful
　　　4) Spinning Song, Op. 67, No. 4 (C Major)—fast, brilliant, difficult, a good partner to go with one of the lyrical ones. Book 6 and beyond

　3. Schumann

　　Traümerei—short, lyrical

　4. Grieg

　　Notturno—Book 5 (good reader) and Book 6. Appealing, expressive. 2 against 3 skills required.

II. First concertos to study (Book 5 and beyond)

　1. Haydn

　　D major Concerto (All movements are excellent)

　2. Mozart

　　Concerto, K. 414 (All movements are excellent)

III. Collections of good supplementary literature

　1. Applause, Vols. 1 & 2 (for Book 4 and beyond)—a tape of this music is also available (Alfred Music Co.)

　2. Young Pianists Guide to Bartok (or Kabalevsky)—an audiocassette tape is included (Studio 224)

IV. Twentieth century music

1. Pinto, Run, Run!—Book 6 and beyond. Fast, brilliant, fun!

2. Kabalevsky, Sonatina in C—Book 4 and 5. The third movement is a student favorite

3. Villa-Lobos, Polichinelle—late Book 4 or beyond. Short, flashy

4. Kabalevsky, Etude (A minor)—Books 4, 5 or higher. Short, fast, easy to read

5. Bartok, 3 Rondos (No. 1 is my favorite)—Book 5 or beyond

6. Tauriello, Toccata—Book 6 or beyond. Brilliant! Easy to read, but technically difficult

V. Impressionistic music

1. Debussy, Arabesque No. 1—Book 6 or 7, contains much 2 against 3. Difficult to read. Beautiful and rewarding to study

2. Debussy, Dr. Gradus ad Parnassum from Children's Corner Suite—Book 6 and above. Dramatic, rewarding

3. Debussy, Golliwog's Cakewalk from Children's Corner Suite—late Book 5 and above. With omission of a few octaves, quite usable for small hands

VI. Duet repertoire

1. Bastien Duets, levels 1 to 4—appealing. Both parts can be played by students. Fun and light. Early level readers can use

2. Classical Album—music of Haydn, Mozart, Beethoven, Clementi, Kuhlau, Weber, Book 4 students and above (Kalmus)

3. Dances Espagnols, Op. 12 by Moskowski, Book 5 and beyond. Colorful music

4. Waltzes, Op. 39 by Brahms—No. 15 is of special appeal, Book 4 and beyond

5. George Gershwin Piano Duets—arrangements of favorite Gershwin music. Fun! Tricky rhythms. Book 4 and above (Chappell Music Co.)

6. Six Children's Pieces, Op. 34 by Arensky. Waltz (No. 4) is especially beautiful. Book 4 and above (Powell)

Here is another list of supplementary literature:

- Book 1: none

    Book 2—for reading:

    Small, Basic Timing (Alfred)
    Ayola, Winning Rhythms (Kjos)
    Frances Clark, Music Tree (Summy-Birchard)
    Frances Clark, Contemporary Piano Literature 1

    Book 3:

    Anna Magdalena Bach Notebook, Musette, Minuet in D, March in G
    Contemporary Piano Literature 2
    Aaron, Buzzing Bee
    Nevin, Toccatina.

    Book 4:

    Schumann, First Loss, Sicilienne
    Contemporary Piano Literature 3
    Dello Joio, Lyric Pieces
    Gillock, Lyric Preludes
    Schumann, Strange Lands
    Seuel-Holst, Singing Balls
    Persichetti, Little Notebook
    Tchaikovsky, Rêverie
    Goldston, Adventures of an African Boy

Book 5:

Bach, Invention in F major, Little Prelude in C major 939
Chopin, Prelude in A major, Mazurka in F major
Heller, 50 Studies
Bartok/Kabalevsky
Albeniz, Malaguena Op. 165 #3
Kabalevsky, Variations on Russian Folk Songs

Book 6:

Bach, Little Preludes (F major 927, C major 933, C minor 934), Invention in A minor
Chopin, Waltz in C# Minor, Mazurka in A Minor
Haydn, Concerto in D
Bernstein, Birds
Nin-Culmell, Tonadas (Book 2) Seguidilla Murciana
Mozart, Rondo in D
Beethoven, Rondo in C
Pieczonka, Tarantella
Khatchaturian, Sonatina in C
Kabalevsky, Sonatina in C, Variations Op. 40
Turina, The Circus

Book 7:

Chopin, Fantasie Impromptu
Tcherepnin, Bagatelles
Bartok, Rumanian Dances
Albeniz, Sonata
Grieg, Papillon, Nocturne
Tauriello, Toccata
Scott, Lotus Land
Turina, Danzas Gitanas
Schumann, Fantasie Pieces
Ravel, Sonatine
Debussy, Maid with the Flaxen Hair
Mompou, Cancion y Danza 1, 5
Mendelssohn, Scherzo, Rondo, Capriccioso

Bach

12 Short Preludes (C major 939, F major 927, C major 924)
6 Short Preludes (C major 933, C minor 934)
Invention No. 1 in C major

Inventions No. 8 in F Major, No. 13 in A minor, No. 14 in Bᵇ major

12 Short Preludes (D major 925, F major 928, D minor 926)
6 Short Preludes (D major 936, E major 937)
Inventions No. 6 in E major and No. 4 in D minor

Invention No. 10 in G major
French Suite   No. 6 in E major, Gavotte, Polonaise, Minuet
*   No. 3 in B minor, , Minuet, Trio*
English Suite No. 3 in G minor, Gavotte 1, 2

Well-Tempered Clavier I, No. 2 in C Minor, No. 5 in D Major
*   No. 6 in D Minor, No. 9 in E Major*
*   No. 1 in Ab Major, No. 21 in Bᵇ Major*
Well-Tempered Clavier II G Major

French Suite, No. 6 in E Major
Fantasia in C Minor

French Suite (No. 5 in G Major)
Italian Concerto
B♭ Partita

Concertos

Haydn, C Major

Haydn, D Major, movements 3, 1, 2

Bach, F Minor, 2nd movement
     G Minor, 1st movement
     C Minor for 2 pianos, 2nd movement

Mozart, K. 414 A Major
     K. 488 A Major
     K. 459 F Major
     K. 453 G Major
     K. 407 C Major
     K. 415 C Major
Beethoven, C Major, No. 1, 2nd movement
Mozart,   D. Minor, 2nd movement

Kabalevsky, Youth Concerto in D Major, 1st movement

Shostakovich, No. 2, 3rd movement

Beethoven, No. 1, 3rd movement
     No. 3, 1st movement
     No. 2, 1st movement

Schumann, 1

Grieg (ed. Grainger), 1

Chamber Music List

Taylor, Chamber Music Primer	*Piano, violin, cello*	*Book 2*
McSpadden, Twenty Triolets	*Piano, violin, cello*	*Book 2-5*
Alt, Red Clouds	*Piano, violin or flute, cello*	*Book 3*
McSpadden, Sonatina Concertata		
(Clementi, Kuhlau, Beethoven)	*3 violins, viola, cello, bass*	*Book 3, 4*
Blanchet, Petites Pièces en Trio	*Piano, violin, cello*	*Book 3-4*
McSpadden, Kabalevsky (Kammermusic)	*Piano, violin, cello*	*Book 3-5*
Chamber Music for Beginners (Musica Budapest)	*2 flute or oboe, 2 clarinet, bassoon, cello, 2 violin (any or all)*	
Haydn, Concertino in C (Peters)	*2 violins, cello*	*Book 4*
Chamber Music Sampler, 1-3 (Kjos)	*Piano, violin, cello*	*Book 4-7*
Rowley, Trio on English Tunes	*Piano, violin, cello*	*Book 5, 6*
Schostakovich, Three Violin Duets	*Piano, 2 violins*	*Book 5, 6*
Trios (Early Chamber Music) (Budapest)	*Piano, 2 violins, cello*	*Book 5, 6*
Johanson, Greensleeves (Willis)	*Flute, violin, cello, piano (big hand)*	*Book 4*
J.C. Bach, Quintet in G	*Flute, oboe, violin, viola, piano*	*Book 5*
Schwartz, Little Trio (MCA)	*Violin, cello, piano*	*Book 4*
McMichael, Rose Quartet	*2 violins, cello, piano*	*Book 4, 5*
Carse, Minuet/Rondino	*Violin, cello, piano*	*Book 4, 5*
Martin, Cakewalk/Paso Doble/Rumba	*Violin, cello, piano*	*Book 5, 6*

Violin and Piano

Johnson, Accompanying the Violin	*Piano, violin*	*Book 2-4*
Persichetti, Masques	*Violin, piano*	*Book 4*
Kabalevsky, 20 Pieces	*Violin, piano*	*Book 4*
Peter Martin, Little Suite, No. 1		*Book 3-4*

Accompanying the Suzuki Piano Repertoire
McSpadden, Piano Score for Triolets (2nd Piano)
Meixner, Book 1, 2, Selections from 3, 4 (1, 2 pianos)
McMichael, Book 1 to 3 (1, 2 pianos)
Anson, Second Piano Parts to Anna Magdalena Bach
Timm, Second Piano Parts to Clementi Sonatinas Book 1 (Op. 36 No 1) Book 2 (Op. 36 No. 3)
Lancaster, Für Elise, (Alfred) (2nd Piano)
Kuhlau-Riedel, Second Piano Parts, Book 2 (Op. 55 No. 1)
Burgmüller, Op. 100
Butler, Two Pianos (Boston)
(Koppelman)

While recommending the use of supplementary repertoire, one respondent pointed out the necessity for being careful in using other non-Suzuki material.

- *Care must be taken not to overshadow the basic Suzuki repertoire with too much momentum. While students should not feel a competitive urgency to move to the next book, they should have a sense of progress. Too much supplementary material has the tail wagging the dog. I personally have no problems with finding and using appropriate supplementary music; however, I would support any effort to include more styles in the Suzuki repertoire. (Harrel)*

Review

Importance of review

In the Suzuki® Method, students keep up all their pieces. Once pieces have been learned, students are expected to keep polishing them. This is seen as the key to learning the language of music.

- *The Suzuki review process is an add-on approach where students accumulate repertoire by building on the past; they continue to polish known pieces while learning new ones, just as they employ previous vocabulary as they learn new words. This results in sharpening skills and deepening acquired knowledge. (Schneiderman)*

All respondents stressed that review is an essential element of the Suzuki® Method and explained why they feel this element is so important.

- *Review of repertoire is basic to the method. It is through the continued study of pieces already learned that a child can truly develop musicianship, technique, and confidence in performing. I tell parents that in the daily practice the review is most important. (Fest)*

- *Reviewing is important because it permits the student to polish the music and be at home with it. It is necessary in order to bring the playing to a higher level of musicianship and ease. Having nothing ready to play is a discouraging feeling. (Koppelman)*

- *An essential element in the Suzuki® Methodology is the repetition of literature. As students progress through Book 1, we review earlier pieces and work on musicianship skills (shaping phrases, balance of hands, understanding of line, and form). (Adams)*

- *Reviewing is one of the most valuable tools built into the Suzuki® Method. Just as in speech we continue to add to our vocabulary, so too in building music skills we need to add to our base vocabulary using familiar notes and rhythms to help us be able to add the learning of dynamics, phrasing, musical line, tone production, etc. (Williams)*

- *For Suzuki students, review must be an essential part of their musical experience.... It is with review pieces, especially at the early levels, that we can refine skills and work on new ones. With Book 1 pieces, I very often use the review pieces to work on musical refinements such as dynamics, phrasing, shaping of the melodic line, tempo, mood, and balance. It is also with these comfortable pieces that the child can better concentrate on technical issues such as hand position and posture. (Liccardo)*

- *I consider review to be one of the Suzuki® Method's most valuable assets. It not only strengthens present playing skills of the student, but it also can be used to introduce new skills. (Powell)*

- *The role of review is extremely important, especially in Book 1. Internalization is the goal of repetition in the areas of listening and physical execution. Constant review sets in concrete the kinesthetic patterns of the review pieces. As new skills and ideas are learned in current pieces, they are demonstrated to be universal as they are applied to all the appropriate review pieces where the notes are already in place. Self esteem is also high when students have a large repertoire they can perform at any time. (Harrel)*

- *The importance of the review process cannot be over-emphasized. Just as in language acquisition, it is only through accumulation and frequent usage, an add-on process, that vocabulary is learned, maintained, digested and integrated into the deepest levels of knowledge.*

  Review, along with nurturing, listening and repetition, is vital to our method. (Schneiderman)

Some respondents really emphasized the importance of living with a piece for a long time.

- *Until becoming a Suzuki teacher, I don't think I had any idea just how intimately and well one could really know a piece, but after almost twenty years of living with the music of Books 1 to 6, it is very clear to me just how shallow the learning is of any piece that has only been played, say, for three or six months. (Taggart)*

- *Most pianists have had the experience of expending so much energy on a major work and reaching the highest degree of perfection they could attain at that time. If we review that work regularly, our fingers become more comfortable. After six months we have grown technically and musically, and can return to add more polish and expertise to a piece that has become easy. (Harrel)*

Here is a more detailed explanation of the benefit of reviewing the pieces already learned for some time.

- *If the students keep their old repertoire, and are encouraged particularly to do so with favorite pieces, they will be reminded, even on bad practice days, why they really do love music and love to play the piano. If they only work on their new projects, or current recital piece, there is too much work and not nearly enough play (pun intended) in the mix.*

  There are also other equally important reasons to keep pieces to review. Science tells us that the repetition-review process is a primary factor in brain development and coordination skills. Each time the same stimulus and same request for a specific action travels down the neural pathways, the synapses (electrical impulse connections) bridge the gap from neuron to neuron more efficiently. Unwanted connections are essentially pruned out, leading to inhibition of actions opposed to the desired activity. (This assumes that the playing activity is not allowed to become sloppy or inaccurate just because it's an old piece.) The development of inhibition—not turning on any actions other than the minimum necessary to do the job—is the essential building material of good coordination.

  Another reason is the importance of review and repetition in building the music vocabulary. Dr. Suzuki uses a comparison to language learning: the child does not cease saying a word once he learns it. Rather, he uses it over and over, incorporating it into his daily vocabulary.

  Our musical vocabulary for sound quality, articulation and melodic and harmonic patterns begins simply in Book 1, with the physical manipulations required to bring the music to life. Building upon these, the vocabulary grows best when the old words are reused, reiterated, repeated, thousands of times. Any experienced teacher has had at least several "little geniuses" who whiz through Book 1 superficially while the parents beam with pride, in spite of the teacher's best efforts to slow them down and ensure that details are correct and basic skills firmly established. When these students meet the challenges of Book 2, the lack of firm imprinting of Book 1 skills usually causes a sudden slowdown and frustration for both the students and parents—and a valuable lesson for the teacher. (Taggart)

Parents and students are informed very early about the importance of reviewing pieces.

- *Parents are told of the importance of review and the reasons for review at their first parent meeting. (Powell)*

- *I explain that one of the keys to success in Suzuki® Method is the repetition of literature. The more each piece is played, the better it sounds. The better each piece sounds, the more the students want to play it. The more they* play each song, the better their skills become and the better they feel about themselves. It becomes a wonderful cycle of learning and encouragement. (Adams)

- I tell my students that the musical mind is like a magic closet: the more you put into it and keep there, the more it can hold. (Taggart)

The analogy of learning a new language is often used to explain why students have to review their pieces.

- I would point out to parent and student that we must develop repertoire just as a child develops vocabulary in order to have command of the language. I want the Suzuki student to speak the language of music, to become comfortable and fluent with this language. All of this comes through review of familiar material. Review pieces allow the child to feel comfortable at the instrument as the technical difficulties have already been mastered. With this comfort comes confidence, poise, self-assurance and a feeling of achievement. (Liccardo)

- I present this concept to parents during our orientation through reading, discussion and observation, emphasizing its importance by explaining the mother-tongue analogy. I also describe the process very early to students, that they will be learning music the way they learned to speak when they were babies—by continuing to use and enjoy and improve familiar words as they learned new ones. (Schneiderman)

Review and weekly lesson

The percentage of time spent on review at the weekly lesson varies a great deal from teacher to teacher.

- Twenty percent of the lesson time should be spent on review. (Adams)

- I spend 60 to 90% of the lesson working with review. (Fest)

Other respondents gave percentages but explained that these amounts vary from lesson to lesson.

- It is difficult to give an exact percentage of time spent on review. It depends on the particular student and parent, how well they can learn new material on their own, how I feel the child needs to be paced at that time in their development, what time of the season it is and whether we are preparing for recitals, auditions, competitions or festivals. As a general rule I would say that I spend about 80% of lesson time on review in Book 1, 50 to 70% in Book 2, 25 to 40% in Book 3 and approximately 25% from Book 4 on. (Liccardo)

- The percentage of time given to review in the lesson does vary, with greater amounts in the beginning as our process is being established and basic skills solidly rooted—maybe one-half or three-quarters gradually diminishing to about one-fourth or one-third. However, these figures are approximate and should not be construed as immutable. It is so important to respond with flexibility to a student's needs on any given day—perhaps more help with reading, technique, motivation, interpretation or performance preparation. I aim to rotate activities from lesson to lesson to be sure that all elements are adequately covered. I periodically use Cathy McMichael's second piano accompaniments for review pieces and the children find them inspiring. (Schneiderman)

Every teacher tries to give some lesson time to review, especially in Book 1. As students become more advanced though, the time given to review during the lesson tends to decrease.

- I check their repertoire regularly. In Book 1, it is at every lesson for usually 10 minutes. In later books, the time varies depending on what we are working on. (Yurko)

- I explain reviewing as refining so we all understand what it's about. It is most important in Book 1 to build up musical recall and establish good habits of body use. At that point, I try to hear everything known so far at each lesson. In later books, I hear at least one piece to give some additional focus. (Koppelman)

- In Book 1, I hear all pieces each week. In Book 2 and beyond, I hear at least one review piece weekly on a rotating basis. Review does need to be a regular part of your lesson plans, but may not always be possible every week especially as the student advances to higher levels and the pieces get longer. I usually ask for a section of a composition at that point every week—it keeps the students on their toes. (Williams)

One other teacher explained that while she considers review very important, she recognizes that it is hard sometimes to fit it into the lesson.

- *The percentage of lesson time spent on review in my studio varies, depending on circumstances. If a graduation recital is being prepared, I often turn the entire lesson over to review for a few weeks. The same is true for the time of the year when we prepare for the National Piano Guild auditions. However, since I am highly committed to preparing my students for success, I tend to spend a lot of lesson time introducing them to new techniques and/or musical points on new pieces. This means that I do not always have time on a weekly basis to hear all the review I want to hear. When I realize I am not hearing enough over a period of a few weeks, I feel guilty and often declare that our next lesson will be primarily spent on review. I also ask periodically that each child play a review piece for the next group lesson rather than a new piece. The more advanced the students' playing becomes, the more difficult I find it to maintain the review, in spite of lengthening their lessons. Ideally, I believe about one-third of the lesson should be spent on review. (Powell)*

Review assignment

The number of pieces kept in review also varies from one teacher to another. One respondent asks his students to keep about half a book in review.

- *I usually divide Book I into two parts,* Twinkles *to* Long, Long Ago *and* Little Playmates *to* Musette. *When the student is playing* Long, Long Ago, *they are also reviewing all of the other pieces they have learned. As they begin moving into the second half of the book, I may begin to gradually drop some pieces. By the time they reach* Musette, *they generally are reviewing from* Long, Long Ago *or* Little Playmates. *I try to keep an amount of repertoire that I feel I can hear at the lesson and have enough time to do quality work. As the child moves into Book 2, I generally retain the last four pieces of Book I until about the Bach Minuet point. From Book 2 on, we usually keep about three to five review pieces in our fingers. (Liccardo)*

But generally, students are expected to keep all the pieces of one book in review. Then a certain number of pieces are kept as the student moves on to the next book. These pieces are gradually dropped as more new pieces are added to the review.

- *Review is a vital part of my program. I expect Book I students to keep all their pieces at playing level as they learn others. Our graduation recitals often consist of the entire book. This allows full familiarization of notes to help develop fluency and ease of playing.*

  Book I pieces are usually kept in a student's repertoire throughout Book 2 and sometimes beyond. (Yurko)

- *Students review each piece until they complete a Book I Recital. Then students choose four pieces they will continue to play for review. They continue to polish these pieces along with the Twinkle Variations as we begin Book 2. (Adams)*

- *Students keep reviewing Book I (plus any supplementary literature) throughout Book 2. Some will gradually replace Book I songs with Book 2 songs as we accumulate them, but I encourage maximal reviewing. Temperament is a factor here, with some children enjoying refreshment more, and others, familiarity. Book I pieces are excellent material for polishing, transposing, consolidating new skills and studying harmony. (Schneiderman)*

- *I carry over key pieces I have selected that I want students to keep reviewing from one book into the next and beyond. (Williams)*

- *After the book concert, I ask them to keep at least three or four favorites from that book going for at least a year as we move into the next book. I will periodically ask to hear these pieces and express great joy that they have kept them in their repertoire and play them so easily and well. (Taggart)*

- *My students continue reviewing Book I until they have learned about one-third of Book 2. At that point, I find most of the parents and students overwhelmed with all they have to do; often, they do nothing when overwhelmed. For this reason, I allow them to add enough pieces from each previous book to the new one to total ten and those pieces become their review assignment. This is something they feel is reasonable and I see a brighter spirit and attitude from them as a result. I continue using the pieces from Book I in as many ways as possible for a long time, however. In group lessons, we transpose, play in modes, and add different accompaniments (such as jazz) to this literature. In the private lesson, we often read Book I, once reading skills are established. (Powell)*

- *I ask students to review the pieces in each book until they complete the book. After that, we jointly choose a few important pieces to continue while working on the next book. We may call back any previous pieces if there is a particular purpose—an upcoming performance, needed reinforcement of some point etc.*

  Advanced students are encouraged to keep at least a program-length repertoire. (Koppelman)

- *Regarding review in upper books, I encourage students to maintain major pieces such as the Beethoven Sonata, Op. 49, the Bach Minuets and Gigue from the B-flat Partita, as well as other pieces they especially enjoy. (Harrell)*

- *I like students to have 20 to 30 minutes of review pieces. I also insist that all public performances be from the review repertoire and not from new repertoire. (Fest)*

Two respondents cautioned about the danger of keeping too many pieces in review. They feel the importance of reaching a balance.

- *A caution, though. As the students progress through the literature, certain pieces are worth keeping and others may, and should, be let go. The sheer volume of notes in piano music, and the time required to play them daily or tri-weekly, or on alternating days, demand that one be selective as the repertoire advances, and keep only the highest quality and best-beloved works. (Taggart)*

- *Repertoire should constantly be developed and maintained as part of their daily practicing. However, the amount of review required should be reasonable so that the student can maintain quality performances of these pieces. (Liccardo)*

Some teachers provided ideas that can help motivate students to work on their review pieces.

- *My students have one sheet each month which includes a calendar, practice list, and lesson assignments which includes their review list. They are expected to play these review lists daily. Some students enjoy having several lists which they rotate so they don't play the same pieces day after day. (Yurko)*

- *I introduce my "Hundred Days of Review Club" as soon as enough pieces are learned and a student is ready for some degree of independence. The student chooses one point from a previously compiled list of goals for improvement, plays all his review pieces for the day with that goal in mind and earns a sticker for his chart. This focus produces results quickly, teaching a student how to work alone and listen mindfully. It also improves concentration and motivation, instills thoughtful, productive study habits and paves the way for the weaning process, when parents' help gradually diminishes. (Schneiderman)*

- *The best teaching tool I have found to make sure that the review process actually takes place is the Book Concert, an adaptation of the Japanese graduation piece concept. The crowning achievement of the early years of study is the Book I concert, and no one in my class proceeds to Book 2 until they have done this. We have a home concert celebration during which the student performs every piece in Book I for an admiring audience, followed by great refreshments—anything from pizza to piano cake to a sit-down catered dinner. The students make their own invitations and concert programs, sometimes with parental help, and decide whether it will be a big party or just close friends and family. The concert is recorded for posterity and a wonderful time is had by all.*

  What began as a requirement for Book I twenty years ago has become an expected tradition for every book for most of the students, so of course they keep their old pieces, because they need them to give the concerts! (Taggart)

Two respondents explained how to make review beneficial.

- *In the lessons, I try to assign specific goals for the review each week; I usually ask that a "one-point focus" be used to improve or strengthen skills (such as balance between hands, steady tempo, good fingering, dynamics). In this manner, I hope to direct the review toward the child's greatest needs and to prevent thoughtless or meaningless review. (Powell)*

- *There are many skills to be learned and maintained in Book I. We all set priorities about which ones are most basic at the beginning. As those basic priorities are internalized, we add new skills such as balance between melody and accompaniment, phrase shaping, dynamics. These new skills are each demonstrated to be universal as they are applied to all the review pieces where the notes are already in place.*

  Review without a focus can be very boring and result in perfunctory playing. The focus could be on reinforcing the main point of the lesson for the week. That point could be technical or musical. (Harrel)

READING

Introducing reading

In the beginning, the focus of the Suzuki® Method is on developing the ear. It is only when the ear and the technical abilities are strongly developed that a third skill, reading, is introduced.

- *A Suzuki teacher develops sensitivity in all aspects of listening in all students as a first priority. This emphasis continues, achieving increasing refinement throughout study. Developing a good ear and good body use is a prerequiste for good reading ability. The beginnings are a necessary "sound before symbol" preparation for reading. (Koppelman)*

- *The teaching of reading skills is delayed until the child's aural and basic keyboard skills are established. (Powell)*

- *Reading music follows learning the basics of playing the instrument. As in a language where a baby listens, imitates, repeats, and reads, so in the Suzuki philosophy a child is encouraged to follow these steps in studying music. Reading is neither discouraged nor neglected; it is just not the first step. Teachers must present learning music following the sequence of listening, playing, and reading. Introducing reading music at the beginning of study is merely using the Suzuki repertoire to teach in a traditional fashion. (Fest)*

When learning to read music is introduced, it is seen as a very important priority by all respondents. The fact that the Suzuki® Method relies on the ear in the early stages of learning music does not mean that reading is neglected; it is just delayed.

- *I place a very high value on reading for musical literacy depends on it. Exploring and befriending the vast world of music, our great cultural heritage, is an incomparable joy for those who learn to read notation fluently. The Suzuki® Method wisely begins with the development of the ear because sound is the essence of music. Once the basic habits are established, the Variations well-launched and the names of the keys learned, we move quickly to the rudiments of reading, using other materials, because Book I is learned entirely by ear. (Schneiderman)*

There seems to be a general trend among the respondents to start pre-reading activities (rudiments of reading or basic theory) sometime during Book 1, and to start a reading method sometime during Book 1 or, more often, in early Book 2. Many respondents feel the need to spent at least 20% to 25% of the lesson time on reading and that figure can often increase to over 50% in the early stages of its introduction. This chart outlines the respondents' basic plan for teaching reading.

Plans for Teaching Reading	Suzuki Book 1	Suzuki Book 2	Lesson time spent on reading activity
Adams	Pre-reading	Reading method	At least 20%
Fest	Theory (group classes)	Reading method	Approximately 30%
Harrel	Pre-reading: early group lessons Reading method (mid- or late book 1)	Reading method continued	
Koppelman	Preparation for reading book	Reading method	
Liccardo	Pre-reading (note reading, rhythm clapping), solfège (in group classes), traditional method book (⅔ of Book 1)	Reading method continued	Between 10 and 30%
Powell	Pre-reading (at home and group classes)	Reading method	In the beginning, 50% of the lesson When reading is established, 30% of the lesson
Schneiderman	Pre-reading and group theory classes, reading and theory books	Continue reading and theory books, group theory classes	As needed
Williams	Pre-reading	Reading method	On an average 50 %
Taggart	Pre-reading in group classes Reading method (end of Book 1)	Serious work in reading method	In the beginning, at least 75 % After a few months, 50% For the next few years, never less than 25%
Yurko	Pre-reading Theory classes	Theory games and reading method	20 to 30%

- *I emphasize reading from the very first lessons. The learning of reading skills is an essential element of the Suzuki® Method.*

  In the early lessons, students spend time learning basic reading skills, then later incorporate these skills as they work through a reading method book.

  At least 20% of the lesson time is spent on reading skills and materials. (Adams)

- *I feel I put a great emphasis on reading. I want all my students to be good readers and have a solid understanding of music theory.*

  In Book 1, my students are in Music Mind Games *theory classes to learn the basics of rhythms, dictation and note placement on the staff and keyboard. There is no actual reading of music at this level.*

  In Book 2 we continue with Music Mind Games *and begin reading from a supplementary book. (Yurko)*

- *The percentage of lesson time spent on reading, as with all elements, is flexible and variable, according to the needs of the individual student. I often rotate activities and reading might involve 5 or 10 minutes or more of a half-hour lesson one week and referred to more briefly at the next in favor of technique or polishing, for example. However, in the active stages of securing reading concepts, the last half of Book 1, I try to touch base with reading progress at every lesson. (Schneiderman)*

- *Reading is of vital importance if the student is to become a good musician and an independent worker. We all know as musicians that the score must be read accurately, understood and interpreted. We need to teach students that the score is the composer's only form of communication with us today and we need to have great respect for it. In order to achieve this, it is important for the Suzuki student to be aware of what is in his music even before he is learning his pieces through reading. Certainly by Book 2, children should know the composers as well as the definition of all musical terms contained in their pieces.*

  I would recommend that about five to ten minutes should be spent on reading in a thirty minute lesson and ten to twenty in a forty-five minute lesson. As the student becomes more advanced, time is spent checking and consulting the score even in the pieces he plays well. This reinforces reading skills that are being developed in their independent reading and sight-reading material. (Liccardo)

- *Because I only start students as beginners between the ages of 4 through 6, I have found that I want children to get ear training and basic technical skills ingrained solidly in the first book. When the child is ready, I begin to do some pre-reading activities in Book I with the idea that students should begin to read when they are beginning to read at school. I have found that to delay this process any longer tends to make students more hesitant to do reading and they become remedial readers. I expect my students to do their reading assignments weekly and I do hear reading at every lesson. How much time is spent depends on many factors. (Williams)*

- *Once I begin reading music with a child, I hear some of it at each lesson. If I do not hear reading, the message I send is, "This isn't that important." Consequently, that attitude will be reflected in the home practice. I spend approximately 30% of the lesson time on reading from a series or from supplementary material. (Fest)*

- *I feel that learning to read music is a vital part of the total development of the student; thus I put a tremendous emphasis on it. I begin pre-reading experiences with my students in Book I, using Book I of* The Very Young Pianist *by Jane Bastien as a workbook to be done at home. In addition, group lessons are used partially for pre-reading experiences. I do not spend any of the private lesson time on it in Book I, however, since that book is intended for building other skills.*

  Actual reading is started at the beginning of Book 2. Feeling that the beginning is the most important time, I take extra lesson time introducing it; in the first few lessons, it is not uncommon for me to devote 15 to 20 minutes of a 30-minute lesson to reading.

  Once the reading is soundly established, I do not need to devote as much time to it; however, I generally spend about one-third of the lesson on reading with the child who is progressing adequately and I make it a habit to begin the lesson with it most of the time. I feel that all teachers need to be giving it this much time, for learning to read is a long and difficult process for most children and it requires our help and attention. I tell the parents that a minimum of four pages (and preferably more) of reading prepared weekly is needed for their child to make progress. (Powell)

- *The ability to read is such an important skill that it ranks right up with ear development, and the two senses involved in reading and hearing can be the clue to making sure no student falls through the cracks.*

  Students who find it incredibly easy to play by ear are naturally channelled toward learning through the ear. Students who are more challenged at playing by ear are probably oriented toward learning through their eyes. Teachers must individualize their instructions.

  The ear-oriented child must be made aware from day one that reading is part of piano lessons. At the outset the parent and child can sit on the sofa as the CD is playing and trace the notes in the Suzuki book with the child's finger. Reading-readiness games which include the staff, rhythm, and pitches can be played. A reading method book could be introduced in the middle of Book I. If the child is very young, one might choose a book with large notes, but the important thing is that the child understands from the beginning that reading is an integral part of lessons. It is dangerous to delay reading very long for ear-oriented children, for they (and their parents) will be so excited about their rapid progress that they may become unwilling to take the time to become literate.

  On the other hand, eye-oriented children will want to read and enjoy the decoding process. However, they need to work on ear development, so delaying reading until the end of Book I is more appropriate for them. (Harrel)

- *Music reading is an absolute must, and every effort possible should be made to ensure that no student leaves or graduates from the program without being a competent music reader. I usually officially begin the reading at the end of Book I before beginning serious work on Book 2. We have also done a lot of pre-reading work with Michiko Yurko's materials in our monthly group lessons. During this period at least 75% of lesson time is spent on reading; after a few months, 50%; then the amount is gradually decreased, but is never less that 25% for several years.*

  In order to meet the goal of every student becoming a competent music reader, the teacher must have a planned curriculum of good reading materials that covers every aspect of music reading skills imaginable and beyond.

  But just having the curriculum is not the solution. The teacher must give it paramount importance—more importance than proceeding onward in the Suzuki repertoire—for whatever time period is necessary for the particular student to demonstrate that he or she is really understanding how to decipher and not just playing by ear. This time period of dawning comprehension can last anywhere from three months to several years, and for the less visually adept it can be a terribly frustrating struggle which requires enormous amounts of understanding and sympathy on the part of the teacher and parent as to just how difficult it is. There will come a time when all students will own their ability to read music with great pride, and we owe it to them to help them get to that point no matter what effort it requires on our part. (Taggart)

This same respondent addressed the fact that Suzuki students often have the reputation of being poor readers.

- *The most often-stated negative questions or comments about Suzuki students are the ones like, "But can they read?" "I hear Suzuki students can't read" "Suzuki students hate to learn to read!"*

  Where does this come from? Partly from a sad state of affairs—there are some Suzuki teachers who don't give reading enough importance and time.

  I think this is a very big problem because the traditional piano teachers and others who make judgements about reading ability, such as church and school choir directors, are used to encountering a "visually selected" group as sight readers. Traditional piano students who sight-read well are the 10 to 20% who were visually predisposed to read piano music even before they had their first lesson. At the first and subsequent lessons with music in front of them, they were successful, so they continued to take visually oriented piano lessons. The fact that the drop-out rate for reading-oriented piano programs is about 80% (in the U.S.) after two to three years (source, a lecture by Marvin Blickenstaff), as opposed to the very low drop-out rate for most Suzuki piano teachers, ought to tell us something about the suitability of a visual-to-hand approach versus an ear-to-hand approach. The visual-to-hand only seems to work well for a small percentage of the population; the non-visually adept students (a large percentage) soon become discouraged and quit. The ear-to-hand approach, however, seems to be the ideal way to make excellent playing and advancement in the skills needed to play well accessible to everyone, not just the visually adept.

  So here we are as Suzuki teachers with nearly all our students playing very well—but with still only 10 to 20% of them sight-reading well. Does it matter? Should we go back to visual selection as the criteria for success? Of course not—but we must take every step possible to help the remaining 80 to 90% become good decipherers. (Taggart)

Teaching pre-reading and reading skills

Many respondents gave us an account of how they usually proceed in teaching pre-reading and reading skills.

- *The first reading tasks, after becoming familiar with the grand staff, involve learning landmarks on the keyboard and their matching lines or spaces on a magnetic noteboard, giving names to each. We start with a description of how the treble clef and bass clef signs evolved from an early form of the letters G and F and learn those landmarks first. As we gradually add six C's, high G and low F (related by the octave interval to the clef landmarks G and F), we also learn to read steps and skips up and down from each landmark, singing as we play "line-space, step-up, G-A" for example, becoming familiar with the sound, labels, feel and sight of a second. (Later we use the terms "seconds, thirds" etc.) Phrases so often revolve about these pivotal keys in the beginning stages and an ability to read relatively is essential.*

  We gradually move on to short tunes or shapes, which we learn to see at a glance (I cover them up), remember and play; then we add 4ths, 5ths, 6ths, 7ths and 8ves starting from each landmark. Along the route of this progression, we learn to recognize notes above or below each landmark and then to read intervals and tunes starting there. For a systematic approach we learn to ask three questions: 1) which hand plays? 2) what landmark (or nearest landmark) is the first note? 3) what is the interval, the direction, or shape of the tune (e.g., 4 skips up, 3 steps down).

  We also introduce theory and lesson collections when a student is ready. I have used a variety of materials including Glover, Frances Clark, Constance Starr's Music Road, Magic Reader, Méthode Rose, Music Machine, Julie Johnson, Resa, Hannah Smith.

  We sometimes play, in a spirit of fun, speed recognition games with landmarks in theory classes (or in lessons). I am always introducing new ideas and materials as I discover them. Both the children and I enjoy the variety and it certainly enhances the learning process.

  We sight-read holiday music and play duets in the lesson and theory classes so the children reap the benefits of their growing skills. I encourage trips to the music store for students to have the fun of selecting appropriate material which attracts them. (Schneiderman)

- *I view Book 1 as a preparation-for-reading book. When the student is listening well, and has achieved the basics of good body coordination, I introduce reading. I separate it into note reading and rhythmic reading at the beginning.*

Rhythmic : During Book 1, I have the student clap or tap beats to the Twinkle Variations *to help establish a strong sense of beat. We do it to other pieces in the book as well, especially* Honeybee *(for rests), and differentiate between* Little Playmates *and* Allegretto 2, *(2 and 4 notes to the beat),* Mary *and* London Bridge *(dotted rhythm) and* Musette *(in 2 and 6). Later we work with the metronome, tapping or playing on the piano 1, 2, 3 and 4 beat notes at different tempos, then 2, 3, 4, 5, 6 (or more) to a beat. The students use* Winning Rhythms *(Ayola: Kjos) and* Basic Timing *(Small: Alfred), playing the rhythms on the piano with the metronome.*

Note Reading: The students use a magnetic note board for basic concepts such as direction, intervals, sighting the lines of bass and treble clefs on the keyboard. They put the notes of music they have played on the board, working by ear, and identify Book 1 songs I put on the board, take dictation, etc. The approach is to add the way music looks in the score to the sound and feel of the music that they have already learned. After this, we use a variety of reading books, such as Music Tree, *putting together all aspects of reading.*

This is followed by what I call "teach it to your ear", where one or more pieces per week that have not been heard before are learned and can be put into repertoire. Here I use Contemporary Piano Literature, *(Frances Clark Library) among other material.*

This is followed by a weekly assignment of 1 to 4 pieces of music from various periods which are to be played appropriately for that period. I hear some reading each lesson. More time is spent at the beginning, since more explanation is required.

We also do short sight-reading pieces, with about 5 minutes to look it over before playing. (Koppelman)

- *Group lesson games are the ideal vehicle for presenting pre-reading essentials such as staff, rhythm, notes, intervals, etc. When a reading method book is begun, the teacher must be active in helping the child relate his pre-reading experiences to the method book presentations. Strong emphasis should be placed on reading intervalically. Once a teacher is satisfied that the child and parent have a successful practice routine for reading established, he or she only needs a few minutes in the lesson to check on progress. When a new concept is presented in the reading method, extra lesson time may be needed to cement that idea in the lesson. The teacher must always be alert to any flagging in reading results, because some parents live in a competitive environment which rewards quick results. They may sacrifice reading time in an effort to produce more pieces.*

  Companies which publish method books usually add many supplementary books at each level. If a teacher uses a method book such as the Alfred Basic Library, I recommend using all the auxiliary books as well. When children learn to read words in school, they read hundreds of books before proceeding to the next difficulty level; thus, competency is insured at each level. Reading at the piano requires not only visual-mental activity, but kinesthetic response as well. A student may be ready intellectually to understand the next level, but the muscles need much repetition to achieve complete ease. Concepts and physical motions are given many extra repetitions by using all the supplementary books at each level. (Harrel)

- *I have discovered that the students who become good readers are accompanying their choruses at school or church occasionally. These students tend to stay with music longer because they really like it and feel the reward of their years of practicing. In turn, they want to continue with the more difficult repertoire. At Christmas time, I have the children play a lot of carols and have found that they are using their ear training to help move them along at a more rapid pace in reading than at other times of the year. (Williams)*

- *Generally I begin using a reading series when a child begins Book 2. However, if the child is only four years old, I may delay starting reading. Prior to starting a reading series, I have the children in theory classes. Here they learn to read rhythms and do simple dictation. I teach the musical alphabet in various forms and apply it to the staves. The students also become familiar with the signs, terms, and notation one encounters in reading music. They become familiar with the names of the keys on the piano. Consequently, students learn rudiments of music reading before they officially begin reading music from the printed page.*

  When introducing reading, I teach the parent and child how to break every aspect of the score into steps; for example, we work with the rhythm first in each piece. Here are the steps we follow as we work with rhythm:

  1) Mark dashes under every note for its rhythmic value—quarter notes get 1 dash, half notes get 2 dashes, etc.

  2) Tap the rhythm as we count it aloud

  3) Count aloud as we play the piece

The other step involved at the beginning of the method book is the reading of notes. Before playing the notes, we discuss: 1) steps and skips; and 2) directions up and down. I write the steps I want followed in the child's method book, and it is understood that every piece learned at home is to be broken into these steps before it is played. As the method books begin adding new musical symbols and concepts to be understood, the student learns to scan the score before playing and to discuss each of these before playing the music. (Powell)

- I spend at least $\frac{1}{4}$ of the lesson hearing what reading piece(s) the child has prepared. As each piece is read at home, the child and parent make a check mark on the page when the piece is played completely. Stickers show how many times the piece has been played without mistakes. When I open the music book, I will know the ability the child has to play that piece.

After I hear the piece in lesson I use a system of colored self-adhesive dots to mark the progress. If the piece is mastered, I put a blue dot near the title. If it needs more practice, I put on an orange dot. If the child tries a brand new piece in the lesson (sight reading), I put a green dot near the title. We all like using these dots.

The important skills we use for reading are:

1) playing a piece hands together from the onset

2) not looking down at our hands—a piece of stiff paper held over the hands works very well

3) not going back to play notes that were played incorrectly

4) rehearsing the hands separately after several initial playings

5) playing the entire piece accurately (Yurko)

Recommended reading materials

The respondents recommended many reading materials (pre-reading, reading methods, supplementary reading material).

Pre-reading material	Adams	Fest	Harrel	Koppel-man	Liccardo	Powell	Schnei-derman	Taggart	Williams	Yurko
The Very Young Pianist (Bastien)	•					•			•	
Winning Rhythms, Ayola, (Kjos)				•						
Basic Timing, Small (Alfred)				•						
Music Mind Games, Yurko (Warner Bros.)			•					•		•

Reading material	Adams	Fest	Harrel	Koppel-man	Liccardo	Powell	Schnei-derman	Taggart	Williams	Yurko
Music Tree/Time to Begin, Frances Clark		•		•			•	•	•	
Music Road, Constance Starr	•	•	•			•	•		•	
The Progressive Pianist, Books 1 and 2, Katherine Beard					•					
Alfred Series	•		•		•			•	•	
Alfred Duet Books					•					
Bastien Series			•			•			•	
Glover Series	•*						•			

* notespeller only

Reading material	Adams	Fest	Harrel	Koppel-man	Liccardo	Powell	Schnei-derman	Taggart	Williams	Yurko
Eckstein Piano Course, Books 1 to 3					•					
Piano Adventures (Faber and Faber)	•									
Now I Can Play, Gillock								•		
Easiest Piano Course, Books 1 and 2, John Thompson					•					
Reading Keyboard Music, C.W. Reid (Demibach Society)			•							
Making Music My Own, Catherine McMichael (Lorenz)										•
Magic Reader							•	•		
Méthode Rose							•			
Music Machine							•			
Julie Johnson							•			
Resa							•			
Hannah Smith							•			

Supplementary material	Adams	Fest	Harrel	Koppel-man	Liccardo	Powell	Schnei-derman	Taggart	Williams	Yurko
Supplementary Solos/ Contemporary Piano Literature, Frances Clark Library	•			•		•	•	•		
Kabalevsky	•						•	•	•	
Music for Millions		•			•		•	•	•	
Encore	•							•	•	
Applause	•							•	•	
Masterpiece Classics									•	

- *I use many reading materials to teach and encourage reading. There are so many basic reading methods, all of which can be effective if taught well. The two which I use most frequently, because I find them particularly effective with very young children, are Constance Starr's* The Music Road *and Francis Clark's* The Music Tree. *(Fest)*

- *If the child is very young and does not read words, I use* The Music Tree: Time to Begin *and a magnet board; if the child reads words, we use the Alfred Series 1A and 1B, magnet board, flash cards, and* Now I Can Play *by Gillock, plus other supplements. (Taggart)*

- *I like* Music Road *by Constance Starr for two reasons: (1) there are a multitude of examples providing physical reinforcement, and (2) the melodies remain in one clef and one hand for several measures, encouraging fluent intervalic reading. Beware of methods that skip from one clef to another every few notes; the mental adjustment needed slows down the reading. The Alfred and Bastien series are well-organized and popular. Although I have not personally used* Reading Keyboard Music *by C. W. Reid (revised), published by Demibach Society, P.O. Box 7092, Stockton, CA 95207, some teachers are very excited about it. (Harrel)*

- The following reading materials are excellent sources:

  Piano Adventures, *Lesson, Theory, and Technic Books* (Faber and Faber)

  Music Road, *C. Starr*

  Thirty Notespelling Lessons, *Primer to vol. 2* (Glover)

  Prep Course for the Young Beginner (Alfred)

  Sight reading materials differ from the aforementioned materials, to include:

  holiday materials

  Sight Reading Unlimited *1B* (Alfred)

  Line A Day Sight Reading, *Vols. 1 and 2* (Bastien)

  easy/big note pop music

  duets

  numerous one-page reading examples from standard classical literature. (Adams)

- *I use a variety of method books for reading instruction. We begin with* The Music Road, *Book I, by Constance Starr. She, a Suzuki teacher, knows the value of repetition; she includes countless pages of reading seconds and then thirds. The large print of the book adds extra appeal. Next, we move into the Bastien Basics and the books that accompany it (Performance, Technic, and Theory). We begin with the primer and continue with Books 1 through 4. Upon completion of these, we move into the Frances Clark Library, beginning with Level 1 and continuing through Level 6 of this excellent series. This series includes Piano Literature, Contemporary Piano Literature, Supplementary Solos (includes jazz pieces) and Piano Technic in each level. I omit the Piano Literature because it contains so much of our Suzuki Book 2 repertoire. I prefer to use the Bastien Intermediate Theory books, levels 1 through 3, while playing in the Frances Clark Library.* (Powell)

- *I use Christmas carols and sheet music by various composers such as Palmer, Olson, Glover, etc. as supplementary reading material for beginners.*

  After level 2 and 3 of the method books, I like to use other classical literature for reading. I often use Kabalevsky Op. 39, the Repertoire 3A and 3B of the Pathways Music Course by Lynn Olson, Burgmüller Op. 100 and various collections such as Essential Keyboard Repertoire, published by Music Millions - Easy Classics to Moderns, edited by Agay; Everybody's Perfect Masterpieces, edited by Watts and Bigler and again various pedagogical pieces written by Olson, Nevin, Rollin, Vandall, Hartsell, Goldston and others. (Liccardo)

- *We have a reading and theory method we use in conjunction with the Suzuki® Method in Books 1 to 7 to try to insure that our Suzuki students are also good music readers and good musicians in the area of theory. But it won't work if not pursued consistently and it should not require me to spend private lesson time on it to any great degree.*

  *Their reading and theory method consists primarily of magnet board, flashcard games, and texts which are the best available ways I have found to enable ways for students and parents to do this work without **me** constantly assigning and checking it. This list is given to all parents every year when they receive the new schedule:*

  Required:

  Early readers and those having difficulty with note identification should do magnet noteboard work and flash card work every day as a normal part of practicing for six months to a year or more.

  After and during initial magnet note work, use Alfred Books 1A and 1B Lesson Book and Theory Book. Do theory workbooks consistently according to the pages they match as directed in the book. Add Gillock: Now I can Play, Books 1 and 2 published by Willis. Also, two books which are great for this level: A Celebration of Notes, by Jane Bastien, Book 1 and 2, published by Kjos. Also try Sticking with the Basics and Dot to Dot. Also possibly Solo Repertoire for the Young Pianist, Vol. II (early elementary level), ed. by Gillock (Willis).

  Continue flash card work until effortless. Go on to Gillock: Accent on Solos, I, II, III. Add Note Speller II, D'Auberge Series (Alfred pub.)

  Next, do Gillock: Accent on Majors, followed by Accent on Majors and Minors. These are the scale and cadence fundamental texts and contain many essential reading puzzles to solve. Continue flash cards if necessary.

  Duet work: basic are Two at One Piano, Vols, I and III, followed by The Joy of Duets. Also use Music for Millions, Vol. 17 for sight reading.

Advanced students:

Every student in higher groups should own and be working in the following two texts, and understand the theory in them in order to get the most from their studies:

> *By grades 7, 8, and 9, the students should be doing the brown book,* Intervals and Chords: How to Use Them, *by MacCarteney and Pabst (Willis).*

> *By high school they should move into the green book,* The Language of the Piano *by Priesing and Tecklin (Schirmer).*

Also, for optional use:

> Supplementary Solos, *level 1 and many level 2, from the Frances Clark Library. (Birch Tree Group)*

> Contemporary Piano Literature, *Vols 1, 2, Frances Clark Library*

> Patterns *by Paul Sheftel & Vera Wills (Alfred)*

For more advanced readers:

> More Classics, Romantics, Moderns, All Time Favorites *No. 103, (C. Fischer)*

> Lyric Preludes in Romantic Style, *Wm. Gillock (Summy Birchard)*

> Applause, *Bk. 1, ed. L.F.Olson, Alfred No. 2537. Cassette available also.*

To explore jazz:

> Jazz, Rags and Blues. *Books 1 and 2 by Martha Mier (Alfred)*

> Sunshine and Blues *and* Swing Street *by Arletta O'Hearn (Kjos)*

For the lighter side, a contemporary sound, with nice harmonies, try things by Robert Vandall, Dennis Alexander, Jerry Ray

For New Orleans sound, Dixieland-type things, look at Wiliam Gillock's three volumes of New Orleans jazz plus other sheet music, blues, etc. (Taggart)

- *The materials I use vary, but I have found success with the* The Music Tree *(Francis Clark), the James Bastien series, the Alfred series, and I use some of the accompanying books from those series. I like to move into the Kabalevsky short pieces after the second level, and from that point I tailor it all to keeping the child motivated through the specific needs and likes of the student, from visual appeal to the actual sound of the music. I include technical study books like* Dozen A Day, Hanon, Czerny, Burgmüller *Etudes, repertoire books such as* Encore, Applause, Masterpiece Classics, *Clark repertoire books, jazz books and* Music for Millions, *which include literature from all periods of music so that the child has a rich diet. I intentionally want to hook the child on liking to read. I always use original works and not reductions because there is so much good literature to use. If students want to learn reductions of popular songs, I encourage them to do this on their own time. However, I ask them to bring the music to their lesson if they have a problem with any of it. My experience is that they find the standard literature overall more rewarding of their time and they are proud to be able to play both kinds of repertoire. I think a lot of this is perhaps because I do keep an open door to their likes in their growing-up stages but will not apologize for not devoting significant time in the lesson for the "popular" literature. (Williams)*

Learning to read the Suzuki repertoire

At one point, students become able to read the Suzuki repertoire. The transition usually happens somewhere in Book 2. This is where teachers expect students to understand certain elements of the written piece. By Book 3, students are able to read a good part of the music and even to read the full piece.

- *It varies when my students begin reading their Suzuki pieces since it is a gradual process. As a general guide, the music is up on the music stand in Book 2 and the child may understand bits and pieces of what's happening. In Book 3, they are reading a good part of their pieces and by Book 4 they are in full swing. The exception is an older student; a 10-year-old in Book 2 will be reading more fully than a 4- or 5-year-old in Book 2. I ask parents to photocopy their Suzuki music when the child begins reading it and to enlarge it to 11" X 17" each page. Suddenly the reading becomes so much easier with big music. (Yurko)*

- *About half way through Book 2, reading of the Suzuki literature is started. Cradle Song and Melody are excellent reading choices. By the time students reach Book 3, all Suzuki repertoire is read. (Adams)*

- *Beginning in Book 2, we learn by a combination of ear and eye. (Schneiderman)*

- *Some of my students begin reading the Suzuki repertoire in late Book 2. By Book 3, I insist that they all use their reading skills to help learn this literature, regardless of their degree of proficiency in reading. I have learned that it becomes too difficult if you wait until the later Suzuki books to make that transfer. (Powell)*

- *By mid-Book 2, I usually have students learning selected sections through reading the music. In some of the Bach minuets for instance, I will ask that they learn the first section with the right hand alone (Minuet 1), or the left hand alone (Minuet 3). Even after they have learned an entire piece by reading, they usually memorize immediately and prefer to make corrections by looking at the keyboard rather than the music. If this is the case, I will usually ask them to find it in the music and read it. I also ask them to do slow, hands-alone practice eyes on the music to keep them in touch with the score. (Liccardo)*

- *It is impossible to tell to what extent a Suzuki student is actually reading Suzuki repertoire, since they have heard it before. I expect my students to be able to identify where different themes and sections are on the page early in Book 2; to be able to track the music and find the fingering by the end of the book. By Book 3, at the latest, they can play wherever I may point. (Koppelman)*

- *Usually by the time students are learning Bach's Minuet 3, they are deciphering a great deal of the Suzuki repertoire. By the first Sonatina in Book 3, we are always using the score for learning as a reference, but still memorizing immediately as we go.*

  A small item, but one which helps a great deal: from Book 2 Minuet 3 on, until Book 4 if not further, students are responsible for finding and highlighting (yellow) every note in the score that is altered by the key signature before they begin to work on that piece. For example, in the G-minor Minuet they must locate and highlight every B and E which is on that page. (Taggart)

- *As with all learning, some children learn to read faster than others. Therefore, I do not have a specific point at which children should use reading to learn the Suzuki repertoire. They begin applying reading skills to Suzuki repertoire as soon as they are able. For most children this happens somewhere in Book 2, for others not until Book 3. (Fest)*

- *I like to start the transition into reading Suzuki material in Book 2. Students are able when they reach Minuet 1 to easily play, hear, and visually recognize intervals. After the child has learned Minuet 1 by ear, I ask them to watch the score and play right hand alone, naming each interval before they play. Now they realize that they have the skills to read their Suzuki material. If the transition into reading Suzuki material is made too rapidly, some visually-oriented students rely on their sight and tend to stop using their ears. That is the reason for insisting that they first learn Minuet 1 by ear and then look at it from a reading viewpoint. The same process can be applied to other Book 2 pieces. By Book 3, students should be reading Suzuki material, although they are never reading from scratch because they are listening to the CD. Therefore, it is essential to continue using other materials which they must read without having heard the sound. (Harrel)*

Sight-Reading

Respondents clearly differentiated between reading and sight-reading and presented those as two distinct abilities.

- *I do differentiate reading from sight-reading although in the beginning they are similar. Reading skills need to be adequate to learn new material with relative ease and accuracy through practice at the current playing ability. Sight-reading fluency is usually around two levels below playing level and requires accuracy and musicality in a first viewing of new material. (Schneiderman)*

- *Sight-reading is begun as soon as the student has some basic reading skills. I distinguish between reading and sight-reading with my students by explaining that the reading assignment involves the learning of new musical concepts, notations, etc., which take more time and repetition to prepare, while the sight-reading consists of musical material at an easier level which the student is challenged to play well in one reading. I use the Bastien Sight-Reading Books, Levels 1 through 4. Once these are completed, I have a collection of many various books that I lend for additional sight-reading. (Powell)*

- *Sight-reading, by my definition, means students have a piece of music placed before them for the first time and they learn how to read the meter, key signature, scan the music, set a tempo by counting and play. That music is taken away and another piece is tried. I begin by using simple two- or four-bar excerpts and gradually build their confidence and skill so that they can feel a sense of accomplishment. (Williams)*

- *There is most definitely a clear distinction between reading and sight-reading. Over the course of a week, a student may be able to accurately learn a new piece that he has never heard. This demonstrates that they can read the notes, locate them on the piano, accurately interpret the rhythm and put the hands together. However, to coordinate all of these skills at the same time on a first reading is very different. Sightreading must be done with materials that are several levels below the student's actual reading level. The most important skill here is the ability to keep the beat, even if it means ignoring mistakes and leaving out some the notes. Accuracy increases with experience. I do give my students time to scan the piece before playing it. (Liccardo)*

- *I definitely differentiate between learning to read and sight-reading. I choose to use the summer as a real focus on sight-reading. The children are assigned a minimum number of pages to sight-read over the summer, based upon their playing level. Rather than lend music for sight-reading, I show the parents appropriate material for the student's level and have them go to the music store and browse. Throughout the summer the children report at each lesson how many pages they have sight-read. I also have them sight-read at lessons. This is a team effort for the studio, as we add together the number of sight-reading pages completed by all the students. This project is not optional. I find the children improve remarkably by using this "Summer Sight-reading Project." I encourage sight-reading throughout the year and we sight-read in the theory classes. However, by making it a top priority for 3½ months, the children are inspired and can see the progress possible by daily sight-reading. This project also impresses the parent and underscores the need for routine in learning to read music. (Fest)*

Another teacher differentiated between a competent music decipherer and a good sight-reader.

- *Every student that we teach has the ability to become a competent music decipherer even if dyslexic or otherwise visually impaired. I use the term decipherer on purpose to differentiate that primary goal from the secondary one, which is to help produce a good sight-reader.*

  To help and sometimes to insist that the student become a good decipherer is always possible; to guide the student to become a very good sight-reader is sometimes not possible to accomplish in the time frame we have in their lives. Mostly this is because all the mechanisms and eye organizations that go on in good sight-reading at the piano are not clearly understood yet. There are lots of theories and excellent drill books and exercises available, and I've tried many of them, with varying degrees of success. The subject of sight-reading is too complex to examine in detail here. (Taggart)

MUSICIANSHIP

The elements grouped under this heading—improvisation, keyboard harmony, transposition, composition, ear training, sight-singing, music history, theory—are not considered to be essential components of the Suzuki® Method. Nevertheless, all respondents seem to agree on the importance of developing musicianship. The following quotations express the feeling of many respondents :

- *I don't think these skills are related specifically to the Suzuki® Method, but rather to developing good overall musicianship and understanding in any music student. (Liccardo)*

- *All of the elements under Musicianship are very important to the development of a complete musician, and I try to weave them into the fabric of the lessons and group classes whenever possible. (Taggart)*

Although teachers recognize the value of developing a complete musician, they differ in the importance they give to each one of these elements. Time constraints are often the primary factor explaining the difficulty in dealing with all of these matters.

One respondent stated her position as follows :

- *Piano teachers can become frustrated by the number of things they are expected to teach. Even worse, they begin to feel inadequate and guilty for not teaching everything. One must make priority choices in accordance with how many varied things can be taught well in the time allowed. This problem is the biggest argument for having a group lesson weekly in which the teacher's time is used efficiently. Therefore, I choose transposition, improvisation and theory as priority choices. (Harrel)*

Transposition, keyboard harmony, improvisation, composition

Transposition is a skill taught by many teachers in the early stages. They ask students to transpose the Book 1 pieces and often use the group lessons for these activities. Improvisation and composition are encouraged but very few teachers systematically teach those skills. They often rely on their students' own interest in initiating and pursuing musical composition. Keyboard harmony is sometime taught, most often in relation to theory. Most respondents say very little about developing those skills after Book 1. A few teachers mentioned, however, that they regularly work on keyboard harmony, transposition and improvisation at the intermediate and advanced levels.

- *Transposition is a skill that I work to develop through group lessons. Making regular assignments, I use the Suzuki Book 1 pieces in the beginning and then we move gradually to harder pieces.*

    Keyboard harmony is taught in the private lessons, primarily with the use of theory books, and is supplemented through group lessons.

    Improvisation and composition get less time than I would like them to get. We do a little in group lessons, but mostly it comes from the attention given them in their theory books. A few of my students who are unusually interested and talented in this area are taking composition lessons with another teacher, due to my encouragement.

    All of these areas are left to the individual teacher to develop in the Suzuki® Method. While they are not considered to be of primary importance to the method, they all relate to it because they serve the purpose of developing the complete musician. (Powell)

- *Some of my students transpose their Book 1 pieces. Each recital I try to have a different theme—it may be that each of the students play their recital piece plus an original improvisation of a Suzuki piece or an original composition. This is always very successful. (Yurko)*

- *I have the child transpose many of the Book 1 pieces into multiple keys and encourage them to make up their own pieces. Our group classes build on these things at all levels. Due to lesson time constraints I probably do not do as much as I could in the lesson but feel that through groups they have the resources to build on these skills. I believe that all of this trains a well-rounded music student, Suzuki or otherwise. (Williams)*

- *Transposition, keyboard harmony, improvisation, and composition are practical skills for the young pianist. All of these skills are included in the TMTA (Tennessee Music Teachers Association) theory portion of auditions. (I was one of the authors of the TMTA Theory Tests.) Instructional materials and study guides are a part of the preparation process.*

    All of the aforementioned skills are related to the Suzuki® Method, in that they are necessary skills for the well-rounded musician. The goal of the Suzuki® Method is to produce complete musicians and human beings, not contest winners or piano prodigies. (Adams)

- *Transposition of Book 1 pieces gives children many different kinesthetic experiences and a knowledge of keyboard geography. It helps to prepare them for the jump in difficulty level which occurs in Book 2.*

    Improvisation is especially important for Suzuki students, because we require such a high level of perfection in the playing of their Suzuki pieces. The repetition needed to achieve that perfection can result in a loss of spontaneity and freedom at the keyboard. The antidote is improvisation where anything is allowed. (Harrel)

- *I give minimal time to transposition, keyboard harmony, improvisation, and composition. It is not that I dismiss these skills as unimportant; there is simply not enough time to do everything I would like to do. I do work with* transposition in Book 1 and also in the reading series. I work with keyboard harmony in theory classes so that students learn to read chord symbols and also to play simple pieces by ear with various styles of accompaniment. Occasionally I work with improvisation in theory classes. I do little with composition. However, if a student is interested, I certainly encourage it. All of these activities enhance a student's musicianship and therefore are valuable in the Suzuki® Method or any other method of teaching piano. (Fest)

- Transposition: In their musicianship classes we use a movable do system. As soon as they learn how the staff works they immediately begin writing in many different keys. The instructor marks do with an X anywhere on the staff and the student has to recreate what they hear based on that do. As far as transposing at the keyboard, I don't do too much of it too soon. By working constantly in the key of C with the early Suzuki repertoire, children begin to tune in to those pitches as many string players can sing an A. I think it helps develop perfect pitch. I do have students transpose some of their reading songs later on, usually into all of the keys they have been exposed to up to that point.

  Keyboard Harmony: From the very first chords we play, we identify them as I chords or V chords, etc. At this early stage we do not discuss the theory that explains this labelling. However, at the sonatina level, they begin learning how these chords are formed in their musicianship classes. They then proceed to harmonize melodies with basic I, IV and V chords in the keys of C, G and F. As they become more advanced they deal with more advanced chord progressions.

  Improvisation and Composition: Both of these skills are touched upon lightly in their musicianship classes. They do some work with improvisation on the xylophones used in their classes. They may compose question and answer phrases and harmonize them. We do offer classes in both improvisation and composition for more advanced students. (Liccardo)

- I encourage literal transposition to other white keys in Book 1, and make sure they transpose at least two or three songs, if they have not already discovered transposition on their own, which many do.

  Improvisation comes next, which brings with it both composition and an unconscious use of keyboard harmony. It is important to let the parents know that you officially approve of the students making up things and that this activity is also an excellent way to have the student start the practice session for the day on their own, while the parent is getting ready to come in to do practice on the regular work.

  I have been really amazed at the results of the permission and encouragement to fool around in the early years as the student advances. I have seen some wonderful, complex, advanced pieces which have been notated on computers; jazz and rock combos which get paid to perform, arrangements and original compositions performed by school bands—quite a harvest considering that all I really did as a teacher was encourage it and help with the musical tools needed. The inspiration and hours of perspiration are totally student-generated. (Taggart)

- We do some transposition of the Twinkle Variations and a few Book 1 songs that lend themselves to this activity. When a child shows particular interest in transposition, improvisation, keyboard harmony or composition, I pursue it more vigorously to provide the stimulation and information for fuller development. It is important to be sensitive to such inclinations, for we may be in the presence of a future conductor or composer, if not concert pianist. Some students will naturally vary the ending of a song, for example, to express their creative spirit. Within reason, I welcome these excursions, and see them as signs of originality and musicality to be encouraged.

  In later phases, we transpose cadences to many keys, starting simply and progressing through gradually more complex chord sequences. I include keyboard harmony regularly in our workout project to help establish a feeling for harmonic logic. We thoroughly explore one tonality with scales, triads and their inversions, progressions and arpeggios, including improvisation. I like the children to become very familiar with the terrain of a key, feeling a muscular as well as cognitive and aural familiarity.

  Even such a simple improvisation as hand-over-hand triads up to four octaves can sound delightful if played musically. It offers the opportunity to explore all the stuff of music as students experiment with the many ways to vary these three notes—melodic order, phrasing, legato/staccato, blocked/broken, pedal option, dynamics, shaping, tempo and combinations of all these. Then they have insights to bring to their perceptions of "what the composer did with A Major" for example. This process opens the student's mind and ears to the details of other people's music in a fresh way, with more depth, understanding and appreciation.

  One of the Suzuki® Method's essential features is development of a fine ear for music. Students absorb music to an unconscious level where it is deeply and naturally integrated into their lives. These creative skills and activities are *logical outgrowths and extensions of the inherent spontaneity Suzuki students feel with their instruments and with music. They take students farther along a road they already travel, providing cognitive, imaginative and aesthetic windows into the workings of the music which has already been deeply engrained aurally, tactilely and emotionally. (Schneiderman)*

Ear training and sight-singing

In the early stages, the Suzuki® Method is based on the ear, and teachers all agreed on the importance of developing a strong musical ear. While some rely on the learning-by-ear approach to develop ear training skills, others add specific listening exercises like interval identification, dictation, etc. While some teachers ask their students to sing, very few actually teach sight-singing.

- *Ear training is the key to starting a child before he can read and is the main focus of the Suzuki® Method. Therefore the teachers must always be on the guard for themselves and the parent to not slip into rote teaching. I have children sing steps and skips back to me, sing the melody of pieces and later on sing printed intervals which eventually become four-bar phrases. (Williams)*

- *The Suzuki approach is ear training. I teach basic solfège, movable do. I wish I had more time or available classes for this. (Koppelman)*

- *We regularly practice taking melodic dictation as part of our* Music Mind Games *theory classes. I feel this is the most valuable tool to understanding how to read music. (Yurko)*

- *Ear training is an essential element of the Suzuki® Methodology. A University of Tennessee professor of music (and father of one of my former Suzuki students) developed several ear training programs exclusively for our Suzuki piano students. This is a favorite class in our group lesson offerings. These computer programs are available for sale to the students in our program and to the general public. (For further information about Kid CAT Curriculum for Aural Training contact Mark Boling, 4915 Westover Terrace, Knoxville TN 37914.) (Adams)*

- *We sing all the time, especially inner voices and RH parts while the LH plays, but we don't really do sight-singing per se. The ear training seems to take care of itself because of the listening. (Taggart)*

- *Our students develop ear training skills in their very first musicianship classes. They learn to use their voices to match pitch, begin singing and identifying basic melodic patterns using solfège and eventually do more advanced sight-singing and dictation. (Liccardo)*

- *I work with ear training, but not sight-singing in the theory classes. In working with fundamentals of music, I want the children to hear as well as play and write. Consequently, scales, chords, intervals, melodies, harmonic progressions, and rhythms need to be taught and comprehended aurally, and not taught only through writing or playing. Playing, writing, and hearing complement one another and work toward developing a deeper understanding of music. These abilities are not taught as mere abstractions or exercises, but are used in learning, memorizing, and performing repertoire. (Fest)*

- *Suzuki students' ears tend to be wonderful because it is a listening-based approach. In addition to listening to tapes or CDs of the literature, we also help them listen more acutely through a demonstration-imitation approach in our teaching. Since I am aware that the finest pianists (and musicians) are those who listen to themselves when they play, I feel that good ears are extremely important. One of the most important reasons for the follow-the-leader game that I play with my students in Suzuki Book I is to train their ears to hear intervals. I begin with simple five-finger patterns for them to imitate; initially it is done with eyes open, but later the students close their eyes so they are dependent on ears only to imitate my playing. It is fun to make the patterns harder and harder as time goes by; I never cease to be amazed and delighted at what Suzuki students can hear! Ear training is also done at every group lesson without exception. We learn to hear: 1) all the intervals; 2) major scales and natural, harmonic, and melodic minor scales; and 3) major, minor, diminished, augmented, natural, diminished seventh, dominant seventh, major seventh, and minor seventh chords in root position as well as inverted. While we do not do sight-singing, we do melodic and rhythmic dictation, beginning this very early in the group experiences. (Powell)*

- *We play listening games (i.e., ear training) from the very first lesson and we continue later in noteboard work and theory classes to emphasize the sounds of the various elements we study (intervals, major/minor) as well as their names, their visual appearance (on staff and keyboard), their feel on the keys and the ability to reproduce them (dictation), at first with magnets on the board and later drawing them with pencil on paper.*

The children also learn in theory class to sing a major scale—using do re mi, 123 and CDE, etc.—and also intervals, singing: 1-2 is a second, 1-3 is a third, 1-4 is a fourth, etc. as I accompany on the keyboard. We do much singing and "signing" tunes (based on 5-note scales) from do to sol, using a simple variant of the Kodaly hand signs, moving vertically up and down in the air. The students imitate my sounds and signs in echo fashion and learn them readily. This large muscle parallel to the rise and fall of the lines deepens their intuitive understanding of melody and captures bodily the essence of music reading.

One hears that pianists are inclined to develop lazy ears because our pitches are provided for us. To play our instrument we don't need the keen pitch perception required, for instance, for accurate intonation on a string instrument. Singing insures that we learn to hear with precision sufficient to actively reproduce pitches.

We also learn to identify parts of Suzuki songs from the magnet board staff, requiring an inner audiation similar to sight-singing. Later our ear training advances to distinguishing major, minor, perfect, diminished and augmented intervals, inversions, cadences, the four qualities of triads, seventh chords, progressions, three kinds of minor scales, etc.

In a sense, technique and all other aspects of music-making rely on the ear and develop the ear because we can only produce on the keyboard what we are capable of imagining inwardly. Tone quality depends on an aural fine-tuning as we hone our sound and listen for shades of difference. Similarly, interpretation with subtlety and nuance, and even concentration itself equates with listening refinement. One can only be attentive to slight gradation and variation in detail with intense focus and concentration. Asking students for this kind of careful listening helps them develop it. (Schneiderman)

Music history

All the teachers recognized the importance of acquiring some basic notions about musical styles and forms in order to develop good musical interpretation. Some provide that information at the private lessons as students are introduced to new pieces, others teach the subject more formally in the group class. Studying the different musical periods and the life and music of composers are the most common ways of approaching music history.

- *Understanding music history and style is important in musical interpretation, so I begin early having my students learn about them. Using my group lessons, we study a different period of music each year. First, I present a story about the period being studied, trying to give them some basic understanding of historical and stylistic characteristics of that time period. Before the next group meets, I give the students a study sheet of all we learned so they can be prepared for a game and quiz about that period at the next group. Later in the year, the students bring in reports about composers of that period; I also try to take them to see and play period instruments when possible. To further heighten their awareness, I ask that the students announce the title, composer and music period of the pieces they are playing at group lessons; after they perform, we often discuss why that piece sounded like the period to which it belonged. As they mature in their knowledge and understanding, I frequently play a piece unknown to them and have them guess the correct period. The parents frequently express their excitement and pleasure in all they have learned about music through our study of the periods; they feel they can now listen to classical music and understand and appreciate it more fully. (Powell)*

- *The introduction of music history and general music history facts is necessary to help complete the students' curriculum. The understanding of the musical period of each composer, historical events surrounding the years of the composer's life and his compositions, the development of specific forms indigenous to the period, and the style of composition for each era are all necessary elements which help to formulate an understanding of each composition.*

Rebecca Stout, a teacher in our Suzuki program, has written two books entitled Previews, Books 2A and 2B, *which are excellent supplements to Suzuki Book 2. These books include materials on each composer, musical period, historical period, forms, terms used within the book, and general practice aids. These books have added a new dimension to my teaching and to the knowledge gained by my students. (For further information contact Rebecca Stout, 5416 Holston Hills Rd., Knoxville TN 37914. Call 1-800-367-2109 to order). (Adams)*

- I would like the younger student to know who the composer is, know that a Minuet is a dance and some very basic facts about the composer. Realistically, their understanding of style will not come from reading, but through listening. However, where it is appropriate, I give information that will better help them understand why they are playing something in a certain way. For instance, discussing the type of dress worn when dancing the minuet will give them a visual picture to help them understand the appropriate tempo.

  For older and more advanced students, it becomes more important and more relevant to know something about the composer and about the times in which they live. We sometimes play the game Musical Jeopardy to encourage them to learn more about the pieces and composers they are learning. (Liccardo)

- Because fine interpretation requires a comprehensive knowledge of historical context, I value music history very highly in my program. It is important from Book 2 on for students to be increasingly aware of the keyboard styles of various periods and composers, and their historical, social and artistic milieu. We begin immediately to immerse even Book I students in these subjects in our monthly workshops. I believe learning to be a layering process, with each subsequent exposure to a concept deepening and securing more a person's understanding. Each month we highlight one period and one or two composers. In the Baroque period, for example, we discuss features such as counterpoint and ornamentation; the favored keyboard instruments, organ, clavichord and harpsichord, and their characteristics; the importance of the church and the nobility in music of that era; colorful events in composers' lives of particular interest to children. We illustrate how people dressed, and how their houses looked, and we discuss the art, architecture and attitudes of the era.

  The children also read a variety of books on history and composers' lives which are displayed in my studio, and they enjoy crayoning in coloring books on the same subjects. At the workshops I provide large pictures of composers along with descriptive information for younger students who would like to take them home to color or paint. We often display these on our bulletin board.

  We also discuss composers and periods, as well as stylistic and interpretive details derived from these topics as we work on repertoire, both in beginning a piece and throughout study. This information is relevant, helpful and often inspiring to a student, and we probe more deeply at intermediate and advanced levels. I encourage students to write school reports based on a composer or other musical topic. In theory class, we play with composer card games which are both enjoyable and instructive. (Schneiderman)

- I include music history in the theory classes of the more advanced students. Prior to that time, I have found the "Composer of the Month" to be helpful in introducing the various musical periods. I have provided each family with a timeline showing when composers were alive and composing. I also give each family a subscribtion to Clavier's Piano Explorer. This is a fun and age-appropriate way for children to learn about music history, composers, and different musical instruments. I provide video tapes for families to borrow, and I also have a supply of children's books about composers which are available to the students. (Fest)

- Very important. I teach it as I go along, in each book, with increasing detail. Period and composer are closely studied so students learn to "read the composer's mind" and can make more of their own decisions without depending on teacher or tape. My students participate in Music Teachers Association of California annual evaluations, including theory, reading and ear training, and use those materials through the year. (Koppelman)

- We discuss the composers, the type and mood of the piece, the appropriate sound for the period, both then and now, but not until about Book 4 do we formally do any music history. Then we use the My Music History materials as a repertoire list compiler, and discuss and add to these lists periodically. (My Own Music History by Karen Koch is available from The Music Studio, 442 N. Maple St. Trenton, IL 62293. It is an imaginative notebook with timeline and musical period repertoire sheets color-coded by period.) (Taggart)

- This is important and helps the child key into style and creative thinking about a piece. Children love this part of their learning—what was going on in the world at the time the composer lived, what they ate or wore, what school was like, etc. Most of the work in this area takes place in our group-class curriculum. This past month the six concerts for our piano students had a Baroque period theme. Parents and students both got involved with the display of historic pictures, some wore authentic period costumes and played period compositions. The concerts had a narrated script telling about composers and period instruments. Parents and students said they learned a lot and had a lot of fun. (Williams)

- This area is not emphasized in my program although I occasionally take time in theory class to read about composers from Katherine Kendall's book Stories on Composers for Young Musicians. In all honesty, I feel this *area is overlooked in my program. I've often thought about developing a music history program similar to the one I created for music theory. So many ideas, so little time. (Yurko)*

Theory

The study of musical theory is seen as indispensable for all piano students. All the teachers insist on spending time on theory, often in both private and group lessons.

- *Music theory is treated seriously in my studio. I teach it both in the private and group lessons. Written theory is done weekly and checked during the private lesson. Group lessons are used for developing aural skills and for strengthening skills learned in the theory books. To make certain that my students are relating their theory knowledge to the music, we constantly examine their reading books as they begin each piece for key signatures, familiar chords, inversions, scales, etc. I use the theory books from the Bastien Basics series; first, we go through levels 1 through 4, and then we do the three levels of their intermediate books. (Powell)*

- *Music theory is an essential and integral part of learning to play the piano. It begins with a student's first exposure to the piano, to the staff and to rhythmic notation and continues into the study of Bach preludes and fugues, Beethoven sonatas, etc. The basics of theory such as intervals, key signatures, chords, circle of fifths, understanding meter, being able to count a variety of rhythms, and appreciating the basic form and structure of piece are essential for students even in the sonatina level. These skills must be taught, reinforced and reviewed numerous times in both group classes and the private lesson. (Liccardo)*

- *I've already referred to the importance of theory throughout, so I'm sure you know that I believe it to be very important. Theory needs to be incorporated in the lesson continually if the student is really to understand why scales, arpeggios, cadences, phrases, form, etc., are important. Repetition is essential because the student has a hard time putting this all together, in fact it may take years. I use some theory workbooks occasionally but find that it is best to combining keyboard and paper simultaneously. This process is built into our group class curriculum continually as well. (Williams)*

- *Theory is enormously important in my eyes. It makes us literate, helps us to read, and most importantly, justifies our decisions on interpretation. I do it in group lessons and use my own materials. (Harrel)*

- *Again, if time was not an issue, I would have theory classes weekly and not just monthly. However, I have learned to be very efficient in the monthly theory classes. Theory is very important, but not very helpful if simply taught abstractly. Therefore I reinforce theory in the weekly piano lessons so the students can see theory knowledge practically applied. Mostly I use my own materials and ideas. However, I do have several commercial games I have purchased which make learning theory great fun! I am always working at theory with the goal of "hear it, play it, write it." (Fest)*

- *Theory can be thought of as the science of music. It is a fascinating and exciting topic intrinsic to music education. A deep knowledge of theory is essential to understanding the design, the compelling dynamism and momentum of music, and projecting it coherently. Theoretical knowledge can lead to the deepest musical understanding and artistic playing, where every phrase is given appropriate weight and meaning proportionate to the whole. In each musical event one feels an organic sense of the entire work. Even the emotional fulfillment, which we value so deeply and which ultimately remains wonderfully elusive and magical, is related to musical facts we can study and appreciate.*

  Theory is a requisite of musical literacy, the ability to read music fluently, and it aides in interpreting, memorizing and performing confidently. The ability to analyze a piece of music, to perceive each phrase and region in a logical relationship to others in order to follow the narrative, is based on knowing theory. Such components as intervals, harmonies and meter, and concepts such as tonality, texture and structure are the basic materials of music. This cognitive awareness is vital to an integrated approach to music making, where all facets of the person are functioning in harmony.

  In lesson time, I work regularly with students toward a thorough understanding of the circle of fifths. From the early observation that G Major, the first sharp key, is a perfect fifth up from C while F Major, the first flat key, is a perfect fifth down from C, we gradually build a clear mental picture of the whole circle with majors and relative minors (cousin keys), demonstrating its beautiful symmetry visually with a chart and playing through the scales at a student's current technical level. For students who study chemistry, I compare it to the periodic table which fascinated me equally when I came upon it as a youngster. Since the circle of fifths presents an overview of all the traditional tonalities and their interrelationships, we value this knowledge highly. It provides students with a framework for perceiving a particular key they may encounter as a feature of a clearly organized system rather than a floating fragment of knowledge.

I help my students relate the harmonies in their pieces to the tonality, to analyze the chords at cadences, starting points and as much as possible elsewhere. This is an invaluable aide in memorization as well as providing a deeper understanding of the music. (Schneiderman)

- As a professional musician and performer, I think knowledge of music theory is indispensable both to an understanding of how the composers did what they did, and to a security in memorization for performance.

That said, the problem remains as to how to convince the students that this information, which most of them feel is dry as dust and boring, can be of immense value to them. In the early years, it is not too difficult to sneak the basic information in, at group lessons and with the parents at home, using the multitude of excellent theory games available. But later, for a clear understanding of scales, key signatures, the circle of fifths, the chords, etc., some drills and difficult, repetitious work is required—and this is when many of the advanced students balk at doing the work consistently. My attitude, arrived at over many years of trying to get them all interested and educated, has become one of presenting the information as best I can, using materials that are comprehensive and self-teaching and don't require too much lesson time explanation, and letting their interest dictate how much of it they actually absorb. For the advanced students who play and read well and enjoy those aspects very much, but are not going into music as a career, I feel that the study of theory beyond the basics can be their choice. They have been introduced to the information and know how to get more if they choose to. However, for the advanced student who is going to major in music in college, theory is a must. With those students, even if reluctant, I insist that they do theoretical workbooks and analyze their music for chord progressions, etc. It probably isn't fair, but piano majors are required and expected to know a great deal more about theory than, say, string or wind players, both when they enter college and in subsequent years of study.

I recommend in particular a text called The Language of the Piano by Preising and Tecklin (G. Schirmer) for high school students going on as college music majors. If they complete this, and understand it, they will be very well prepared for any freshman theory program and also gain a lot of analytical skills to speed up the learning process for new works at the piano. (Taggart)

Musicality and Good Performance

Respondents were asked to define their notion of musical performance and to explain how they develop good and sensitive playing with their students. Their answers are rich and inspiring.

- Musical playing means being able to play with a beautiful tone, shape phrases, achieve a balance between hands, honor tempos and style, and have an understanding of the form of the piece so that it can make a musical statement. I think this process needs to begin in Book I and develop, just as all other aspects of piano training. In developing this in students, I must hasten to say that for some students it comes more naturally and for others it can come painfully slowly; however, if the teacher is persistent it does come in varying degrees with all students.

I teach by demonstrating on the piano, asking students to listen; asking them to draw phrase lines in the air, to walk, run, march, etc., to the mood of the piece; and almost anything else that I can think of that will create imagination. Sometimes I have them feel many different types of textures. I ask them to paint tonal pictures after writing stories about the piece and their feelings in the various sections. If no story is forthcoming, I make up a story for them and ask them to finish it by the next lesson—the young student will frequently draw a picture. For feelings of intensity (big tone, sforzando, crescendo/decrescend accents) we sometimes push on the wall, drop books and do physical-resistance-type exercises, just to have the student experience the energy needed. Students think they are making contrasts, but are surprised to find that they actually are doing them at a minimum level. They gradually realize that it can make a big difference in what the audience actually hears in their playing. I make tapes for them and have them listen to different artists. I record their playing so they can hear what they are doing, and frequently will keep an ongoing tape so students can hear where they started and what the progress really is in their playing. This quite often spurs them on to greater achievements. Repertoire classes are good places for students to test their budding efforts at developing musically good performances. (Williams)

- Musical playing is expressive playing that reaches beyond mere accuracy. Musical playing affects the soul of the performer. This results in conveying an inner sensitivity and awareness that draws the listener and moves the listener to respond to the music.

  Primarily I develop musicality through listening to fine performances. A student who is surrounded with great music develops a sense of style for specific composers as well as a sensitivity to truly beautiful playing. Without this exposure, musicality is much more difficult to teach.

  I also train students to listen to themselves and evaluate concretely what they hear. This begins with Book I in listening to one's tone, control, voicing, and touch. Students must learn how to listen carefully to themselves. If the parent or teacher simply tells the child, the child develops the attitude that "I don't have to listen; someone will tell me."

  I teach musicality by demonstration. If children are taught to listen critically, they will be able to imitate what I am doing to shape the music. Imitation is simply a beginning. Once students have more experience, they learn what possibilities there are in being creative with their music and offer their own original interpretive ideas.

  However, the heart, the key, to beautiful playing is to listen, listen, listen. (Fest)

- Musicality refers to playing music with understanding and effective communication of the composer's ideas. This includes good tone, sensitive phrasing, rhythmic vitality, personal involvement.

  Providing students with good role models is very important. This means first of all, always playing as beautifully as you can for the student, from the first moment, and demonstrating a great deal, especially during the first years of study. Hearing other students playing musically is also important. CDs and concerts are important too. Living in an environment of musicality is what is best.

  Expressing some musical idea is the purpose of what we do, so it always takes first place. We need to use our bodies well to be able to communicate musical ideas, so being as well-informed as possible in this area is of great importance in being able to develop musical playing in a student. If students are not playing as musically as I and they would like, I believe it is most likely due to interference with the way the body is designed to be used. I try to find the difficulty and help them correct it. Everything I have described here from the first lesson on is devoted to developing musical playing. I don't view it as a separate category. (Koppelman)

- Musical playing is the ability to express one's feelings at the keyboard, to include execution of phrasing, tone color, dynamics, variety of touches, voicing, pedaling, nuance, and general style awareness.

  Musical playing may be developed in students through the following procedures:

  1) Student knowledge and understanding regarding phrasing, dynamic control, tone color, and voicing

  2) Successful demonstrations by the teacher with respect to the above skills (correct and incorrect demonstrations to improve listening)

  3) Listening to professional recordings of literature (to include genre other than piano; vocal and orchestral recordings for style, sound and tonal production)

  4) Singing by student and teacher with respect to phrasing and nuance

  5) Tape recording the student's performance for critical listening

  6) Exposure to other teachers' perceptions through private lessons, master classes and recitals

  7) Viewing video taped performances of master classes of comparable literature. (Adams)

- I define musical playing as playing that portrays moods and feelings, touching the soul and the heart. It comes from an inner source in the performer and carries to the listener.

  Practically everything I do in my studio contributes to musical playing. I am aware that I, as a teacher, can only go so far in developing it, for one student will take what I offer and play acceptably while another will exceed my highest expectations. I never doubt that every child can play musically, however, nor do I ever give up until I get it. Here are some of the ways I work toward it:

  1) Developing fine pianistic technique so that each student is physically able to create the music.

  2) Constantly emphasizing the various aspects of musicianship that lead to musical playing, such as good phrasing, dynamics, tempo and rhythm, and beauty of tone.

3) Stressing the importance of listening at home so that the child constantly hears musical playing in his environment.

4) Using good teaching techniques that lead to successful results in creating beautiful music. These include demonstration-imitation teaching, the one-point focus, stop-prepare techniques, clear parental instruction, a positive psychology, specific instructions (both in the lesson and in the home assignment), and the use of small steps when needed.

5) Being creative through descriptive words and/or stories to bring the music to life for the child.

6) Putting the child first and the music second. Children who sense that a teacher genuinely cares about them usually respond more positively to both the teacher and the music. (Powell)

- Musical playing is the ability to touch your audience an emotional way. Sometimes the simplest reading of a piece can be the most profound, and the innocent approach of a small child can have a great impact on an audience. There are many elements that go into the performance that reaches an audience. A good-quality, singing tone is very important. The performer must also have a sensitivity to the phrasing, must be able to shape a phrase, end a phrase beautifully and must breathe with the phrase. The performer must have a sense of the style of the piece, should be able to control the balance between the hands and convey the mood of the piece. They need to have dynamic contrasts as well as a sensitivity of touch and control of different touches. They must be able to project and communicate to the audience as well as listen intensely to the sounds that are being produced and adjust accordingly. They also need to choose what I call "living" tempos—there needs to be a natural flow to the music, a technical ease, and an emotional involvement and understanding of the music they are playing. This type of understanding can be reached at all levels of development in a way that is appropriate to the age and maturity of the performer.

The first and most natural way to develop musical playing in students is through listening. We cannot expect them to play with a beautiful tone if they have never heard one. They should listen to recordings, not only of their Suzuki repertoire, but all great piano music and attend live concerts whenever possible. This should include not only professional pianists, but recitals given by more advanced students.

Singing is the next step in the progression of desiring to make music. Encourage your students to sing as much as possible—yes, even the teenagers! Since most of the songs in Book 1 are folk songs, I think it is very appropriate to put words to them and have teacher, child and parent sing them. Singing allows the child to feel the music internally and helps them realize that the music can be a part of them.

Demonstration is also a valuable tool for teaching musical playing. There is nothing quite like seeing and hearing the music being produced right before your eyes. It is also a wonderful teaching tool to demonstrate the difference between a good performance and a bad one. Invariably the child will choose the better performance. It is also a painless way to make a correction in their performance.

At the piano, the first thing I try to achieve with my students is the production of a simple, pleasant tone. I don't try to do too much too soon. The tone should be appropriate to the size of their hand and body and should be tension free. Demonstrating good and bad tone helps the child learn what to listen for in their own playing.

The first nuances I ask for are simple dynamics, such as echoes. I may also ask for a pretty ending and through demonstration teach them how to relax the tone and tempo at the end of the piece. Many phrases end on the thumb, so I would ask for a gentle thumb to create a sense of the phrase. I would then add simple crescendos in the middle sections of songs like Lightly Row and Cuckoo. I would also use pieces like Aunt Rhody and Long, Long Ago, where phrases end on long notes, to teach them to "breathe" between phrases by lifting the hand (and physically breathing).

As their control grows, I begin to ask for more sophisticated dynamics and shaping of melodic lines. Pieces in the second half of Book 1 and Book 2 offer many opportunities for expressive playing. We also practice timing, such as ritardandos and fermatas in pieces such as Allegro and Musette. Usually in the second half of Book 1, I try to first sensitize their ears to listen for correct balance between the hands. This is a difficult skill and usually takes some time to develop. I regularly place my hands on top of theirs to let them feel the difference in touch between the two hands.

I begin getting the body even more involved in tone production by asking the student to "swing" up to the high notes, letting the arm get behind the tone. Allegretto 1 is an ideal song for this type of motion. I continue it with Musette and Ecossaise and with the first two songs in Book 2, we begin working on a basic down-up motion with the wrist for two and three note slurs. I continue to refine this motion with the Mozart Minuet.

Rhythmic stability is also an essential part of good music making. This is something that I work on with my students from the Twinkle Variations on. However, with the Bach minuets I ask them to practice with the metronome. For students who have difficulty with this, I limit their use of the metronome to the lesson only. After I feel confident that they are comfortable with the beat, I ask them to do it at home as well.

With songs like Arietta and Melody, I start teaching what I call wrist circles. Sinking into each long note, this circular motion helps to produce a beautiful round and resonant tone that is never harsh. Keeping the arm in motion this way also helps to create a beautiful creamy legato. This motion is an extension of the arm swings that we do earlier with Allegretto 1.

Finally, it is most important that as performers we are able to communicate the mood or character of the piece to the audience. Through the use of imagery, a child of any age can have a mental picture of the piece. I think having this kind of feeling for the piece is possibly the most important element in a musical performance. (Liccardo)

- Musical playing is the ability to take the essentials of music learning—notes, rhythm, fingerings, tempo, pulse and balance—to a higher level so that the performer and the listener are transported to a high level of experience. This can happen at any level of playing and depends entirely on the ability of the performer, which of course in the case of students, usually goes back to the ability of the teacher.

Musical playing is developed from solid listening skills. I feel that the essentials of each piece of music must be mastered completely first. This includes accurate notes, rhythms, fingerings, and phrasings. I help my students reach these steps by using the game I've developed called Incredible! The game helps students repeat the music in small steps so that they will move the piece from an outer awareness to an inner awareness. Once the piece begins to be internalized, the student is more free to relax and be expressive. When the student does not have to focus entirely on finger changes and which notes to play, the concentration can be directed to play with sensitivity and feeling.

Listening to fine music, whether recorded or live (this is the best!), promotes musical playing since this gives the ear a model.

Frequent performance in lesson, practice and home concerts, student recitals, and competitions (for older students) gives practice in presenting a piece musically. I encourage all these activities.

Here are a few ideas for training musicality:

1. Tone: Tone is the ability to have a pure singing quality to each note. Playing to the bottom of the key helps. A relaxed arm, hand and fingers also contribute to the beauty of the sound. Many years ago I heard Dr. Suzuki's clever way of illustrating tone to his students. Although intended for violin playing, it transfers easily to producing beautiful piano tone. I demonstrate on the piano as I talk.

   Spider tone: "Have you ever seen those bugs we call water spiders? In warm weather they hurry along the top of the water in ponds or a slow moving stream. This is tone that is on the surface of the note."

   Fish tone: "Since fish swim under the water and not on the surface, this is tone that is a little better than spider tone, but still it's not very deep."

   Hippopotamus tone: "Hippos like the water, too. They like to swim deep in rivers but of course they must come up for air. They will stay in the water with just their ears and noses showing. This is tone that sometimes goes deep but is uneven and becomes shallow." This is the most common tone.

   Tuna tone: "This is the only tone to produce whether the music is played softly or loudly. Tunas don't swim in ponds, lakes or rivers. They swim in the ocean which is very deep. They don't need to come to the surface for air either. So tuna tone is deep. It's the best."

   Shark tone: I added this tone level since sometimes students try to make their tone too deep and it becomes harsh. "Listen carefully so your tone is deep like the tuna."

2. Shaping of the musical line

   After the child has learned Musette in Book 1, we restudy the RH pieces to learn how to shape a melodic line. I use an analogy with color, asking the child to choose a favorite color. "Let's use blue as our example. I ask the child to imagine that the keys are colored and the lowest note (D) is a light shade of blue. The highest note (A) is dark blue. The keys in the middle change gradually from light to dark." To illustrate the point, we look around the room, finding all the shades of blue.

I play the first line of music, demonstrating how the line can be shaped. I usually play it incorrectly the first time—loud on the lower notes and softer on the top. Then I play it correctly. I ask the child to listen and choose the one that sounds naturally musical. Both parent and child will easily choose the second one. Then the child tries the first phrase of Musette (RH) until it's mastered.

This is usually not difficult because I have waited until the end of Book 1 to introduce this concept. "Now you can do this with all your other Book 1 pieces—listen to how beautiful they can be." I don't aim for an exaggerated shaping, but this generalized approach does improve their tone. We will then add color to all the melodies in their new pieces and it sounds naturally musical.

3. Balance

Another important musical improvement which is added at the end of Book 1 is playing so the melody sings out more than the accompaniment. If a child is asked to play with balance too soon, it is difficult to do. However at this time, it is quite easy for a child who is listening to a fine CD. If it is tricky, I ask the student to ghost (play on top of the keys, no sound) the LH and play the RH. (Yurko)

• Musical playing communicates, evokes emotions and images, demands that you listen to it, has something original to say and is never boring. There is something unique about the sound of every note because to the player every note is important—as it is to the listener. Musical playing is like light scattered through a prism, hundreds of ever-changing colors before your very ears. The Scarlatti and Mozart of Horowitz, Bach and Mozart of Gould, the Mozart of Uchida, the playing of Sviatoslav Richter, Yefim Bronfman, Garrick Ohlsson—when they play you have to stop whatever you are doing and listen. These are just a few of the pianists who have this towering musicality, and to whom you must expose your students as much as you can. As the Suzuki® Method makes clear, music is first and foremost an aural art, and the ears need to hear the best possible models of what can be done in order to imagine how to do it by oneself.

To develop musical playing with one's students is a long process that requires carefully planned steps. For most students it doesn't just happen but is a result of educating their ears to first hear the possibilities and then train their bodies to have the skills necessary to realize these. I frequently give a presentation to piano teachers on this topic, and it is on videotape. (The two-hour videotape, Teaching Musical Playing, lecture and demonstration for the Suzuki Piano Teachers' Association of Syracuse, N.Y., is available for $25.00 by contacting Marilyn Taggart).

Given the time and space limits here, I will try to touch on the main elements of a plan for developing musical playing.

Book 1: Focus on tone quality, a clear, round sound for every note, no fadeouts or shallow sounds on 4th or 5th fingers. Absolute evenness rhythmically, with a discernible pulse on downbeats. All sound in a mezzo-forte range. No echoes or balance as yet—don't smother the left hand before it has had a chance to grow. A clear distinction between the upward separated sounds of staccato and repeated notes, and the downward walking sounds of legato. No dynamic contrast or ritards except at endings of pieces—where this can and should be done to give the student a specific safe area to try out this new and difficult skill. In Book 1, one must be very careful to be sure the basic skills are solid before piling on requests for balance or dynamics—which paint a pretty picture but may destabilize the technique and cause slowdowns, mistakes and bodily tension. Build the basement foundation first, then the rooms on top. Decorate last!

Book 2: Lots of emphasis on the two-tone phrase, ask for mf on the first note and pp on the second. Continue emphasis on endings but extend this to phrase and section endings within the piece. Begin serious work on balance and singing tone, particularly in Cradle Song and Melody. Introduce pedaling in supplementary pieces and make sure the student always has a pedal piece in his current repertoire. Pick specific places in pieces to ask for exaggeration of articulation, phrasing or dynamics, just one or two per piece but be relentless about them—until they are always there. If there are too many places, or the dynamic contrasts are too spread out, the effect is dissipated and meaningless to both the student and listener at this point in his development.

Books 3 to 4 and on: The student is now ready to begin to pay attention to the musical content on two levels simultaneously: (1) the larger whole of the piece itself—where the phrases are going, where the climax is, the changes in musical and emotional content from section to section; and (2) making up the whole—the details of articulation, phrases within a phrase, dynamic shadings, balance, etc.

Articulation is a word that looms very large in my teaching, and I think (I hope) that the students understand it as is the essential element in communicating in the language of music. Without clear, intentional articulation—choice of length, sound quality, emphasis within a group of sounds—music, like speech, is garbled and messy and boring to listen to. Like any good public speaker, good musicians exaggerate their articulation, slow down their tempo to make a point, use pauses and dynamic contrast for emphasis. Like an artist with a large picture in mind, the good musician still paints with a very small brush while the work is in progress, attending to every detail.

I have always worked, and ask the advanced students to work, from the small to the large when learning and polishing a piece for performance. First, the notes and technical areas must be mastered, the fingering chosen and mastered, the basic articulations worked in, all the while collecting musical ideas to try but not implementing them as yet. Then, when the basic structure is solid, I and they begin trying out the endless discovery process of "What if we did this here? Or there?" with musical details. We also work on imagery a great deal, even to the extent of finding actual pictures of what a certain part or piece might look like. We talk about the composers' thoughts, what words might go with certain things; what mood is being conveyed. I encourage them to think of themselves as transmitters of these ideas—their own and the composers—into sound. In order to transmit to the audience they must send very clear signals, no fuzziness or static.

I have often wished the Suzuki books from Book 3 on would eliminate editing and dynamic marks altogether and let the students and teachers find out from the music itself what the music wants to say. Yes, even the composers' marks would be eliminated in my ideal scores. Their messages are still there and the adventure for us is to find them. Perhaps we may even find different messages than the composers originally intended—this happens, in art forms. (Taggart)

• Musical playing recreates the qualities inherent in the music itself—qualities that reflect its nature, that indeed bring it to life. It is not mechanical or dry, but energetic and spontaneous, not superficial but in touch with the essence, the inner drive of the music. It displays personal concentration, expressivity and physical freedom. Musical playing involves the whole person, demonstrating emotional commitment, vitality and imagination. We see a natural "becoming" of the music, a one-to-one identity of the performer with the music, in touch with the momentum and logic of its narrative. Musical playing has a feeling of flow and a lively sense of pulse, rhythm, timing and pacing. It is communicative and inspiring with beautiful tone quality, sensitive touch, and appropriate phrasing, dynamics and shaping that express the character of the musical gesture.

I believe that a feeling for and understanding of music is natural for human kind. It is in all of us, but it will not automatically express itself on an instrument without sensitive guidance. As teachers, it is our privilege and our responsibility to draw forth this natural gift (education comes from the Latin educare which means to lead forth or draw forth). We enable our students to discover their own routes to a unique expression of their native musicality; we give them the skills and confidence to unfold it.

In our search to sensitize our students to fine music-making, we might keep in mind several areas for growth, the artistic, emotional, personal, cognitive and physical spheres.

We can develop artistry by teaching our students to hear musical ideas, not notes or measures, as the basic unit of musical language; to sense the forward direction of the music—how it flows toward and away from goal notes, with a feeling of arrival of the goal notes. We can help students to be open to the changing moods of the music and feel these emotions speaking through their fingertips. We can use imagery to heighten their personal responses and create meaningful associations. Dynamics and shaping emerge naturally when we hear where the music grows more exciting and where it is calming down. We hear the story-line, sense the punctuation, let the music breathe.

Teachers can underline harmonic progressions by playing along with a student so they feel the urgency and fulfillment of the harmonies more intensely. We can keep developing our own skills to demonstrate ever finer tone quality and subtleties of shading. To produce musical results, students need to be able to hear and feel the fine-tuning of sonorities, to do them, to understand and personalize them.

We can ask: What is the mood of this piece? How does it make you feel? Does it change in the next phrase? How? We learn that there is not just one way of playing a phrase, that imagination and understanding grow through experimenting with different coloring. We honor a student's choices and respectfully discuss interpretation so he feels valued for his individuality, his uniqueness. We learn to think and talk about music with descriptive words that capture the meaning of concepts such as "home note" for the tonic. We learn to notice patterns, to think structurally, to analyze music for the exciting discoveries we make. We learn a sense of flexibility and give in the body, to interact with music as a whole person.

We learn early to listen for fine-tuning of our sounds—in Little Playmates, for example, **how** short are the staccatos? Musical playing is very often a matter of degree, and touch is so important for portraying the essence of a musical event. We need to imagine an infinite variety of touches as a palette to choose from as we interpret.

We discuss emotions to match the dynamics: "What kind of forte or piano do you think this is?" Personal involvement intensifies when a student's own choice and feelings matter. We need to validate the creative spirit, to find a balance between the order necessary for a healthy process and the freedom that permits a budding artist to grow.

Once we have thoroughly digested the basics of a piece and it is accurate and secure, we are ready to find the poetry in it. Once we have learned our theory and the pleasures of analyzing music, we can appreciate unexpected harmonies and surprises in rhythm or meter or phrase structure. Once we know how to get centered and have learned the habit of composure, our minds are clear and our spirits free to enter the flow of the music, to experience it deeply and color it richly. Our Suzuki philosophy of honoring the inner lives of children while they learn their skills will help them develop a healthy belief in themselves which they need for artistic growth, for confident performance in both music and life, for staying the course. Our Suzuki® Methodology provides a treasured foundation for ripening into musical maturity and artistry. (Schneiderman)

TECHNICAL SKILLS

In the section dealing with technique, each respondent was asked to answer several questions ranging from their conception of a good piano technique to the way they teach the *Twinkles*. Because their account of the work they do in teaching technique makes a block of information so tightly connected, we decided not to break down their answers, but to reproduce each presentation in its entirety.

Adams

Elements of Technique

Technique is the overall music making process. It is the connection between the soul and body, the avenue by which sounds heard inwardly are realized.

Posture: students and parents must be taught that correct posture at the keyboard is the foundation of piano playing. The arms must be parallel to the floor. Body cushions and foot stools are arranged so that the arms find this comfortable position. The back must be straight and relaxed and tilted slightly toward the keyboard.

Hand position: the hands are extensions of the arms, and are not to be elevated or lowered. The bridge of each hand (the roof of the hand) is the most elevated point, with arched, rounded fingers extending from the bridge. I illustrate to my students that the fingers should not be in a "straight back chair", and not lying down, but in a "reclining chair." Each finger makes gentle contact with the keys on the fatty cushion located just behind the tip of the finger.

To demonstrate a good example of the proper placement of the fingers on the keys, one might play a 5-finger pattern in the key of E major. The longer fingers numbered 2, 3, and 4 are slightly extended outward while the "trouble" fingers 1 and 5 are closer inward. Care should be taken to assure that the thumb is also elevated onto its side pad. The 5th finger is also arched and round.

As the fingers play, weight is shifted from one finger to the next. Each finger is supported by a relaxed wrist and arm.

The above technical aspects must be demonstrated, not verbalized to the students. Teachers should demonstrate again and again, in order to establish a relaxed but firm hand position. This skill may take many months to learn. The parents need to understand the proper technique, and must be able to demonstrate as well.

The Beginning

After learning to clap the rhythm of *Variation A*, we work to play individual notes of *Variation A* with proper hand position, good tone and correct rhythm. I focus on one point at a time to watch and listen to. I play, the student plays. I praise, and demonstrate again. This is repeated over and over until the desired basic skills are reflected in the playing.

In the first few weeks we strive for proper hand position, good tone, correct rhythm, and relaxed, happy children enjoying their first musical experiences. As the students progress through the first year of study, we continue to work on the aforementioned basic technical skills.

The *Twinkles*

The *Twinkle Variations* are the ABCs of piano. In learning these four *Variations*, students learn the basic technique used for the beginning study of piano. The *Variations* are taught in the order that they are published. We use the fingering found in the book and have the students play each variation at an "mf" dynamic level. The average tempo is a quarter note = 68. The student learns the *Variations* with the right hand and then with the left. The *Twinkle* theme is eventually played hands together. We continue to play all of the *Variations* as warm-ups and technique review for all other books.

Variation A (Pepperoni Pizza)—this variation is a basic arm staccato with a rich, round tone. Each note of the variation is a staccato touch with the motion coming from the entire arm, not the wrist. The arm is firm but not tense or stiff.

Variation B (Bounce, Roll, Bounce)—this variation is a study in the use of the flexible wrist. Each note is played three times: the first note is a staccato eighth note, the second a legato quarter note with a gentle roll-up of the wrist, and the third a staccato eighth note. The goal is to learn how to use the flexibility of the wrist, and to achieve a rich tone on this longer note.

Variation C (Run, Mommy, Run, Mommy)—this variation is very similar to *Variation 1* with each note being a staccato touch. The "run" eighth note is a high bounce, while the "Mommy" sixteenth notes are shorter bounces. The staccato is from the whole arm but with a differentiation between the high and short staccato. The student strives for a rich, round tone on each staccato tone.

Variation D (Twinkle Theme)—this variation is a study of legato line. Each note is legato and is hooked to the next note with a gentle roll-up of the wrist at the end of the phrases.

Students vary greatly in their initial learning of the *Variations*. Some may learn them in one month, while others may take several months. We do not advance to *Lightly Row* until basic concepts of the *Variations* have been learned.

Technical Exercises

Students are introduced to 5-finger patterns mid-way through Book I. They learn these patterns as an introduction to scales and to the difference in the terms major and minor. These exercises may also be used to work on hand position, tone, and legato in addition to the *Twinkles*. The study of scales is started at the end of Book 1. Exercises such as Hanon or Czerny Op. 777 and Op. 823 are useful for additional work on hand position.

Time Spent on Technique

Since technique is the skill needed to play each variation, about 90% of each lesson is used to teach technique. As the students progress, more time is spent on the musical aspects (i.e. phrasing, dynamics, balance of hands) of the pieces. In subsequent books, time spent on technique varies widely from student to student. The home practice time for technique should be proportionate to the time spent in the lesson.)

Elements of Technique

A good piano technique allows one to play fluently, accurately, and expressively, and with a beautiful sound. The technique needs to develop in a natural way which does not strain or injure the body.

Good technique begins with good posture at the piano. At the first lesson I show the parent how to seat the student properly and emphasize that the parent must constantly monitor this in the practice sessions. I have the child sit at a height which allows the forearms to be parallel with the floor when the child is in a playing position. The feet need to be supported with footstools, allowing the feet to be completely flat, not dangling. The student should be sitting tall, but not rigid, and leaning slightly toward the piano. From this point we look at hand position. The hand should be relaxed as the fingers rest on the keys. I find it helpful to ask the student to drop the hand to his or her side. From that relaxed position I place the hand on the keys. The fingers now rest on the pad of finger, not the very tip. Neither should the fingers be fully extended nor rigid. The wrist and arm remain relaxed, beginning from the shoulder. I teach students to play by moving the finger from the third joint (where the finger joins the hand), playing on the pad of the finger. The thumb plays at an angle to the keyboard and makes a very slight movement inward, toward the hand.

Elements of technique are monitored and corrected over the years; this is a process, not a one-time event. I am reluctant to try to verbalize something that needs to be seen and heard. This reduces piano technique to a cookbook approach, which is rarely effective.

The Beginning

In the first lesson, I work with the rhythm found in *Twinkle A*. Some children will only work with the thumb; others will use all their fingers. I do this with a preparation, then say, "Ready, go". There is a pause after each repetition of the rhythm. We listen for the tone quality and watch how the fingers are moving, which of course, are related elements.

There is a long-range goal in developing technique. Every child is different; therefore it would be unwise of me to set short-range goals applicable to all children. We simply keep working toward the goal of a fluent, accurate technique which helps to create a beautiful sound without stressing the body.

The *Twinkles*

The *Twinkles* are the foundation for building technique. I teach all of them in the sequence given in the book. I teach right hand alone, beginning left hand only when the right hand is approximately at *Little Playmates*, and I never have the students play *Twinkles* hands together. The children work on *Twinkles* consistently throughout Book 1. In Books 2, 3, and 4 I use the *Twinkles* as necessary to help with technical problems. After that I rarely refer to them.

How long does it take for students to learn all the *Twinkles?* My answer is always, "As long as it takes!" This is not the place for "shoulds" or preconceived ideas as standards by which parents and students can measure progress. I have seen children take anywhere between two weeks to one year. I can only encourage; I cannot make it happen. Children and parents need to feel comfortable with the idea that it takes as long as it takes.

For all the *Twinkles* I use the following fingering: 14543211
4321
4321
14543211

With *Twinkle A,* I work for an energetic sound with active fingers, as described above.

I see *Twinkle B* as an introduction to long, legato sounds. The eighth notes are played like the eighth notes in *Twinkle A.* The quarter notes are played with the same finger movement but with also a slight wrist movement. The wrist drops as the finger falls into the key, then rebounds by smoothly moving back into position. Again, I am reluctant to verbalize this without a demonstration. Many people have misunderstood, thought of this as "drop-roll," and teach a very exaggerated, unnatural way of using the hand and the wrist.

Twinkle C is very much like *Twinkle A,* except smaller. I teach the same finger movement as in *Twinkle A,* but the sound should be much gentler than that of *Twinkle A.* *Twinkle A* is more of a forte sound; *Twinkle C* is piano.

Twinkle D elaborates on what was learned in *Twinkle B.* I teach this *Twinkle* in two steps. First I ask the child to simply play all long sounds, listening especially to repeated sounds. It is helpful to "walk in" on the key for the repetition, rather than attempting to play in precisely the same place on the key. When this is easy for the student, I work on the second step which is playing legato from one key to another. I call this walking, as opposed to hopping. We listen for the differences, and I sometimes find it helpful to demonstrate on the student's forearm, enabling the child to feel what it is like for the fingers to "walk" or play legato.

Technical Exercises

I begin teaching scales when a student starts Book 2. The scales are practiced only hands alone until around Book 4 or 5. Around Book 3 or 4, I add selected Czerny and Hanon exercises. We transpose the Hanon, varying the touch, the articulation, and the rhythm. I add chords, arpeggios, and octave scales as I deem appropriate for each student.

Time Spent on Technique

Early Book 1 is primarily the *Twinkles,* so I spend nearly 100% of the lesson working on technique. By late Book 2, I spend 25 to 30% of the lesson on technique. I recommend the same for home practice. In Books 2 and above I recommend about 25% of the practice be spent on technique.

Liccardo

Elements of Technique

At any level, the student should be relaxed and tension-free. My primary goals at the lower levels are to have a relaxed, comfortable sitting position; a relaxed, rounded hand position; a level, relaxed wrist position; the ability to keep the finger joints firm, not break in; the ability to play scales and passagework comfortably and smoothly with good thumb crossings; and the ability to produce a pleasant tone.

To develop a natural and relaxed hand position, I take the hand from the lap or from a position hanging loosely at the side and place it on the keyboard. To help build the firm front joint, I start with a one-finger, detached touch and continue with this detached touch, or bounce from the arm, for first half of Book 1. Besides building the hand, it teaches the student from the very beginning how to use and control arm weight for tone. It also enables the body to stay relaxed as it is the arm and not just the fingers that produces the tone. Next, a portato touch can be added to the bounce, allowing the wrist to sink and provide a cushion for each tone. I then go back and start connecting pieces when I feel that the hand position is secure. We practice walking from finger to finger in simple five-note patterns and then select pieces like *Cuckoo* and *London Bridge,* which do not contain too many repeated notes, to start playing legato. The earlier portato motion can develop easily into a basic down-up or drop-roll, two-note slur motion which can be used in *Ecossaise* and *Short Story* and later in the Mozart Minuet. I also work quite a bit on wrist circles for beautiful tone production and legato playing. This can start in a song like *Allegretto 1* where we can swing out to the high notes and can develop further in songs like *Cradle Song, Arietta* and *Melody* where we can use circles on each long note to produce a nice round tone and singing legato.

The Beginning

The first technical work we do is one-finger bounces on the *Twinkle Variation* A rhythm. This is always done with my physical help. If they are playing with their right hand, I place my left arm underneath to help them with the bounce and use my right hand to help shape and support the finger we are using. I teach the parent how to do this as well.

I first want them to be able to produce a pleasant tone and to be able to balance comfortably on the fingertips. I constantly provide physical help to make sure their bodies are tension free and so they can better feel the type of sound I want them to achieve. Later on I would like them to be able to coordinate their hands when they are doing different things such as melody and accompaniment. This is a difficult and important step in their technical development. By the middle of Book 1, I want them to be able to control basic dynamics such as an echo effect, diminuendo and small ritardando at the end of a piece. By the end of Book 1, they should have enough tonal control to do more sophisticated dynamics, some melodic shaping and phrasing and have some degree of balance between the hands.

The *Twinkles*

I feel the *Twinkle Variations* are valuable for shaping the hand (the repetitions on a single note) and for the development of rhythmic patterns. I do not feel they are of much importance beyond this and use them as a stepping stone to the next pieces in the book.

I usually teach *Variation* A first, followed by *Variation* C, the Theme and then *Variation* B (the most difficult because of the rhythm). If a child is able, I often teach the first phrase of *Variation* A and *Variation* C simultaneously and may even take them through the entire *Twinkle* theme (with my help) in the first lessons. We are just using one finger, usually the 2nd or 3rd to start, with me or the parent often physically guiding them through the pieces. As the first phrase becomes secure and more independent, I will add the middle and ending, still with just one finger, using the right and left hands alone.

I use a simple arm bounce on each note for all the variations, including the theme, and add the real fingering when the individual fingers are secure. I always use finger number 4 on G (right hand) and use the thumb twice consecutively on D and C in the first and third phrases when we run out of fingers. I use this same fingering for all of the variations (with opposite fingers in the left hand) and it does not affect the *Twinkle* theme, since my students are not playing legato yet.

Technical Exercises

I usually start scales when we are several songs into Book 2. We always use a metronome with scales and usually start with quarter-note and eighth-note rhythms. I also assign a down-up exercise (for slurs) in the beginning to middle of Book 2. We do slurring patterns in groups of 2, 3, 4 and 5 notes. I sometimes assign Czerny-Schaum at the mid-Book 2 level. It serves as both reading and technique practice. I also assign an exercise for wrist circles. To feel the motion better, the student first does four circles per note, then two and finally just one circle per note.

Around the Book 3 level, I usually assign Hanon exercises, which we do with the metronome in rhythms of eighths and sixteenths as well as various dotted rhythms, triplets, etc. We are still practicing scales and I may also assign hand-over-hand blocked and broken chords. I also give an exercise in thirds in a five-finger position playing major, minor and diminished patterns. When the hand is bigger, I will assign four-note chords and inversions as well as arpeggios in diminished 7ths, dominant 7ths and major and minor positions. I also like to use Czerny Op. 299 with students playing sonata literature.

From Book 2 on I feel that the student should always be doing some kind of independent technical work. The amount assigned should be realistic so that the student will practice these exercises and still have time to enjoy making music.

Time Spent on Technique

At the Book 1 level, my students get all their technique from the literature. From Book 2 on, I spend 5 to 15 minutes on technique in lessons ranging from 30 minutes to an hour. It is important to do independent technique work, but we must not lose our focus on wanting our students to enjoy making music. For a very serious student who may be practicing two hours a day I might expand the assignment to 15 to 30 minutes a day of independent technical work.

Koppelman

Elements of Technique

I am currently completing a book on this topic, which is the least that this question deserves. I feel that anything less is pretty worthless, especially without any visual reference. However I will try to summarize.

Good technique is the ability to communicate musical ideas as the performer wishes to. It involves using our fantastic system of body coordination as it was designed to be used. Our body works as a sensitively coordinated whole. Various tasks require differing responses from our body. Playing the piano doesn't require the kind of effort that lifting a heavy piece of furniture does. Extra effort interferes with good use and can cause fatigue and pain, in addition to preventing us from sounding the way we want.

As a teacher, I look for smooth, flowing movement without unnecessary effort while listening for the musical result. The ideal is for every movable part of the body to be free to move throughout its whole range of possibility as needed by the particular task. I want hands that are flexible, subtly changing position in response to the demands of playing the music. I want fingers that are alive to their very tips: movable, sensitive and responsive. I want a wrist that is a sensitive part of the chain of action, free to respond with whatever movement is necessary.

All this is achieved by working with the entire body, with special emphasis on back and shoulder area, to eliminate extra effort and promote coordination. This is accomplished in many ways. One way is by the teacher's example: visual, aural and hands-on. An example of the latter is that the student places her or his hand lightly on teacher's back, shoulder, arm, wrist, etc., while the teacher demonstrates difficult or easier ways of moving. The process can be reversed with the teacher, through a gentle, knowledgeable, hands-on approach, helping the student to find a more comfortable, less stressful way. This approach requires special study, both to be able to give a good example and to know how to help others.

In general, I work for low-effort, coordinated, alert movement. Position of any part is continually and subtly changing in carrying out an activity, and is the **result** of good body use, rather than the cause. Therefore my emphasis is on improving whole body use, rather than in prescribing particular positions. I think of "weight" as your whole body being there, as in walking, rather than as something heavy. I prefer to think of letting go of extra effort and being ready to do anything easily than to think of relaxation. The latter seems too passive.

The Beginning

I begin with playing clusters lightly with a loose fist on the black keys in various directions in the *Twinkle A* rhythm. This is followed by playing that figure with the RH thumb. I will ask for other fingers also if this is done well.

I want to achieve easy, coordinated, whole-body use, including freedom of arms, back, shoulder complex, etc. I want to hear clarity, good tone, lively and even rhythm.

In the first months, I want the student to achieve the ability to play using ballistic movement. This refers to initiating a movement and letting it continue on its own momentum, like throwing a ball. I particularly focus on the *Twinkles* for this. I also want to achieve the kind of body balance that is best shown by freely playing repeated notes closely connected and legato.

By the end of the first book, I want the student to be able to do all the above easily and confidently. Also I expect voicing with a full, expressive tone in the melody and deep, soft tone in the accompaniment. I expect a range of dynamics, and even scalework as in *Little Playmates*, and facility with hands together at fairly fast tempo as in *Allegretto 2*.

The *Twinkles*

I use the *Twinkles* as the material for developing good body use. This provides the student with the physical basis for the development of every aspect of musicality. Each of them serves a particular musical purpose. I teach them all, in order, each hand separately, to every student. Which fingering in the book is used is immaterial. (I use two thumbs at the end).

It is impossible to adequately describe the motions to be used in this amount of space. I can say it is the result of coordinated whole body use. I do not teach any particular position or movement. What happens to hands, arms, wrist and fingers is the result of using the entire body in the beautifully coordinated way it is designed to be used. There is continual, interconnected, ballistic movement with much happening internally throughout the body. What movement is happening can best be discovered by gently touching the student's upper arm, back, wrist, etc. The result seems flowing, loose and alive. There is no pressure on the wrist, which does not lead any particular movement but moves easily as part of the whole. Fingers seem long, flexible and alive.

I am looking for lively, ongoing, even rhythm at a lively tempo with pleasant tone and equal facility with each finger in *Twinkle A*.

Twinkle B needs differentiation of long and short notes and special attention to the length and quality of sound of the long note, as an introduction to true legato. The long note takes a coordinated body with it, but no special movement originating from the wrist.

Twinkle C has a more delicate, ongoing rhythm. It needs to move easily to the first note of the next finger.

Twinkle D teaches legato and it is important to flow easily, with the whole body, from one note to the next, leaving as little discernible space as possible between repeated notes. This is the test of the ability to balance easily with the whole body on each key—a most important basic skill. It is important not to leave one end of the hand behind when moving from note to note, but to be centered on each.

Since I use *Twinkles* to teach basic technique, that is, to give the student the ability to express whatever musical ideas they want to express, this is a tremendous subject, which I cannot do justice to here.

Students work on *Twinkles* throughout Book I, refining and developing their skills. Some students can learn them all at a first stage almost immediately. Students who have considerable tension and bad habits of use may learn more slowly. The range is great.

Technical Exercises

I make up little exercises from the beginning, as I see the need. These could be, for example, playing each two adjoining fingers into the keys legato, or skipping fingers, or 5-finger patterns. I create them as I need them, but don't do the same things automatically with each student.

I introduce scales with Book 2 and do them one octave at first in all keys, then 2, 3 and 4 octaves, 2, 3 and 4 to the beat. I introduce simple chord progressions at Book 2 followed by the same type of expansion. I teach arpeggios later, at Book 3, beginning with a non-legato touch if the hand is very small. Coordinated body use increases range of movement, so this is a temporary, not widely necessary situation.

I often make exercises taken from the piece being studied.

Scales, arpeggios, chords, octaves, etc., are part of every student's musical diet. Lists of what to do at different levels can be obtained from standard sources. It seems unnecessary to list this all again here. The significant information is how to teach our students to do them using their bodies well and easily.

Time Spent on Technique

I don't see technique as something apart from music-making. Part of every lesson time is devoted to using the body in a way that makes it easier to express musical ideas. I usually begin the lesson with some form of warm-up, such as *Twinkles*, or scales. There is more content, scales, arpeggios, chords, octaves, etc., as the student becomes more advanced, so more time is needed. Since exercises are continually being devised from the pieces being studied, a good deal of practice time is spent on this.

Harrel

Elements of Technique

A good piano technique must meet the musical requirements of the music through the natural use of the physical mechanism of each unique person. This means that each hand is different and must be analyzed individually. Essential elements :

Playing the piano is a natural down motion through the use of gravity

The arm is strong. Its connection to the hand and fingers must always be maintained. The following wrist motions disconnect the strong arm from the fingers:

a) Excessively low wrist
b) Excessively high wrist
c) Twisting laterally to the left or right

Loose, flexible wrist

Fingers basically move from the bridge (the knuckles closest to the hand)

The hand position should look very much like the hand looks when the arm is hanging at the side of the body. A quick survey of several people in this position will reveal a significant difference in how curved the fingers are naturally.

The Beginning

My first technical goal is to lay a natural hand in different places on the keyboard, keeping the arm, hand, and fingers in alignment. I seat children so that their right arms can hang naturally at the side. This may necessitate adjusting the seat or bench to the left. I physically move their hands to the keyboard and trace with my finger a line from the elbow to the bridge knuckles. At the keyboard area around one and one-half octaves above middle C, the fingers pretty much parallel the direction of the keys. Around the area of Middle C, the fingers are at an angle to the keyboard. It's all right to play at an angle to the keyboard, but it's not all right to play at an angle to the arm (twist at the wrist). Now the students must demonstrate that they can do this alone. Between each attempt, the arm returns to hanging position. (In a later step it will be done from the lap).

My next step is to physically control the arm, hand, and third finger and use gravity to drop into a key. We then proceed to other fingers. The goal is gravity, hand position and alignment of arm and hand. As the students can achieve this, I ask them to match my tone.

Lining up the fourth or fifth fingers with the arm requires a slight adjustment. Once one can draw a line from the fourth-finger knuckle through the middle of the arm to the elbow, the arm will support the fourth and fifth fingers. No other adjustment is needed for the fifth finger. If one is made, a dangerous twist may occur at the wrist.

Clearly, this activity cannot last too long, because it takes a strong focus. It must be relieved with fun things such as pitch matching or improvisation or finger numbers.

When the gravity drop is comfortable, I teach a tiny movement that achieves complete relaxation. By moving forward on the pad of the finger ever so slightly (1/4" or less), all downward pressure is immediately released. The wrist does not rise; it simply moves forward with the rest of the mechanism. The drop-forward now becomes one continuous motion. The steps above which are learned with the right hand are immediately presented to the left hand. After much experience, I no longer believe it advisable to allow the left hand to lag behind at all.

At no time are the fingers spread over five adjacent keys. The fingers move most efficiently in their natural resting position, i.e., with no extra space between them. It is important to inform parents of this matter during orientation. In their effort to execute their responsibility for correct fingering, they often ask the children to cover five keys.

During the first months and first year I would expect to achieve the goals mentioned above.

The *Twinkles*

To achieve my technical goals outlined above, the first *Twinkle* is D. It is an ideal vehicle because (1) the children love it, (2) gravity drop-relaxation can be easily taught, (3) alignment of arm-hand-finger can be achieved as long as it is played with long notes non-legato for a considerable period of time. Only after the above is thoroughly internalized would I move to legato.

Twinkle B is next in order.

The pieces are initially played non-legato to (1) continue the process of lining up the arm and finger, (2) ascertain just where the student can play on the pad of his finger without the first knuckle caving in, and (3) experience the freedom of coming out of the key as well as the gravity drop. As these elements are internalized, we move to legato.

Somewhere in the middle of the Book 1, I introduce *Twinkle* A. After much experience, I have decided that *Twinkle* A is the most difficult of the *Twinkles* and that it is probably placed first because it is the first bowing exercise for the violin. Violin technique is not remotely like piano technique. By beginning with something this difficult, we teach the student at the outset that playing the piano is hard, and by delaying the pieces until all *Twinkles* are learned thoroughly we run the risk of flagging interest and lost momentum on the part of the student. I believe that technique is taught continuously in the pieces and not only in the *Twinkles*.

By the middle of Book 1, the gravity-drop is thoroughly learned, the hand position is established, the knuckles are firm, and arm-finger alignment is set. Now the student can easily play *Twinkle A* with a relaxed arm, good tone, and focus especially on finger movement both from the bridge of the hand and also at the first joint.

Technical Exercises

While students are working on *Twinkle D, B*, and non-legato pieces, I introduce legato as two-note patterns with various finger combinations (3-2, 4-3, 2-1, 5-4, 2-3, 3-4, etc.). The second note always ends with a slight move forward on the pad of the finger to release any tension. This is not only the beginning of legato but also the beginning of phrasing. Two-note patterns graduate to three-note patterns, etc.

Scales should begin towards the end of Book 1. Arpeggios can be started in Book 3. Hanon exercises provide a concentrated vehicle for a specific technical need of a particular student. Simple études are often good reading pieces and give students more playing experience before moving on to more challenging Suzuki pieces.

Powell

Elements of Technique

Good piano technique involves the ability to use the body skillfully and freely to attain musical results.

The hand is one of the essential elements with which we must work. The hand I demonstrate to my beginners is the same hand we have when it hangs naturally and loosely beside our body. When this type of hand goes to the keys, the result is fingers that touch on the pads. I do not use the words "hand position" with my students, for it can lead to a fixed, stiff position; instead, we practice dropping what I call "loose hands" on the keyboard. Since the hand moves into many shapes and positions as it plays, it needs primarily to be loose.

I teach the fingers to move from the large knuckle; this is the knuckle closest to the palm of the hand that moves when we wave our hands. In this way, we are moving the fingers from the short flexor. Fingers curved tightly at the nail joint move the long flexors which connect into the arm and are a leading cause of tension and hurting in the lower arm. In my studio we often wave our fingers and talk of loose fingers.

The wrist must also be loose. Its movement involves the use of the upper arm, which is so important to good piano playing. Use of the wrist also affects the tone quality, for it serves as the shock absorber and takes away the impact of the blow. A flexible wrist is something I stress heavily and I teach my students to use it purposefully. Closing the piano lid and pretending to do trampoline jumps with all the fingers falling into the lid, the wrist dropping slightly and then riding upward, is the first way I initiate this movement.

Arm movements are taught to my students before I stress fingers. I feel that arm movement is essential to good playing, for movement is initiated at the shoulder girdle and involves both fingers and arm working together for best results. For example, alignment of the arm behind the hand provides support and strength for the fingers when playing. Learning specific movements of the arms—such as riding the wrist upward, circle technique, rotation, sliding in and sliding out of the keys—all involve incorporating the arm. Work with proper alignment of the hand and arm begins on the *Twinkles* by demonstrating how the large knuckles are parallel to the fallboard when aligned and then preparing our hands in this manner before playing; sometimes we add visual aids such as small stickers on the keys, marking them in order to maintain that alignment as we play. Movement of the wrist, which involves the upper arm, begins with *Twinkle B*. Other techniques are gradually added as the student advances through the books.

I am an advocate of weight-based playing; most pianists skim the top of the keys and do not use their bodies properly to gain proper weight. Work in my studio includes stressing good posture and using the body properly to attain weight. Demonstration techniques of tones based on weight-based playing versus playing without weight help the students hear the difference. I also have the students and parents feel the difference by playing on their arms with weight and without; the student, in turn, plays the same on my arm and then takes the feeling of weight to the piano.

I have a stuffed frog who sits at my piano and demonstrates loose, relaxed arms to my beginners; his arms are totally relaxed and swing freely from his shoulders. The students love to swing his arms to test for looseness; I then test their arms at the keyboard for the same relaxation. Every week after this test, I tell them that "loose arms and bodies are important to good piano playing." We frequently drop my frog from the air into our hands to experience how we let go (or use gravity) to produce a tone; this is often followed by holding our arms above our head and letting them fall loosely to our sides. Relaxation of the body is stressed through emphasis on good posture. When I see tension in any part of the body (for example, the elbow or the jaw), I have children intentionally tighten that part and then relax it. In this way, they can understand how to let go of the tension in that area while playing. In addition, I often build in rest points (stop-prepare) for practice on difficult passages to allow the students to stop, check themselves for an especially tense area, relax, and then continue. Through this kind of practice, the students are gradually able to let go of their tension.

The Beginning

My beginners' first lessons are taught away from the keyboard to do some preparations for playing. As soon as we move to the keyboard, we learn to play *Twinkle* A rhythm up and down the five-finger pattern on C; I consider this their first technical exercise.

Technical achievements I work to gain during the *Twinkles* are as follows:

1) Good posture, including feet, body, hands, arms, and head

2) Concepts of good tone

3) Good use of arm movements

4) Ability to play with speed

5) Ability to play legato (*Twinkle* D)

Technical achievements stressed by the end of Book 1 are as follows:

1) Strong concept of legato

2) Strong concept of good tone

3) Good posture

4) Ability to balance between melody and accompaniment

5) Ability to change dynamic levels

6) Good independence of the hands

7) Ability to shape phrases

8) Ability to play pieces at musical tempos

The *Twinkles*

The *Twinkles* are treated with the greatest respect and care in my studio; parents are told that they are the foundation of the children's technique and they should expect to spend a great deal of time on them. I teach all of the *Twinkles* in the following order: 1) *Twinkle* A; 2) *Twinkle* C (because it is more like Twinkle A in technique); 3) *Twinkle* B; 4) *Twinkle* D.

Twinkle A techniques are as follows:

1) Forearm motion

2) Sixteenth notes played close to the keys
Eighth notes played with slightly higher motions

3) Speed emphasized

4) Beauty of tone emphasized

Twinkle B techniques:

1) Eighth notes are forearm bounces, as in *Twinkle* A. Played almost staccato for lightness

2) Quarter note uses a flexible wrist; the wrist drops slightly, then rides up and forward. This syncopated note is stressed, using weight from the arm

3) Beauty of tone emphasized

Twinkle C techniques:

1) Speed is emphasized

   a. Requires small forearm motions, very close to the keys. (A slight use of the wrist is permissible if it is natural to the child)

   b. Must be played very lightly, almost whispered

2) Stress difference in note durations—big, short, short

3) Beauty of tone emphasized

Twinkle D techniques:

1) Stress legato on all notes, both moving and repeated notes

2) Wrist movements are used

3) Eveness and beauty of tone emphasized

The fingerings I use are as follows:

A section—(RH) 1 1 4 4 5 5 4 3 3 2 2 1 1 1; (LH) 5 5 2 2 1 1 2 3 3 4 4 5 5 5

B section—(RH) 4 4 3 3 2 2 1 4 4 3 3 2 2 1; (LH) 2 2 3 3 4 4 5 2 2 3 3 4 4 5

An exception to the fingerings of the A section is made on *Twinkle* D; in order to maintain the legato, we change fingers on the next to the last note (the D). The fingering now becomes:

(RH) 1 1 4 4 5 5 4 3 3 2 2 1 2 1.

(LH) 5 5 2 2 1 1 2 3 3 4 4 5 4 5

The majority of my young students spend on an average of three to six months learning their *Twinkles*. We review them mostly through Book 1. Beyond that, I tend to use the rhythms from them for various purposes rather than the *Twinkle* melody.

Technical Exercises

In Book 1, I use the tonalization (which is shown in the original books right after *Twinkle* D) as an additional exercise. It is a word adapted by Suzuki from the singer's term "vocalization". I saw the value of it through my own sons' study of the violin and have found it tremendously valuable for my piano students as well. It is a study in beautiful legato and tone. My students practice it daily at home and we never miss doing it in a Book 1 lesson. Through this exercise, they have become stronger and more confident in playing with depth of tone, evenness of tone, and beauty of tone. I make a game out of it so they do not become bored with the process; thus it has become one of their favorite parts of the lessons.

Book 2 brings the addition of several new exercises. One of those is scale study in which we learn to play one octave to the quarter note, then two octaves with eighth notes, three octaves with triplets and four octaves with sixteenths. These are all done hands alone and with the metronome. By the end of Book 2, the majority of my students can play their right hand with all these rhythms at a metronome setting of 100 to the quarter note; left hand is often slower. We work for many skills through these scales. Some of the most important ones are as follows: 1) Playing to the key-beds; 2) evenness of sound; 3) fingers moving from the short flexor (large joint); 4) good alignment of the hand and arm; 5) proper passing under of the thumb; 6) proper passing of the hand over the thumb; 6) beauty of tone. I see each book as a preview to the next; and these skills are preparing them for the sonatinas of Book 3.

In Book 2, I stress a second technical exercise I call "Book 2 tonalization." This uses the same five-finger pattern as the original tonalization, but it now uses the wrist (and upper arm) motion for groups of notes. Students play two-note, three-note, five-note groups allowing the wrist to ride up as they play. Through this, the arm takes all the notes in one physical gesture.

Scales are continued indefinitely through the books. While in Book 3, many of the students are able to bring their scale speed up to a MM 120 or beyond (4 notes to the tick), done in the same procedure as Book 2. Using the circle of fifths, we complete all the major scales and then add the harmonic minor scales, all hands alone. Once these are completed, we repeat the same process but with hands together this time. Each student moves at his or her own pace, but regardless of the pace, each scale is played with much proficiency before another is learned.

Arpeggios are played in the same manner as described for scales; these I delay until the later books, for passing the thumb under the hand on these is difficult for small hands.

Most of my students' technique is gained through their Suzuki repertoire. For example, circle technique is presented through left-hand, broken chords initially; rotation is presented through the broken left-hand octaves of the Bach *Musette*; and numerous exercises are created for difficult passages.

Time Spent on Technique

The amount of time spent in the lesson on technical work that is not in the literature varies. If I am presenting something new and difficult, then I might spend a good amount of time on it; otherwise, I seldom spend more than a few minutes. For home practice, I tell my students and parents to spend approximately five to ten minutes daily on their scales and arpeggios. Time spent on technical exercises created from the literature varies widely from piece to piece and from child to child.

Schneiderman

Elements of Technique

Good piano technique is the ability to translate with natural ease all aspects of the music into sound that projects the intention of the composer—portraying both the concrete details and the essence. It is often described in terms of strength or speed but equally imperative are skills such as songfully projecting the melodic line in a series of chords, defining the voices of a complex texture with appropriate balance or creating a tender, shimmering yet clear pianissimo.

Good technique requires foremost a comfortable, graceful, effortless, natural coordination of the entire body and a sense of fluid interplay with the instrument. The body already knows what to do; we need only permit the motion without tension, tightness or forcing ("let it happen, not make it happen"). We learn to know the difference between intensity and tension—to express the former without the latter.

This flexible comfort of the body in balance and alignment depends on a clear state of mind, that sense of healthy wholeness and oneness we achieve in rest position. So many aspects of piano playing are predicated upon an integration of our human resources. Here we are discussing technique, but such integration also serves emotional involvement, meaningful touch, musicality, communicative interpretation, posture, performance confidence, singing tone, effective practicing, structural coherence. We return again to the fundamental beginning steps where we teach centering—that all-important moment of peace and composure. This harmony of body, ear, thoughts and feelings can become a habit that enhances practice as well as performance, enabling one to be in touch with the source of one's best ability. I emphasize the inner content of rest position with my Suzuki students, with adults, teacher-trainees and musicians in workshops and classes. It can work wonders! I have seen dramatic changes in levels of confidence and ability when students digest this training.

Some further elements:

1) Awareness of the state of muscles and joints (mental application, imagery, exercises)

2) A mental model of the desired sound is a high priority; physical proficiency at the keyboard depends on the ear, imagination, judgment and taste as much as muscle—a particular sound for each musical idea; technique is "in the ears" (demonstration, imitation, active listening and calibration of elements such as equality, clarity, steady pulse, tone, legato/staccato: technique in service of the music)

3) Efficient movement (getting from point A to point B, from key to key, with the least effort and the most beautiful sound; as close to zero-work as possible)

4) Command of touches; using appropriate movements of finger, hand, wrist, arm, torso and an appropriate amount of force as required by the music (e.g., more arm involved in longer, cantabile note values; close to the key, very sensitive touch and warm weighted pad needed for legato; individual finger action more on the tips and moving from the bridge for sparkling scales and rapid passage work; all coordinated and informed by the intent and momentum of the music)

5) Fluid, cooperative relationship of all parts is essential (coordinated movement of a natural hand; strong, independent, freely-moving fingers, flexible wrists and hip joints, buoyant arms, easy shoulders; the hand, wrist and arm coordinate fingers into groups as suggested by the phrasing)

6) Buoyancy, ease, flexibility, naturalness, fluidity are preferable terms to "relaxation". A comfortable alertness of the neuro-muscular system is our ideal, not total relaxation.

7) Natural hand position (a sense of ease inside the hand itself, the muscles feeling soft and free)

8) Fingertips very sensitive and secure with a meaningful touch, personally expressive; ("We speak through our fingertips", "Imagine a direct line from your heart to your fingertips"). Of course, for tone production as well as musical playing, this is essential.

9) The notion of balance (ready position; play a single note with ease and freedom; while centered and resting comfortably in the key afterward, check for an easy sensation of the arm buoyantly floating up and over the point of repose in the fingertip; check all parts of the arm from tip to shoulder for ease—muscles warm and light, joints flexible and free; then learn to shift weight from finger to finger in a legato five-note scale, checking after each for this awareness of balance)

10) An ability to analyze and solve technical problems is necessary (find the specific troublesome area; verify notes, rhythm and phrasing; check for comfortable fingering, ease, most efficient movement; re-train neuro-muscular system by intelligent repetition of separate hands and then together with the detailed correction in ear and mind; apply a variety of practice techniques; weave the improvement into preceeding and following passages)

The Beginning

Since all ability at the piano depends on mental, physical and emotional ease, I cannot emphasize too much that the harmony of body and mind we instill with our beginning steps is really the first technical as well as musical exercise we teach. Also, since technique requires muscles without tension, thoughts that are clear, feelings that are stable, even the trusting relationship a teacher has generated from the first meeting with a student might be called an early exercise.

Standing before we bow involves the first explicitly physical activity at the first lesson. From neatly lining up their feet to feeling strong but not tight in the legs, tall through the middle and "soft" at the top (shoulders) children learn to know balance in their bodies—centered, secure and comfortable, feeling "good all over". Much else is learned as well, by both teacher and student, as they stand before the bow, a gesture of mutual respect.

A teacher needs to have a clear understanding of how a comfortable body looks and later how a natural body works for tone production so the ideal is always in mind. We work with what each child presents, compare that with the best model we can imagine and sculpt this given system toward the highest standard one step at a time—always selecting the most basic point and working until it is effectively digested: trust, attention, emotional security, concentration, responsiveness to directions, centering, posture, a fluid relationship with the instrument, easy integrated movement of all parts without any roadblocks to the natural motion of the whole.

We need to observe first whether there is balance and ease in the body at large—legs, hips and torso—then in the shoulder area, the arm, elbow, wrist, hand and fingers. It is important not to start with fingers and move backwards, and to continually emphasize with parents that they observe the whole body at home, not just the fingers, which might appear to them to be the main focal point.

Since we are always striving for a balance of pleasure and progress, we need to proceed sensitively in synchrony with a student's needs, abilities, propensities, personality and learning style—an interactive, dance-like experience. We also need to be tuned into the home process and the relationship of child to parent. One is constantly evaluating the development of each student, ready to shift gears or emphasis if required.

It usually takes a few weeks to a few months to learn the beginning steps well, though we continue permanently to reinforce and deepen them. During this time, we are also trying to secure general good habits, motivation, trust, knowledge of keyboard and finger numbers while developing the ear for tone quality, direction, register, volume, note values, articulation, etc. Technique is based on the ability to audiate—to imagine the kind of sound one aims to create.

If a student's tone, body balance and beginning steps are reasonably good, we move to playing tunes as early as possible and gradually introduce the *Twinkle Variations* for a natural hand, independent fingers, floating arms, easy shoulders, flexible wrists and hip joints. Warm sound and a student's delight are early goals. We learn to create a basic tone that is mellow and pleasant.

Then we gradually hone the physical apparatus for improving tone, and the ability to hear and produce subtle variants in sound. We improve the gently rounded finger shape (not a rigid form but always moving according to musical needs), work on the value and comfort of playing on the tips, further sensitize the touch, refine hand ease and the relation to the arm, develop the flexibility of the wrist. We continue to enrich a student's technique as we proceed through Book 1.

During the first year, we begin to learn scale skills—"walking fingers", individual finger action with a quiet but natural, buoyant arm. The finger joints are flexible but ready to be firm when needed for the very brief work of producing a tone. Before and instantly afterward, we feel free (see notion of balance above), and even during the stroke, we feel as close to a "zero-work" state as possible. We want the best sound with the least effort; graceful, efficient movement.

The *Twinkles*

The *Twinkle Variations* are extremely useful for teaching individual finger action, the ability to play repeated staccatos rapidly and equally with a natural hand, developing cantabile technique and quickly alternating between the two touches. They represent a laboratory of basic skills to which we refer often, returning to the familiar motion to demonstrate a move in a new piece or to improve balance on a finger, interval or chord.

I teach all four variations and vary the order according to a student's needs. The details of technique are as follows: *Twinkle A* and *Twinkle C* are basically the same; the finger is the leader with a small, flexible brushing motion, the fingertip catching the tone with each brush. The hand is flexible, soft inside and free, slightly more engaged as the thumb plays while the other fingers move from the bridge. The arm is buoyantly floating over the fingers; just as in walking, the body balances comfortably over the legs. (Sometimes we demonstrate the wrong way to do it, showing how difficult it is to walk with our torsos down by our legs, gorilla style. This makes the point vividly!) The shoulders, back, and hip joints are free.

Twinkle D cultivates a singing legato with rich full tone quality. We feel more weight in the pad and the fingertip acts along with a wrist bounce and forearm action in tone production—team work. We use more arm to translate these long note values and fuller sounds. I call this action a swing, as the wrist descends and springs back up, acting as a shock absorber in a very free motion. *Twinkle B* teaches the student to differentiate the two strokes clearly by alternating them, brush-swing-brush, and develops the ability to shift gears quickly.

We study the variations only with separate hands. Occasionally, a child will enjoy accompanying their right hand with the appropriate left-hand chords, learned by ear. I congratulate them for this accomplishment and recommend that they treat it as dessert, after practicing the variation with separate hands first. Sometimes, when *Twinkle D* is proficient, a student will play it unison, but only if this can be done beautifully.

The fingering I suggest is RH 1454 3211 and LH 5212 3455. The length of time to master the variations varies greatly from student to student, but they take several months to learn and a year to refine. We review them all through Book 1, sometimes transposing them for variety and understanding of tonality. I sometimes use twinkle movements on scales in different keys in Book 2.

Technical Exercises

It happens during the course of study that I create many individualized exercises for students according to their particular needs and the requirements of particular pieces and passages. These are in addition to a core program that all will share. In the early months, for instance, if a child seems stiff in the hip area, I recommend a gently rocking motion of the torso, forward and back, to develop freedom. Or if the shoulders are locked, we do a train-engine, in-and-out movement of the arm, freely bent at the elbow. If the arm muscles are persistently tense, we do contract and release exercises with arms hanging at the side to learn awareness of both states. Here too, we need to emphasize the value of our beginning steps. Before a note is sounded, before a move on the keyboard is made, we give pure, undivided, systematic attention to the comfortable condition of the whole body. Then in graded steps, we retain this natural sensation as we learn to float up gracefully and get ready on the keys. If awareness of ease throughout the body is cultivated early and refreshed regularly, less remedial work will be required.

Balancing on one finger in the key is helpful for centering, for developing a floating arm and for tip security without pushing or tightening. The tip becomes a focal point, a point of repose while the hand and arm balance buoyantly over that finger—balanced, centered, natural, comfortable. Then we learn to shift that gentle sense of weight in the tip from one finger to the next, legato. This leads to five-finger patterns in scales and broken triads, major and minor, beginning for most children toward the end of the first year and advancing at the student's own rate.

We learn eight-note scales usually at the beginning of Book 2 but occasionally in Book 1. Before we ascend the full octave, I use a thumb-tucking exercise that engenders a timely glide of the thumb under, light as a feather, as the second finger plays comfortably in balance. We start chord inversions in Book 2 but the idea has already been introduced in Book 1. The children enjoy and benefit greatly from hand-over-hand triadic arpeggios (Book 1 or 2) in conjunction with improvising, but they are also useful for technique and for understanding the concept of primary and secondary triads.

In Book 2 or 3, we begin our workout key program, with activities all in the currently chosen tonality: scales gradually working up to four octaves, all triads, inversions of primary triads, progressions, improvising and arpeggios and later, scales in thirds, sixths and tenths. Some advance to the grand scale and octave scales. Here too we need to be responsive to the varied life patterns of our students while adhering to the highest standard possible. We hold the ideal in mind and try to help each student develop his or her abilities to the maximum while maintaining a sense of balance.

In scales and arpeggios, we use my adaptation of the technique of the Russian pianist and pedagogue Isabelle Vengerova, passed along to me by Sidney Foster and Norma Bertolami Sapp—for which I am most grateful. It is a wonderfully thorough technical system which can be applied to challenging passages in any piece. The technique cultivates a very secure, comfortable, close-to-the-key legato which, used as an accurate base, can then be honed into other degrees of detached touch.

I find Hanon very useful and introduce it with many students in Book 2 or 3. I recommend the Czerny *Études* for some youngsters, anywhere in Book 3 and beyond, and some of the Burgmüller studies as well. Later of course the Chopin *Etudes* are outstanding musical as well as technical material for dedicated students.

Time Spent on Technique

Piano (and music) instruction in the broadest, deepest sense is an integrated system of activities with much overlapping of purpose and mutual effect. Categories such as technique or review help us discuss and analyze the process but we must be careful to avoid oversimplification, recognizing that piano playing at its best is a refined, imaginative art form involving all human faculties, that piano pedagogy is a sensitive interactive process and that both teacher and student are complex, individual and highly variable human beings.

Thus, we might need to consider including the beginning steps (whose technical value has been described), and review (which undeniably develops technical skill) in calculating the percentage of lesson time for technique in early Book 1. During review, a student is digesting a diverse vocabulary of movements, the physical substance of the musical language, while developing essential features of technique: flexibility, coordination, versatility. Since we are laying a foundation in the neuro-muscular system for a lifetime of relating to the instrument, a teacher's attention is properly directed to physical activities in this stage.

In early Book 1, the proportion of time devoted to technique is increased when one includes the beginning steps which involve much time even though they are not exclusively technical. The sense of harmony they instill forms a foundation not only for physical ease, but for the musical and emotional connectedness that support artistic interpretation and performance confidence. Similarly, the work on review is multi-faceted in nature and purpose.

In Book 2, 3, 4 and beyond, the amount of time spent explicitly on technique varies from student to student and lesson to lesson, as we often rotate material. It also fluctuates with current goals: polishing a piece for recital or other special event (maybe only a brief warm-up or none), introducing a new concept in another area (10%), digging into technical problems or issues themselves (maybe 80%). I would estimate that technique per se usually involves around one-fourth of the lesson time but if one includes discussion of technique in repertoire and as it is incidentally involved in theory work (circle of fifths, chord progressions, etc.), the amount grows considerably. Late Book 1 is roughly similar in proportion.

In general, the percentage of practice time at home is parallel to the the lesson. Review is an exception, involving increasing amounts of time at home as the pieces accumulate throughout Book 1.

Taggart

Elements of Technique

I would like to make several points very clear about what I believe and teach every day:

1) The fixed hand position with fingers curved and playing on the tips is the primary cause of tension and lack of ability to play easily and well. The more the teacher insists on this, the less chance the student has of ever discovering the joys of fluid technique.

2) Understanding and applying the principles of single and double (retake) rotation as found in the work of Matthay, Taubman and Seymour Bernstein, to name just a few, is absolutely essential to fluid piano technique. Teachers are cheating themselves and their students if they do not explore these concepts. The rotational influence is always at work in piano technique because of the structure and placement of the radius and ulna from elbow to hand—it is not just a theory to be discarded at will. One can learn to work with it for oneself and the students, or ignore it and continue to play and teach in an often incoordinate way.

3) I agree wholeheartedly with Gyorgy Sandor and others that one of the most prevalent practices in piano technique is also one of the most damaging to a fluid technique. This is the widely taught put-the-thumb-under preparation motion. Not only does having the thumb under with the joint bent in create a rotationally incorrect relationship of hand to arm, the sudden thumb-tucking motion also causes a reflexive pull downwards on the tendons of both the index and third fingers—effectively tightening the entire hand for a split second. Some peoples' hands are more affected than others, but the freedom and speed of the fingers has always been markedly diminished when doing the following experiment. With the thumb loosely straight beside the second finger, flutter the fingers as fast as possible. Notice the rate of speed and sensation. Then, bend the tip of the thumb and put the thumb under, to approximately the third finger. Keeping the thumb under, observe the second and third finger—are they pulled or bent? Did they react at all when you put the thumb under? With the thumb under, tip bent, try fluttering the fingers. Notice the sensation and speed. Now try the flutter with the thumb out from under and loosely straight again. Do you feel the difference?

Teachers, do not teach "put the thumb under." Do just the opposite, in fact. To counter the intellectually anticipatory action of putting the thumb under too soon, which causes so many problems, please teach a slight lift of the thumb up and away from the note it is about to play, then let the thumb flip the hand as it comes down onto the desired note. Once you and the students learn to do this easily and semi-automatically, you will be amazed at how many problems just disappear from playing.

The Beginning

Over the years I have developed a detailed pre-*Twinkle* routine. Each item on the list has been put there because of something missing in the foundation that I didn't see the need for until the students were further along.

Things to Do	Pre-Twinkle Check-off							Cards																				
	Every activity must be preceded by "Ready-Go." No "Ready-Go" means no go!							1 set of finger cards, 1-5 1 set of things to do cards 1 set of number of repetitions							Some activities need only one card. Some may use all three.													
	Remember: left hand or hands together, and hands slap knee between repetitions																												
1. Bow																													
2. Finger grab, finger on head, nose, floor, ear, etc.																													
3. Thumb stand freeze, count age																													
4. Feet freeze, fingers walk, 1-2-3-4-5-4-3-2-1																													
5. Tin man: lift and drop shoulder, elbow, wrist. Feet still. Check posture.																													
6. Finger feelers: 5 soft things. Pumpkin pie rhythm																													
7. Octopus with tissue																													
8. Octopus with lift-off and stroke back of hand																													
9. Open - shut 1-2, 1-3, 1-4, 1-5, 1-4																													
10. Walking fingers Stand on each																													
11. Bunny sniffing at piano																													
12. Black key twins, triplets. Do high-low, up-down. Finger 2-3 or 2-3-4																													
13. Fingers and letters. Find all Cs. Add other letters																													
14. Singing 3 songs																													
15. Horses'hooves (stand on thumb)																													

(See full-size chart, Appendix 1.)

I don't think of them as technical exercises but rather as activities designed to awaken parts of the brain and body that until now have been unstimulated and under-utilized. Many of them involve proprioception—the body's way of communicating with itself through special nerve endings and sensors in the tissues—to awaken the connection with the feel of the piano, piano sound, and the motions of the hand and arm. These include: stroking soft objects with the fingers, picking up scarves or Kleenex tissues with elongated fingers, opening and closing the hand like an alligator's mouth, floating the wrist upward with the hand dropping downward and the elbow low. These motions are then transferred to the piano itself as we play single keys at first, then incorporated into the early pieces.

I am trying to achieve ease of motion in a natural way, with no part of the playing mechanism held rigidly or tensely in a position by muscle contractions. We are trying to feel, from the very beginning, that each finger and each note has a place unique to itself for the best playing angle to the piano, and that each finger is aligned to the arm and capable of standing comfortably on its own. We find that certain fingers (2 and 3) respond very well to commands to play, and that others (4 and 5) need a lot of practice "answering the phone" because they are harder to "talk" to. I try to have the children develop an almost parental attitude to their fingers (the children) and to become both fascinated and amused at the vast differences in the children's behavior. Since they are the parents, it is their job to teach and help their children, and never get mad or sad at what they do—just try again!

As the children's fingers get smarter, better connected to the ears, and more used to playing the piano, we can ask more from them. Our job, and goal, is to get maximum ease of playing for minimum muscular effort, to learn to use the piano to help support us, to learn to push off from it and land on it without clutching in mid-air, to change seamlessly from upward notes (staccato, repeated) to downward notes (legato, walking) and back again just because we hear the demand for this coming in the music before we actually play it.

For example, the RH melody of *Lightly Row,* just the first line, demands:

Down up down, down up down,
down down down down up up long up....

This is very complex, especially when placed against the LH's continuous downs with big swings. The brain and body want to do things symmetrically, so of course the LH thumb on G wants to go up along with the RH's lifted E!

Book 1 and early Book 2 are where and when such basic things as the example above must become thoroughly mastered and an unconscious part of the technique. Piano playing is not symmetrical, it is not predictable physically, things do not stay in a fixed position. Each student brings to it the same basic physical equipment but widely variable neural pathways—some wired for use but many not connected or used at all—yet!

I find the first couple of years of study to be fascinating. Each new student is like a complex series of packages to be unwrapped, or an onion with many layers. You never know, as you go from box to box, or layer to layer, what will happen next. You do know it will be challenging for everyone involved (student, teacher, parent). A crucial part of the teacher's job in the early years is to make technique so interesting that both the student and parent come to see that without good technique, nothing of high quality can be accomplished—no matter how many notes and pieces one acquires in a given time period.

The *Twinkles*

Fingering

	C	G	A	G	F	E	D	C
RH	11	44	55	4	33	22	11	1
LH	55	22	11	2	33	44	55	5
Middle RH	55	44	33	2				
Middle LH	11	22	33	4				

I think the *Twinkles* are very important, but not as valuable for pianists as they are for strings. Most of the variations deal with leaving the piano (staccato) and ignore the equally important aspect of walking on (legato) the piano. For this reason I introduce the last *Twinkle* variation first (walking and slow repeated notes) and then go to *Twinkle A*. *Twinkle A* can be very tiring, so we do it in very small bits at first. How they do it— with ease, fingers moving, wrist flexible to move upward at—is of much more importance to me than how much of it they do at once. At the same time they are working on both the last and first *Twinkles*, they will work on *Honeybee, Cuckoo, Lightly Row* and *Mary.* This group of pieces, with perhaps a few more such as *Go tell Aunt Rhody,* will make up the bulk of the study for at least the first four months. They will continue to do the *Twinkles,* perhaps one type each day, for as long as they are in Book 1.

Technique Exercises and Time Spent on Technique

I consider every note that is played (after the first try at finding the notes) to be time spent on technique. As the student advances, even the first try at a new piece is already involved with technique—choosing the touch, exploring the fingering, noting the difficult areas and planning what practice strategies will be required.

My students do no technical exercises as such, ever. All the technique is available through piano literature, so we study it there, intensely. They do play scales and chords, but as practical music theory, not drills.

In this age of very limited practice time, it is both wasteful and unnecessary to spend time repeating patterned exercises over and over when a much greater benefit can be found by studying the technical problems as they actually occur in say, Beethoven, and then finding similar problems with similar solutions, in say, Chopin.

Technical exercises usually present the same problem, over and over. Real music, other than études, jumps rapidly from one type of playing to another—the changes themselves are the technical problems.

Williams

Elements of Technique

I emphasize a natural and relaxed body and hand position. This means good posture at the keyboard with the right height adjusted for each child's feet and seating. The forearm and wrist are level. The upper arm hangs naturally by the side of the body. The goal is to watch carefully in those beginning months to have children feel and look comfortable so that they can concentrate on small motions with the fingers (not pushing and collapsing the first joint of finger) and yet are able to produce a good tone, and accurate melodic and rhythmic patterns. I try to teach the natural weight of the arm coming into the key bed with a small motion of the finger on the key, so that the child is almost picking up the sound of each note, rather than pushing into the key with an almost certainly collapsed first joint of the finger. The shoulders, head and back must be free of tension with the energy supporting the body ultimately over time coming from the feet. The hand itself should assume the relaxed look of the hand at the side of the body, with fingers close together, a good knuckle ridge, an upright 5th finger and a thumb held in line with the overall alignment of the 2nd finger. This is all very difficult to do but keeping the hand soft will go a long way toward establish good habits when the young child's hand is very malleable.

The Beginning

I use the *Twinkles*, a finger at a time, as the first exercise.

The *Twinkles*

I teach all of the four *Twinkles* hands separately at each child's own pace. I have children use them continually to reference the staccato, legato or combination of both as they encounter it within the compositions of all books. This makes an easy transfer of information for them.

Technical Execises and Time Spent on Technique

I introduce the chromatic scale first and then some major and minor scales (C, G and F major, A and E minor) at the end of the first book and spend time working on passing the thumb under, keeping the fingers independent. Keeping the three tall fingers close to the black notes with the thumb and 5th finger to the center of the key is also important. Chords, cadences, and arpeggios are put into place as the child's hand and development comes into place. I use Hanon and Czerny as the child is ready. I require a high percentage of practice time on these technical exercises and work out with each student what that requirement is for them individually. I always listen to these in their lessons weekly.

Yurko

Elements of Technique

Piano technique must be individualized for different students. At each lesson I carefully study my students to determine what I can ask of them. With some I can develop technique from the very beginning. And with others, I am permissive and wait before guiding them too much. This depends on the child's hands as well as the temperament. However, there are similarities. I am looking for

1) relaxed arm weight

2) flexible wrists which are not drooping

3) supported, rounded hands

4) round, flexible fingers

5) fingers which touch the key with the pad or the tip (This position depends on the music and the size of the hand.)

6) finger weight that produces a variety of touches

7) relaxed shoulders

8) solid support for the feet

The Beginning

My beginners are usually very young, so in the first lesson I am pleased if we finish drawing the feet paper, introduce the bow and learn rest position while sitting at the keyboard.

Should we accomplish these things and the child is still focused, we learn to play a little with the thumb. The technique I impart is to play with a slanted thumb so the wrist is as high as the hand. "Your thumb can look just like a little slide," I tell them. The first sound is a nice staccato. Using just the thumb, we may do one bounce or the whole *Twinkle A* rhythm.

In the first few weeks, the priority is to keep the wrist up, the fingers relaxed and achieve a nice staccato. In the first few months, we concentrate on the position of the wrist, relaxed fingers, the staccato and not letting the hand turn when finger 5 plays. In the first year, it is important to watch the wrist, the hand and not let the fingers collapse. To help them know that their fingers are naturally strong, I ask them to make finger circles. We form ovals and circles with each of our fingers and the thumb. By squeezing a little, the finger will either collapse at the first joint or remain strong. They can learn how to control the first joint when making finger circles which then is transferred to playing the piano.

The *Twinkles*

I use all the *Twinkles* and hear them at the beginning of every lesson during the study of Book 1. They are very important in my teaching. The students learn them in order as they hear them on the CD. First we learn the RH and then the LH. Some students learn all the RH *Twinkles* and then learn the LH. Others go back and forth, learning each of the hands. They are never played hands together in a parallel position since parallel keyboard playing is tricky and not so necessary in beginning study. At the end of Book 1, my students figure out the LH accompaniment and play them this way on their graduation recital.

Fingering

I use the fingering originally taught in Japan in the early 1970's. Since it is very simple for children to remember, they are more free to concentrate on their technique.

1) RH: Finger 4 always plays only G and the thumb plays both D and C

2) LH: Finger 2 always plays only G and Finger 5 plays both D and C

The only piano key the students need to practice finding is G. Then the rest of the piece plays itself. If the fingering is simplified then the child can turn his attention to rhythmic accuracy and technique.

Rhythm

A priority is the correct rhythm of each *Twinkle*. It must be very accurate. We study this carefully with lots of imitation games.

Stop—Prepare—Go: This is used for discipline and to help the hand from becoming tense from playing too many repeated notes in sequence. At first the discipline is for the child to listen to me. Later it becomes a discipline to listen to themselves and can be used when learning any new finger patterns at any age.

It works this way: After a child plays the first rhythm of *Twinkle A* with the thumb, I say, "Stop." I wait for the preparation on G then say, "Go" when the child is ready. This is used for each note of the *Twinkles*. This helps the child play more accurately by preparing mentally and physically first. If a child is very young (2 or a young 3), I may introduce this a little later otherwise the child may simply refuse to play. It is an individual thing.

To help find G we play a variety of games. A favorite is putting a little animal on G. I take away the animal and the child puts another animal on G. This is repeated over and over. Soon the child is able to find the G accurately, but it may be helpful to put a little animal between the black keys surrounding G for awhile.

Sequence

Since my beginning students are very young, I expect them to learn only the first phrase of *Twinkle* A before going on to the other *Twinkles*. We learn all the *Twinkles* with only the first phrase. At some point in the children's development, their attention spans increase and without effort, they can play the whole *Twinkle* pattern. Usually this happens with *Twinkle* D, often with Mom singing along. Obviously, many accumulated hours of hearing the CD helps make this easier.

Twinkle A

Since this is the first *Twinkle*, many of the disciplines such as stopping to prepare, technique of the fingers and hand, and the fingering of the piece are learned here. I use a great deal of imitation. I am usually on my knees playing with the children, letting them ride on my hand, practicing just one bounce over and over, and helping them finding the notes. I want a clear, nice-sounding staccato with a relaxed, bouncing hand. If the child holds the notes rather than making them staccato, we play with a bright rubber ball, bouncing it on the closed keyboard cover.

As a contrast we talk about a little doll who is sitting and not bouncing. We say that she is sticking to the sound and we want bounces in *Twinkle* A. We try to bounce, over and over, keeping score with little animals if the child bounced or was sticky. This gets the idea across!

Twinkle B

This one has nice staccatos like *Twinkle* A and the middle note is held. I want a beautiful singing note and demonstrate a slight upward wrist motion as the note sings. The children imitate this motion. Later on we practice making the staccatos light and soft.

Twinkle C

This variation is all staccatos. It is easier to play if the hand is a little closer to the keys when it bounces. It's also easier if played softly. If any *Twinkle* rhythm is tricky, it will be this one. Lots of imitation is useful. Children may inadvertently use a legato motion between the notes due to the quickness of the rhythm. This is corrected by practicing with a Stop between the notes. It must be corrected immediately or it will become a habit and hard to change.

Twinkle D

Twinkle D is where legato is learned. With very young children, I may let them play *Twinkle D* for a short time without legato. When they are ready, we learn legato this way:

With our thumb on C, we play two long, singing notes using a flexible wrist. Without letting go of C, we play one G with finger 4. Two notes are being held. This is practiced until it is easy. Then we do it the same way, except after we check to see that both keys are down, we let go of the thumb but still hold onto G. With many repetitions in the lesson and at home, this soon becomes smoother. We practice this technique with fingers 4 and 5 and then it is usually easy to do a regular legato on all the fingers. After that we watch very carefully to catch any fingers which are not legato. If we hear one, the child stops playing. This way the child learns to be careful and good habits form from the beginning.

As D and C are both played by the thumb, I don't worry too much as long as the legato is fairly good. However, I always demonstrate with a silent finger change to finger 2 after playing the D twice. When the children are able, they imitate me without much formal teaching. This way I know I'm not overtaxing their concentration level.

Once all the *Twinkles* are learned and the hand position is fairly steady, we play a shortcut version of the *Twinkles*. This consists of the first phrase of *Twinkle A*, *Twinkle B*, *Twinkle C* and *Twinkle D* all hooked together without any pauses. Sometimes we play all of *Twinkle D* when we play the shortcut version, if the child needs the practice. I always play a rhythmic accompaniment on my piano. This is a great accomplishment when the child can play the shortcut version without help. The accompaniment sets the tempo, establishes the pulse and helps the child play rhythmically.

This is more fun for the children, since they play all the variations in a much shorter time. Since the shortcut version takes less time to play, the parents tell me this helps with playing the *Twinkles* daily at the home lesson as well. This holds true for the lesson too. If we play all the *Twinkles* in their entirety with each hand there's hardly time or energy to do much else!

Technical Exercises

I introduce scales in Book 2 or 3. We begin with one octave for the sharped scales, hands alone. I use a rhythm of a quarter note on the tonic followed by eighth notes on the other notes. This helps with accuracy and tempo. We practice to achieve MM = 76 in the beginning. Once hands alone for two or three octaves is fluent, we put hands together. When the child can ghost (play on top of the keys with no sound) one octave hands together with the correct fingerings, then she or he plays them with sound. This helps the child master the fingerings. We progress to four octaves hands together, parallel and contrary motion in all keys, major and minor, although I must admit I am a little too lax on scales.

I don't use any other exercise books. The pieces are loaded with wonderful techniques. Since the children are anxious to play their pieces, they will more likely practice a technical exercise this way than following a list in a book.

Time Spent on Technique	Lesson	Home
Twinklers	almost all	almost all
Early Book 1	1/2	1/2
Book 1 and subsequent books	1/4	1/4

LESSON PLANNING

First Lessons

The description of the first lessons provided by the respondents illustrates the specifics of the Suzuki® Method at the beginning.

Some respondents like to start students in small groups where each child has some individual time at the piano and spend the rest of the hour observing other students or their parents. Others prefer to start their students in private lessons immediately.

First Lessons	Small groups	Private lessons
Adams	if possible	
Fest		•
Harrel	•	
Koppelman	•	
Liccardo		•
Powell		•
Schneiderman	in some cases	•
Taggart	preferably	•
Williams		•
Yurko	•	

For most respondents, the elements covered in the first lesson include all or most of the following:

1) Bowing

2) Sitting correctly (foot stools and cushions)

3) Posture (balanced body, relaxed arms and hands)

4) Rest position/focus

5) Names of keys

6) Finger numbers

7) Introduction of variations (usually rhythm of A)

8) Various activities: pitch matching, echo games, improvisation, etc.

9) Answering parents' questions and offering guidance

10) Parents' lesson at the keyboard

One feature that characterizes the Suzuki lessons is the participation of the parent. Not only are parents present at every lesson, but many respondents emphasize that in the beginning stages teachers need to devote a portion of the lesson time to the parent. Part of a teacher's responsibility is to answer parents' questions and discuss practice, but also many respondents mention the importance of working individually with each parent at the piano.

- Students begin in small groups (two or three to a class) or in overlapping 20–30 minute lessons. Small groups or overlapping lessons allow students and parents to observe others in the beginning stages of learning, which helps to reinforce individual details. Students absorb materials more easily in a group setting and become accustomed to performing for others. Early basic theory materials and reinforcement games and activities are easily presented in groups.

  The first lesson involves the following:

  1) Bowing
  2) Getting to know each other
  3) Posture/foot stools and bench cushions
  4) Rest position
  5) Finger numbers
  6) Recognition of a few primary keys on the piano
  7) Clapping of the rhythm of the Variation A
  8) Playing Variation A on at least the C and perhaps proceeding to additional notes, G or A
  9) Answering parents' questions
  10) Reinforcing a format for home practice and guidance. (Adams)

- I begin students with private lessons, although there is always someone observing the lesson. At the first lesson, I want the child to actually play the piano; that's why they have come. I precede the playing by teaching the child how to bow. Then I show the parent how to seat the child correctly at the piano and explain that he or she will be responsible for doing this at home and at all future lessons. I play games with the child to teach finger numbers and assign this as part of the practice. Next I work with the child on playing the Twinkle A rhythm with the thumb. For many children this is enough; for others I continue with the other fingers. The child and I bow to finish the lesson, and then it is the parent's turn for a lesson. I work with the parent on the same things I have done with the child, answer questions, give encouragement, etc. (Fest)

- For young children (ages 3-5) I recommend starting lessons twice a week in a group of three children and their parents. Very young children recoil from being the sole focus of adult attention, so a group lesson is easier for them. If the teacher begins with the most outgoing child in the group, the others notice that the first child was safe at the piano and had a good experience. They then are more willing at the outset to take their turn. Each child and parent learns from observing the other lessons. The teacher works with each child individually for as long as his or her attention span lasts.

  Lessons are intentionally very focused. After the short individual lessons are over, the teacher may choose to do some less-structured group activities with the children, such as pitch matching, improvisation, or movement. However, time must also be saved to work with the parents individually at the piano. A parent who has the opportunity to experience a physical technique at the piano or to discuss the main point of the child's lesson will carry through better at home.

  Inevitably, some children will have longer attention spans than others. During that all-important initial orientation, parents must be led to understand why the group lesson is the best environment for young children and also to understand that you are not doing the child a favor by keeping the child at the piano after his ability to focus is finished. On the contrary, at that point you are teaching the child that he does not like being at the piano. Learning is taking place for all during the entire hour—not just when a parent's own child is at the keyboard. A teacher may also subtly arrange to add a few extra minutes to the keyboard time allotted to a parent whose child has a short focus.

  Generally, at age 6 and above, the child and parent come twice a week—once for a private lesson, and once for a group lesson. (Harrel)

- We start with individual lessons in a small group whenever possible. This is especially important with very young students. Parents and children learn much from observing other lessons. Parents are more relaxed when observing other children and find it reassuring. Children see others their age doing similar things, which excites their interest. They can more easily picture themselves doing those things too. There is an alive atmosphere with other children present. We begin with short lessons. As the attention span increases, lessons get longer. This leaves less time for observation.

What I do at the first lesson depends on the student's responsiveness. I cover many things while the student and parent are observing before starting lessons (which is compulsory), such as getting the proper equipment for sitting (chair and footstool), how to bow and sit well, how the parent should take notes and work with their child. At the first lesson I review all this and do what I described in the section on beginning technical skills. I also do some Simple Simon-type activities to encourage the student to be attentive to me and to listen. My usual beginning student is 3 to 4 years old, so lessons are short. If the student is older and responsive, I do as much as they are able to absorb. This is very much an individual matter. (Koppelman)

• *I begin all of my Suzuki piano students with a one-on-one private lesson, but in conjunction with weekly group classes in performance and musicianship. I think it is critical to their success and to the longevity of their study that students have a group experience.*

I will teach the students to bow and set them up at the piano in order to show the parents how do it properly at home. I also test them on right hand and left hand, count finger numbers, tap rhythms (leading up to the rhythm of Variation A) and then we usually play a phrase of Variation A, sometimes Variation C and play through and sing the Twinkle theme. All the playing is done with me physically guiding around the keyboard. However, for the first several lessons especially, I leave at least half of the time to work with the parent at the keyboard. The parent gets a crash course on playing the piano for the first month or two, and I also spend some lesson time with parent and child together at the keyboard to supervise their playing together. (Liccardo)

• *I begin my students in private lessons. Most of the first lesson is done sitting on the floor rather than at the piano. There are four areas I cover at that lesson:*

1) Work with Twinkle A *techniques through clapping games (floor)*

2) Work with loose hands and arm (floor)

3) Seat student at the piano to show the parent proper height for the bench and feet

4) Teach the bow. (Powell)

- I start my students with private lessons after an orientation process that includes the parents' reading, observing and taking several lessons, the children listening to the tape for several months and observing workshops and lessons to become familiar with the setting, with me, and with the idea and reality of studying piano. They have seen and heard other children playing and, I hope, have shown enthusiasm for beginning. The shared atmosphere of the workshop and the opportunity to meet the children they have been observing provide a feeling of immediate community. The social aspect of the experience is very important.

At the first lesson, I try to initiate a sense of friendship and trust between the child and myself and also encourage interaction (brief, warm introductions) with the students before and after. We make as much progress as we can on our bow, learning a poem to help remember a natural, balanced feeling in the body. We are already focusing on the all-important matters of concentration and quality as we learn to follow directions and work on details.

I hope to encourage a healthy sense of self with my words and tone, and hope also to convey my own love of music, suggesting that it can become a very special friend in one's life. We always begin and end the lesson with a bow, a satisfying "container" because it introduces and closes each lesson peacefully. I ask parent and student to do the same at home. I have already established with the parent the importance of the beginning steps and how to work at home.

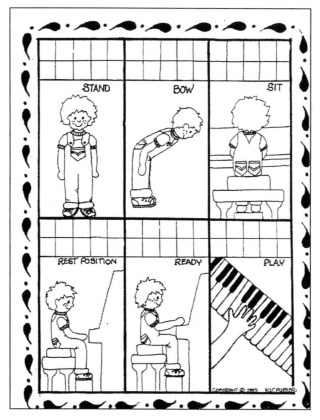

(See full-size chart, Appendix 2.)

We go to the piano and, depending on the student's maturity, do an appropriate amount of rest position training (also with a short poem). I like Kathy Purser's beginning steps chart (see above) and this visual aide is colorful and motivating in the beginning when a child might need extrinsic reward, encouragement and the sense that learning is fun. Some children who are ready learners or especially well-disciplined will even respond to some float-up-and-ready-position instruction, but we will polish all of these valuable centering skills for months and even years. (In later lessons, I emphasize the inner content of rest position, peaceful thoughts, traveling inward to the source of our strength and truth and wisdom as a person—using language appropriate to the age and maturity of the student.)

We do listening games with high/low, loud/soft, long/short, legato/staccato, going up/down and introduce a little at each lesson. We find white and black keys and learn the pattern of two and three black-key groups counting up the keyboard. I might play a song and ask parent and student to sing along or clap as I play.

If the child's concentration span is shorter than the allotted half-hour, we may play rudimentary music-matching or clapping games on the floor with Mom, or tap rhythms on a tambourine or drum and then return to the work at the keyboard.

Within music instruction and the framework of the Suzuki® Method, there is room for much individualization in timing and choice of materials. Syllabus, pacing and tone are largely influenced by the student I am teaching, his or her learning style, personality, interests, age and maturity. Teachers should feel freedom to respond to each child, to explore all the pedagogical possibilities, to imagine and create new ways, to develop the same confidence in their own ability and uniqueness that we seek for the child. Open to change, they will surely evolve and enjoy the excitement of ongoing revitalization.

The beginning steps (bow, rest position, float up and ready position) are of primary importance for instilling many valuable qualities: centering, concentration, peacefulness, physical comfort, posture, self-discipline, balance, readiness to learn and an integration of mind and body which puts a student in touch with his best ability—a condition fundamental to studying, playing and performing. This integration and sense of personal harmony will influence every aspect of a student's musical and personal growth. I have developed this idea in detail in my book Confident Music Performance: The Art of Preparing (MMB Music, Inc) which describes how a confident performance is built into the study of the music from day one—all human faculties joined in a comprehensive process with depth and breadth. Suzuki's philosophy and principles of learning form an excellent foundation for confident performance. (Schneiderman)

- *Small group lessons vs. private lessons.*

  I have done both, as circumstances of my schedule dictate. I prefer the small group, for the camaraderie and inspiration for each other. Usually, they can stay in a group for all of Book 1, and sometimes into Book 2.

  Very first lesson: Good bow. Number the fingers; play finger identification games. Find two and three black key groups. Find all C's and F's. At the piano, adjust seat height, foot support; teach parent how to judge and duplicate this at home. Practice sitting with straight back and quiet feet, playing one note with a requested finger, holding absolutely still while parent counts up to the highest number child can wait. Learning about and using a Ready—Go signal.

  Over the years, I have developed a Pre-Twinkle and Book I list of many small things that need to be covered, and in the past, have asked the parents to make an ever-growing practice chart of these items, to help them as they practice. Finally, one of the teachers I work with made a wonderful chart which demonstrates very clearly that the longer you teach, the more you realize how crucial every small step in the initial learning process is to success in later years. Even if the child is very quick and coordinated, nothing should be taken for granted as intuitively understood, by student or parent. It is also crucial to establish early the habit of identifying a small section as requiring more practice or repetition than other parts of a piece. All too often at institutes and workshops, we will encounter the child who can only start at the beginning. The teachers of these students have not realized that Book I is where the ability to start at any given logical section is developed—later is too late! (Taggart)

- *Because of limitations in my facility, I either start two (2) students in a shared lesson or one as a private student. The parent comes alone for three to four weeks so that we can continue working on philosophy and methodology. The child then comes to the lesson and the hands-on portion of the lesson with the child grows in length as the attention span of the child grows. I begin with the child's ability to bow. Content in the first lesson depends completely on readiness of the child that day (attention span, the environment and many other factors) but the one-point lesson is my goal so that the child has a base on which to build. (Williams)*

- *I begin students in small groups for one-hour lessons if they are ages 2 to 5, so they can learn from each other. The parents also learn from one another and it's more fun. If a child is a little shy, having other children present helps him or her immensely. We maintain these groups for one to two years depending on the progress of the children. When they have the concentration to focus for 30 minutes and/or have too much music for me to hear in just 20 minutes, we move to a regular, individualized lesson format. But students continue to observe one another.*

At the first lesson we draw the feet paper.

The child stands on a white 11 x 11 piece of posterboard and I trace around their stocking feet with a thick black marker. If the child is too shy to do this, then the lesson doesn't proceed, because it's unlikely that the child is ready for instruction. Thus the drawing of the feet paper becomes an important indication of readiness.

But usually the child has observed lessons and is anxious for his or her own turn. I write the child's first name boldly across the top and the date along the bottom. This makes a nice memento as well as a practical feet paper to use for bowing in lessons, home practice and recitals. It's fun for the child to bring his or her own paper to lessons and provides a sense of personal space as well as a guide for bowing.

After teaching them to smile before and after a slow, steady bow, I teach the parent how to use the adjustable piano chair, and seat the child at the piano. I carefully teach the parent to seat the child with the knees just under the keyboard, feet flat on the footstool and hands at a comfortable height with arms fairly level. This position is something we continue to work on throughout Book 1, since most children are naturally wiggly.

Note: For the past ten years I have been using miniature rubber animals in my teaching. There are over 100 different ones, beautifully designed and in attractive colors. They are small enough to fit between the black notes on the piano. I've created many games which help the children to focus and accomplish steps to learning which may otherwise be tedious for them. Parents in my program have their own sets at home for practice. I've never been big on using too many props at the keyboard (I'm not a puppeteer!) but these little animals are a lifesaver.

Next the child learns rest position while sitting at the keyboard. I put a little animal on the Twinkle C (one octave above middle C).

With the child looking at C, I count out loud as long as the child can hold still and not even move the eyes. My goal is to count to the child's age. If that is not possible after a few tries, the lesson ends with encouragment, smiles, a hug from Mom or Dad and an assignment to practice counting with rest position at home.

If we accomplish a sustained rest position and the child is still focused, we learn ready position. The child is shown the C above middle C and asked to place his thumb there.

The technique I impart is to use a slanted thumb so the wrist is as high as the hand. With the child's thumb in place, I count aloud while the child sits perfectly still.

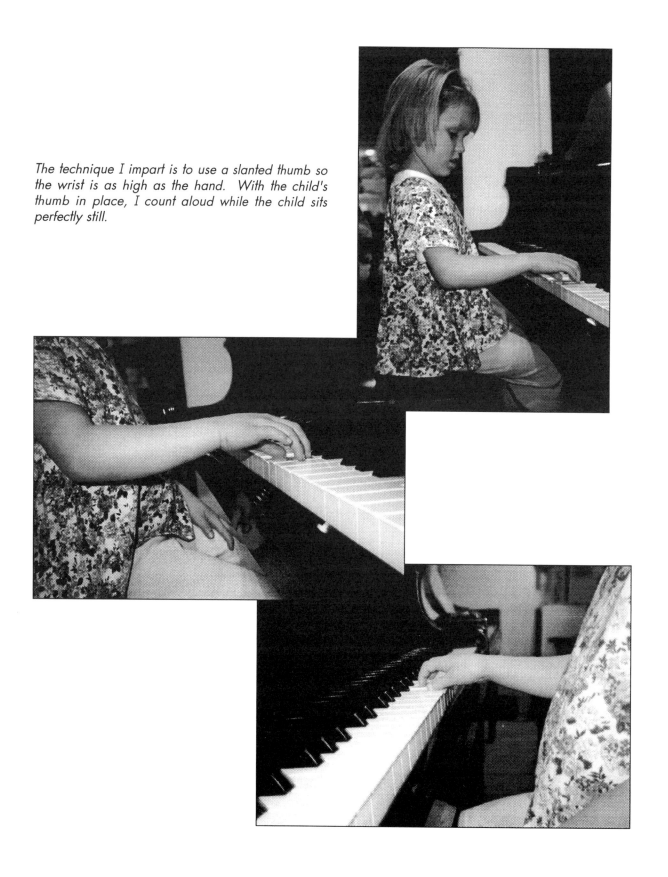

Then it's time to play a little with the thumb. The sound goal is a nice staccato. We can do one bounce or the whole Twinkle A rhythm with the thumb, depending on the child. (Yurko)

Lesson Plans

This section on lesson plans gives a concrete idea of how Suzuki teaching is being done in various studios. Presenting some guidelines for lesson plans offers the opportunity of appreciating the variety and richness of the different teaching styles.

The content of lessons in Book 1 includes the *Twinkles* (each one or part of each one is usually heard at every lesson), review pieces, newest pieces (or working pieces), parental guidance and parental lessons. For some teachers, scales, reading and theory are introduced sometime during Book 1.

In Books 2 and 3, lessons are divided between technique, review pieces, new pieces and reading. Technique now usually includes exercises, scales, arpeggios, and sometimes a technique book (Hanon, Czerny). Many respondents drop the *Twinkles* when starting Book 2 or as they are working through Book 2. The percentage of time given to new pieces (or working pieces) tends to increase as students become more advanced, and the time allowed for review tends to decrease at the lesson (but emphasis is still given to review in home practice). Before the end of Book 2, reading and theory are part of all respondents' lesson plans. At this level, the need to teach parents is not as great, so less time is allowed for that.

Some teachers provided us with a breakdown in percentages of the elements of a lesson. These figures are hypothetical and we all know that plans change with each student as well as from lesson to lesson. But this chart gives us an idea of how teachers try to organize the content of their lessons in general.

Lesson Plans	Variations	Variations and/or other technique	Review pieces	New pieces (working pieces)	Preview	Reading/ theory	Ear training and tonalisation	Parents' lessons and guidance
Beginning Book 1								
Adams	90%					10%theory		
Fest	50–70%							30–50%
Mid-Book 1								
Adams		20%	20%	40%		20%		
Fest	30%		50%					20%
Powell			35%	40–45%			20–25%	
End Book 1								
Adams		20%	60%			20%		
Fest	30%		50%					20%
Powell			65%	17%			17%	
Book 2								
Adams		20%	20%	30%	10%	20%		
Fest		20%	50%			30%		
Powell		20–23%	13%	20–27%		40%		
Book 3								
Adams		20%	10%	40%	10%	20%		
Fest		10–30%						
Powell		8–9%	18–22%	33–45%		35–40%		
Book 4 and above								
Adams		10%	10%	50%		30%		
Fest		10–30%						

- Gradually, all the variations are learned and the students progress through the book, learning right hand, left hand, alternate hands (with a duet partner of parent or teacher), and finally hands together for each piece. A theory workbook is introduced early in the lessons and a reading method book is started when students are comfortable playing hands together on French Children's Song. During the course of Book 1, five-finger patterns are introduced. Each lesson will include technique (five-finger patterns and the Variations), review pieces, working pieces, previews of difficult passages in upcoming pieces, and theory activities or games.

  In Book 2, the same sequence will be followed, but five-finger patterns will be expanded into full one-octave scales and the review will include pieces from Book 1. Theory and reading method books are continued, and expanded into additional reading books.

  In Book 3, the same sequence is used, but more supplementary classical pieces will be added. Scales are expanded into two octaves.

  In Book 4, the Suzuki repertoire is used in conjunction with other classical pieces to include more romantic and contemporary literature. (Adams)

- Beginner: I hear all the Twinkles or at least portions of each Twinkle at every lesson. I begin each lesson with Twinkles and spend most of the student's time at the piano working with the Twinkles. When they play some of the pieces immediately following the Twinkles, I also hear those. The remainder of the lesson time, 30–50%, is spent with the parent at the piano or talking with the parent about practice, listening, etc.

  Middle Book 1: Again, I begin each lesson with Twinkles. It is not necessary to play all of each Twinkle, but I like to hear portions of each one. Approximately 30% of the lesson is devoted to the Twinkles. Then I go to selected review pieces, then to the newest piece, if the review pieces are stable. About 50% of the lesson time is given to the review pieces. The final 20% of the lesson is time with the parent, helping them as needed.

  End of Book 1: I follow the same lesson order as I do for middle Book 1. Often I don't need as much time with the parent, but I am flexible with this.

  Books 2 and 3: I divide the lesson into four sections—technique, review, new piece, and reading. I touch on all these areas in each lesson; I have found that if one of these is not done at the lesson, the message conveyed is that it's not that important. I always begin with technique, taking around 20% of the lesson time. Next I go to either music reading or review. Music reading normally gets about 30% of the lesson time. Review pieces and the new piece take up the other 50% of the lesson time. I definitely put the least emphasis on the new piece; children really learn to develop their musical skills with their review pieces.

  Book 4 and above: Again, I always begin with technique. I may not hear scales, Czerny, and Hanon at each lesson, but I hear some of them. Depending on the student's needs and performances coming up, the time on technique is 10–30% of the lesson. I always hear review pieces. (It is so easy to focus solely on the new piece.) I certainly cannot hear all review pieces at every lesson, but I always hear some. The new piece may be in the Suzuki repertoire, or it may be a supplementary piece. Also, music reading is now a part of learning the Suzuki repertoire as well as learning the supplementary music. Consequently, I cannot so neatly account for the amount of time spent on reading and the amount of time spent on a new piece; they are no longer separate elements. (Fest)

- Focus is best at the beginning of the lesson. Use that time for what is most important at the moment. It might be a new technique, following through on the main point of the last lesson, previews of challenging spots in future pieces, or reading. During orientation, parents are asked to communicate at the beginning of the lesson any problem spots that occurred during the practice sessions, insuring that the teacher has time to step in, diagnose, and remedy the problem.

  Lesson plans must be individualized. If a teacher detects that reading or scales or review is being neglected, he may choose to move that category to the beginning of every lesson as a signal to the child and parent of its importance. (Harrel)

- What I cover is variable, depending on what that particular student needs at that time. But in general, for beginners I do preliminary warm-ups, Twinkles, and RH of pieces they can play, in order. I check to see if they know finger numbers without looking, by my touching them (three-to four-year-olds). I teach the names of the notes on the piano, and anything else that is needed. In middle Book 1, I hear the above points, then pieces they know in order, usually. By the end of Book 1, I hear pieces in any order, teaching polishing points of musicality. I may begin rhythm work with a metronome. In the upper books, I hear technical warm-up, reading, pieces being worked on, review, theory, possibly solfège or any other special study, usually in that order. The order and content may be changed due to special needs or events. (Koppelman)

- 1) Content

    Beginner: Review right hand and left hand, finger numbers, tap rhythms and play the songs that they have learned or are learning. We may do just the first phrase of several of the variations and then add the next sections when the first phrase is secure. I also start them playing the variations with just one finger so the next step would be teaching them the grown-up fingering. We might practice the C to G jump, or just the middle phrases of each variation to make sure they remember to repeat. We also do some singing of the variations and the theme. Time with the parent is also essential to keep them ahead of their child.

    Middle Book 1: Lesson contains lots of review. We play through the pieces already learned and work on a nice sound, comfortable tempo, a good hand position, some basic dynamics such as echoes, and making sure the memory is secure.

    End Book 1: I hear the newest piece, making the necessary corrections and improvements and do lots of polishing and refining of the review pieces. This might include tone, dynamics, phrasing, shaping, timing, tempos and mood appropriate to each piece and possibly some work done on balancing the hands. We also spend time and often start the lesson with reading since I introduce this about two-thirds through Book 1.

    Book 2: In addition to review, I might spend some time reading, where appropriate, some of the new material in the Suzuki repertoire. This usually starts with some sections of the Bach minuets. There would, of course, also be independent reading material that I would check, and I may have them sight-read something new at the lesson. Another new element is scale playing and possibly some Czerny-Schaum towards the end of the book.

    Books 3 and 4: Lesson is divided between reading (Suzuki and non-Suzuki materials), working on the new piece, hearing review and always trying to assign something specific for the student to work on rather than just playing the pieces through, and technique such as scales, Hanon, etc.

2) Order of activities

    Book 1: I like to frame the more difficult task, such as learning the new piece or coordinating a difficult section, with easier, more comfortable tasks. I usually start by having the child play several polished pieces, then spend time with the newer, more difficult material and then finish up again by playing pieces that are well learned. I ask the parents to do this as well.

    Book 2 on: The order of activities and the percentage of time spent on them will often vary from student to student. It will also vary at different times of the season. If we are preparing for recitals and auditions, we might spend much more time on review. During the summer, for instance, we might spend more time on reading, sight-reading and technique. If a child is excited about something I may let them begin with that and then go back into our usual pattern. In general, I like the younger students to start with reading and the older students to begin with technique, but I try not to be too predictable. (Liccardo)

- *A beginner's lessons consists of the following and is done in the order listed:*
  1) *Discussion of correct posture, checking from feet to head*
  2) *Follow-the-leader game (a copycat game)*
  3) *Tonalization*
  4) *Work on the Twinkles (the majority of the lesson is spent here)*

  Secondary in importance, but useful in giving the student a chance to get off the piano bench as well as being helpful to know:
  5) *Identifying notes on the keyboard (A, B, C, etc.)*
  6) *Identifying finger numbers*

  Here is a hypothetical lesson, typical of what I would use, for a middle Book 1 student with a half-hour lesson:
  1) *Posture and seating check (1 minute)*
  2) *Follow-the-leader game (3 minutes)*
  3) *Tonalization (3 minutes)*
  4) *Review*
      a) *Twinkle A (1 minute)*
      b) *Mary Had a Little Lamb (to begin working on the new skill of balance between hands) (5 minutes)*

5) New piece, hands together—Go Tell Aunt Rhody *(7 minutes)*

6) New working piece, right hand alone—Allegretto I *(1 to 6 minutes)*

7) Review

    a) Honeybee *(to improve an existing, low-wrist problem) (3 minutes)*

    b) Lightly Row *(a piece of the child's choice) (1 minute)*

A lesson with a student at the end of Book 1 is similar to middle Book 1 but involves more time spent on review:

1) Posture check *(1 minute)*

2) Follow-the-leader game *(2 minutes)*

3) Tonalization *(2 minutes)*

4) New working piece, hands together—Musette *(5 minutes)*

5) Heavy review to prepare for the graduation recital *(20 minutes)*

A thirty-minute Book 2 lesson is as follows:

1) Reading *(10 to 12 minutes)*

2) Theory *(1 minute)*

3) Technique

    a) Scales *(5 minutes)*

    b) Book 2 tonalization *(1 to 2 minutes)*

4) Suzuki pieces

    a) New working piece *(6 to 8 minutes)*

    b) Review *(4 minutes)*

Note : Since the reading and technique are new skills, I almost always begin the lesson with them; I tend to spend more time with them in Book 2, especially early Book 2, than I do later, for I want to take time to prepare the child and parent to practice them correctly and successfully at home.

In Books 3 and 4, lessons are usually lengthened to 45 minutes. They are as follows:

1) Reading *(10 to 12 minutes)*

2) Sight-reading *(4 minutes)*

3) Theory *(written work is checked while the child is studying the sight-reading; additional time spent is to prepare student for new material presented) (2 minutes)*

4) Technique *(scales) (4 minutes)*

5) Suzuki literature and/or supplementary pieces

    a) Working piece *(15 to 20 minutes)*

    b) Review *(8 to 10 minutes)*

Note: While I have listed the pieces in this order of presentation, I often rotate the reading and the Suzuki pieces so that the Suzuki pieces are not always at the end of the lesson when the child is not as fresh. Since there never seems to be enough time for everything, I often rotate hearing the scales and the sight-reading on a bi-weekly basis. If a child has done more reading than I can possibly hear, I often have the child choose his favorite pieces to show me; in this way, he is rewarded for his efforts and I get to hear a representative sampling of his work.

Books 5, 6, 7 and beyond follow a similar format to Books 3 and 4. Most of my students are taking 45-minute lessons at this level and a few take one-hour lessons. If the students are accompanying for a school or church choir at this point, then I assign much less reading from their reading books; I am willing to give lesson time to these accompaniments if they need me to do so, but as their confidence and skills grow, they do not seek my help as frequently. Arpeggios are added as a part of the technique; we usually alternate hearing the scales and arpeggios on a bi-weekly basis.

In conclusion, I must add that there is a wide variation of lesson structure in my studio at all levels, for I spend the most time with the area that needs the greatest attention. For example, the child who is a weak reader gets more attention in reading; the child playing scales with some technical problems gets more help with them; and the child preparing a piece for a special event gets extra attention on that piece. (Powell)

- *There are numerous elements which need to be presented, followed and developed throughout a program of instruction. As the materials accumulate, we sometimes rotate them over a succession of two or more lessons. Need arises from time to time to delve more intensively into one element or another—reading, technique, polishing or performance preparation, for example. A flexible approach to lesson content permits this responsiveness to a student's needs. It is important to stay in touch with all areas and be certain they are progressing at home.*

  For a beginner, it is essential to work on the beginning steps consistently at every lesson—that is, our bow, rest, float up and ready position. We want to instill a sense of physical, mental and emotional calm through repeated experiences that become a habit—the habit of composure or moment of repose. Practicing is more effective and performance confidence will grow from this learned personal harmony. It cannot be emphasized too much. Another facet of the repose is the intense focus it permits, a clear concentration of all one's faculties on the matter at hand. For the most productive practice as well as the deepest musical interpretation, focus is essential.

  We work on listening games and review what has been learned to date of the early songs and Twinkle Variations. I sometimes teach Mary had a Little Lamb as the first song and gradually introduce the variations interspersed with other early pieces. It is easiest to balance comfortably on the third finger so Mary presents an encouraging beginning as well as being a favored and familiar tune.

  During the middle of Book 1, we continue to refine our beginning steps and deepen that feeling of inner peace allied with physical comfort, a natural feeling in the whole body. As soon as the Twinkles are reasonably well launched, we begin reading readiness with a magnetic noteboard that pictures the grand staff. We continue to include review (Twinkles and songs), work on a new piece, perhaps polish another piece (right hand alone at this point) and start Alberti bass in the left hand (after the LH of unison pieces and Twinkles). Depending on the child, somewhere in the middle of Book 1, we include a series of reading and theory books. We may continue listening games and begin improvisation or composition according to the interests of the child.

  Around the end of Book 1, we emphasize reading more to prepare a student for Book 2, which we will learn by a combination of listening and reading. We continue all other activities: review, variation technique, improving a new piece and polishing another. Somewhere around the middle or end of Book 1, we work on putting hands together on the previously learned melodies once the Alberti bass (two C Major chords alternating with two G Major chords) is secure, fluent, comfortable, sounds beautiful and the child can play correct harmonies by ear while teacher or parent plays the melody. We do some transposing, begin five-note patterns and chords, early study of the circle of fifths and other theory.

  In Book 2, we work on some aspect of technique, selecting from: balance; "workout key" scales in 1 and 2 octaves, triads progressions and arpeggios; Hanon with some students; and circle of fifths. We do review (selections from Book 1 up to our current Book 2 level and perhaps supplementary pieces), a new piece, a polishing piece, reading, improvisation (almost all students), composition (a few), transposition (some), and theory books, with the circle of fifths increasingly developed.

  In Books 3, 4 and above, the content is much the same plus more supplementary material, studies, scales and arpeggios increasing to three and four octaves, more extensive keyboard harmony, etc.

  As I have already indicated, I take a flexible approach to the order of elements, even rotating some as appropriate to a student's current needs and goals. In general, it is helpful to start with technique for its warm-up effect but there is also virtue in beginning with review or a favorite piece for those musical and emotional rewards that provide a boost and a deeper personal association with music. In Book 2 and toward the end of Book 1, I tend to begin with reading (noteboard and theory books).

  The freshness of variety in order and proportion of elements, as long as all are regularly tended to, is beneficial to both student and teacher in keeping the learning process lively and the atmosphere spontaneous. (Schneiderman)

- *Beginner (after four lessons)*

  At the lesson: Introduce and/or review various sensitizing activities; check each one, advise how to improve; check finger number games, note identification games; check posture and feet; check relaxation of upper arm and elbow at the joint, shoulders down; play Twinkle D and Honey Bee; introduce part of Cuckoo or Lightly Row.

  Assignment for home: using practice cards (picture cards for each activity and song section that parent and child make together), they should cover as many items as possible. I make specific assignments for which ones to do every day or three times a week, etc., and how many repetitions to do for each item. The parent tape records the lesson, and listens to it at home either alone or with the child so the assignment is clear to them. Parents are instructed to call me if they have any questions.

Mid/End Book 1

At the lesson: The student plays one or two old pieces to warm up; we work on problem areas if these surface; otherwise pick one or two points to refine, work on this for a few minutes; we move on to latest project. I have the student play RH alone all the way through, singing words or humming, then play RH again, eyes closed (I play LH and check for problems). They play LH—I watch for any hesitation or mix-up with a different LH pattern. More drill on the difference between CEG Bottom Middle Top and CGEG Bottom Top Middle Top may be necessary. The student tries hands together, I evaluate the ease.

Assignment: Based on my evaluation of what we just did, I assign specific areas of a piece to work on, with very specific directions as to how to do it, how to evaluate success, how many times to repeat, and what steps to do next, once a specific comfort level has been reached. We discuss the old pieces, review the schedule and what I want to hear first next time. The parent has taped the lesson and taken notes—I don't write anything at all, but speak directly to both the student and the parent when giving the assignment, both during and at the end of the lesson. If the parent is very involved with the lesson he or she will often forget to take notes, and needs to be gently reminded to please write this down. Once upon a time many years ago, I used to try to make notes for myself about each assignment but I had to stop doing this; it just was too time consuming. The solution is to train the parents to take excellent notes and then give you a quick summary as a reminder at the beginning of the next lesson. For me, this usually does the trick; the previous lesson is suddenly there in my (Suzuki trained!) memory and we pick up where we left off.

Book 2

At the lesson: I always check the reading assignment and reading-skill drills if the student is a new reader. Reading should be the primary focus of at least one out of every three lessons at this level, until they are truly reading happily and fairly independently. Play one or two review pieces. In new work, focus on one specific area. Work through all the practice steps with them until you get at least five perfect rounds; fifteen is even better. How you treat repetition at the lesson teaches them what to do at home. You must take the time, at least once in every four lessons at this stage, to remind them that each repetition needs to be evaluated, and that one doesn't stop when you get it perfect—that's where the true practicing begins! Preview the next new part if appropriate.

Assignment: Specify how far to go on in reading the new pieces and in the workbook. Check the review schedule, is review being done? Assign specific area to be practiced as at the lesson. Give several optional suggestions for further work to be done if time and progress permit.

Book 3/4

At the lesson: Check reading pieces from the students' list, in order. What pedaling piece are they doing? What pieces are they keeping? Ask, even if you can't hear them. If a new piece is to be started, spend most of the lesson on this. If the new piece is in progress, listen and evaluate, work on it. Should they go on to more new material in this piece, or stay where they are and let it cook longer? Decide. Play a duet or improvise for dessert if there is time. Also ask to hear certain scales if they are doing them—we use the Accent on Majors by William Gillock as a textbook for both scales and reading pieces.

Assignment: Every week a student at this level has a basic assignment list which includes

1) Old scales, a new scale. Play all every day, it takes approximately 4 minutes

2) One new reading piece, perhaps more, per week. Learn & polish

3) A duet (1 piano, 4 hands) spread over 2 weeks to a month

4) Review Suzuki pieces

5) New Suzuki work

6) A pedaling piece

7) Book 4 up, sight-reading at least three times a week from Music for Millions volume.

I cannot hear everything at the lesson. They sometimes cannot practice everything on the list every day. But the expectation is that it will all get done eventually, both on my part and the students' and parents' part. From this level on, all three of us in the triangle try to make wise choices and prioritize as circumstances change from day to day and week to week. We decide together what needs to be the focus of today's lesson, this week's practice, next week's, etc. (Taggart)

- *I am not a teacher who has a prescribed plan that must be followed each lesson, but rather, knowing what elements need to be accomplished, I assess each lesson and determine what must be tackled for that lesson to continue building on the base. However, I do start all lessons with Twinkles, scales or other assigned technical work, depending on the level of the student. Elements that are continually before me consist of: posture; body tension; technique whether it is Twinkles, scales, chords or arpeggios; new teaching points; review; reading material; style concepts; dynamics; musicality; and special technical needs that the student has such as fingering, rhythm, ornaments, etc. (Williams)*

- *Beginning of Book 1: Goals are to bow without falling over or doing other silly things, to have a focused rest position, to keep feet quiet and flat on the footstool. For this I put a shiny penny under each of the child's feet. I say, "If I don't see these pennies for the rest of your lesson, they're yours at the end and you may take them home." This works wonders. I observe the child's finger technique, the wrist and the finger position. We learn the Twinkles and work on whatever is needed there.*

After the Twinkles, I introduce Lightly Row. Usually the parent and child have learned this on their own, going ahead to learn a few notes at a time as we work on the Twinkles. I help as it is needed, but I do not teach new notes or fingerings. This is the responsibility of the home teacher. However, if a child needs encouragement, then we may take some time to let the child figure out the beginning notes of a new piece. I have learned not to teach notes in Book 1. Occasionally, parents try to get out of doing the work of learning new pieces, because they feel incapable of doing it, or because they are too busy, or the child is uncooperative at home. Sometimes they are very sly about this. But if I don't teach the parent how to do this work at home, Book 2 will soon follow and the parent will not be equipped to step in and do the necessary preparation for these more intricate pieces. The child and parent must learn these skills in Book 1 if the Suzuki® Method is to work for them.

I encourage the parent to allow the child to sound out most of the notes of the pieces rather than teach them by rote. This is true for the RH melodies as well as the LH accompaniments. A child who is listening enough to the CD or tape will not find this too difficult. The parent must learn to be patient and not rush the child in figuring out the notes. What I've found is that the notes the child learns on his or her own are remembered better. And what a self-esteem builder it is to say, "I figured it out myself!" This skill is best learned throughout Book 1 when the melodies and accompaniments are relatively simple.

Accurate rhythms and playing without pauses is something we work on. I play accompaniments on my piano nearly all the time. I also talk with the parent about practicing and help them learn how to learn and maintain pieces. The parent may need lots of tips in this area. Listening to the CD is discussed regularly.

Middle Book 1: We cover all of the above. We begin each lesson with the Twinkles, usually doing the short cut version. I am generally able to hear most of the child's songs. The hands are played alone. The tone and rhythmic accuracy is important. I ask for nice endings to the pieces with a slight ritardando and decrescendo.

End of Book 1: We cover all of the above. As the child nears the end of Book 1 with the RH, and the LH has learned many RH melodies, then technique, attitude, practicing habits, lesson attention, and posture should be good. At this point, it's time to put hands together

First the child learns the various patterns in the LH of Cuckoo from the home teacher. Next we put the first measure together in the lesson, carefully preparing each note. This is an exciting moment. This measure is practiced for at least one week to develop mastery. After that, I teach the parent how to add one note at a time. Sometimes this takes a few days or several weeks, depending usually on the enthusiasm for the necessary numbers of repetitions.

At the beginning of the third line, I want the child to learn how to play the LH legato against the RH's repeated notes. The normal tendency is to lift up both hands, creating a non-legato sound in the LH. It is not recommended that a student be allowed to play this way. I have acquired transfer students whose teachers took this approach. The child unknowingly does it incorrectly whenever possible so the music has a very jumpy sound. Lightly Row has more than 25 repeated notes in the RH, so you can imagine the sound!

After playing the first RH and LH notes together in measure 9, I demonstrate showing the child how I sustain the LH and release the RH. I say, "Can you hear the whale singing?" We call the B in the LH a whale since it's a low sound and relates to Dr. Suzuki's story of tuna tone, both of them living in the ocean. Then the child learns this and repeats it.

Then we practice keeping the whale singing and connecting into the next note D in the LH. Finally we add the RH note, the repeated D, being careful to keep the LH whale singing, thus producing legato playing. Students and their parents practice lots of whales, making colorful charts or whatever, so this becomes a firm muscle memory.

Mary is our second song with two hands—then the whale is in the RH, or is now swimming on top of the water. The child must keep the RH legato in between measures as the LH chords change. Only occasional reminders are necessary here and there in pieces to make a firm habit of this ability of playing one hand legato while the other is detached.

We continue to add the LH notes to the RH notes in order through Book 1. I expect the child to be able to play hands separately at any time with any piece. This often takes much determination on my part to convince the parents of this important skill. I got tired of asking for this so I made this sign to hold up instead. This has proved to be very effective!

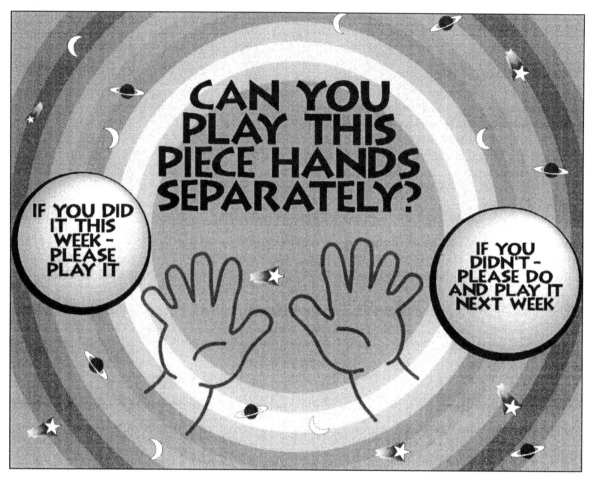

CAN YOU PLAY THIS PIECE HANDS SEPARATELY?

IF YOU DID IT THIS WEEK - PLEASE PLAY IT

IF YOU DIDN'T - PLEASE DO AND PLAY IT NEXT WEEK

(See full-size chart, Appendix 3.)

In a lesson, I continue to hear the Twinkles first, then the newer pieces and an ample supply of the learned repertoire.

At the end of the Book 1, expect the student to be able to play all the pieces with both hands, learn the accompaniments for the Twinkles and Honeybee by ear, learn to control the balance between the hands, use the dynamics shown in the music and heard on the CD, and play musically.

Although the child may begin Book 2, as soon as ten or more pieces are ready we schedule a Graduation Recital during the regular theory class time. This is held in my studio with the parents contributing a reception or dinner. The ten pieces must include Twinkles, Little Playmates, Christmas-Day Secrets, Allegro, Musette and five of the child's choosing. Many children choose to play the whole book. These parties are the opposite of birthday parties; the graduating child gives a small gift to the other members of the theory class. Graduations are repeated for each book.

Book 2: We play the Twinkles at the beginning of Book 2 study but at some point this time is taken over by scales. Reading supplementary music is also added. The pieces become more complicated so more time may be necessary to explain details. Unlike Book 1, each piece in the remaining repertoire is learned with both hands before going on to the next. I try to hear all the pieces in Book 2 at each lesson and those from Book 1 on a rotating basis. If the parent or child needs help in practicing habits, cooperation or whatever, time will be spent discussing these.

At the end of Book 2, emphasis is placed on following the phrasings in the music. Up until this time, most of the pieces phrase themselves without too much effort. But on the Beethoven Sonatina, the student must be conscious of accurate phrasings.

Book 3 and above: Time is divided between scales, reading, repertoire and new pieces.

Division of the lesson: I begin with reading and/or scales, because if I don't I will most likely forget to do it. The new piece is usually next, with repertoire following. However, this will vary depending on specific needs of the student and parent. For example, if new scales are being introduced we may spend half the lesson here. Or if the student has accomplished a lot in reading, we may spend a lot of time doing that. Or if the child is entering a competition or playing at a recital, we may work only on the performance piece. Or if the child is not motivated, we may talk the whole time. (Yurko)

Assigning a New Piece

When a new piece is assigned, some teachers like to preview it at the lesson by pointing out the difficult sections and the special technical elements. Some like to be very specific in the preview of a piece, often going into great detail to make sure that the piece is learned the proper way. Other teachers prefer to limit themselves to a few features in the preview and subsequently, when the child has learned the notes of the piece, the detailed work starts.

Some teachers prefer not to preview at all. Students are then expected to prepare the new piece at home, with parent's help, and bring it to the next lesson. That way, the lesson time can be used to improve and polish pieces rather than to learn the notes of a new piece.

Some teachers like their students to learn as many new pieces as they want, moving ahead at their own pace, while other teachers expect their students to wait until they are told to start a new piece.

Some respondents also stressed that the new piece is not to be learned by rote (i.e., using finger numbers, key names or imitation, where the parent shows the notes on the keyboard and the child reproduces them) but by ear. If children listen sufficiently, they will be able to pick up the song by trial and error. Students will learn to rely on their ears while parents supervise the use of good fingering as well as proper technical and musical skills. Eventually, as students develop their reading skills, they will use the printed music in learning a new piece.

- *Lesson time does not allow for me to teach the new piece during the lesson. I preview portions of new repertoire and point out to the parent any predictable difficulties in learning the piece. The parent actually teaches the new piece at home. In the very beginning stages of lessons, I show the parent how to teach new pieces, so that it is not simply rote learning or memorizing fingerings. If students are listening sufficiently, much can be done independently by the children using their ears. As the students advance and develop skills for reading music, they are encouraged to use the printed music in learning new repertoire. (Fest)*

- *Parents are expected to teach new pieces until the children are advanced enough and old enough to read the music and practice on their own. The parents understand that they are expected to wait until I start them to begin each piece. When it is time to begin, I use the following procedure:*

  1) Previews, if needed, are given on certain passages or sections. This is done in advance of officially beginning the piece. I cover the technical or musical demands of each preview through demonstration, with imitation from the child, stating them verbally to be certain the parent understands, and marking each point in their score; specific suggestions for repetitions are given for home practice.

  2) I divide the score into parts for learning; each part should be learned before beginning the next part.

  3) Stars are marked in the score for places that will require extra repetition. In this way, the main technical and musical points in the score are covered. In Book I, I write the main points for the right-hand melodies in the margin beside the pieces; in the other books, I mark right over or under the notes. (I ask that the parents provide a second copy of the score so that I can make all the marks necessary on one of their copies and still leave them a clean one). Parents are to try to combine the physical gestures needed for the technique and as many of the main musical ideas as possible with the teaching of the notes. All of this is done with great care, for I am strongly committed to preparing them for success. (Powell)

- *When beginning a new piece, we preview difficult passages for several weeks and recommend additional listening. The parents are shown problem spots and the means to solve them through practice. If listening has been a diligent part of the musical experience, and if the parents are guiding the children carefully, then learning is not difficult. (Adams)*

- *In Book 1, students learn new pieces by ear (not by any form of rote learning) at home with their parents' guidance for fingering and systematic practice habits, getting only as much assistance as necessary so the experience belongs to the child. When the notes, fingering, phrasing and rhythm are accurate, they may progress to a new piece. I like beginners to move ahead at their own pace. They may learn other right-hand melodies on their tape as long as parents check that the fingering is correct and let me know so I may hear it. (I like to work with students on separate hands until they are correct even into the advanced levels.) Sometimes a child is spontaneously drawn to a more advanced tune and inspired to work on it (" I have a surprise for you!"). I like to satisfy this sign of authentic musical affinity by allowing them to do so if it is reasonable.*

  Often in Book 2, I will preview details and sometimes in Book 1 as well (the several touches in Christmas-Day Secrets, for example). Of course we work in fine detail subsequently, but in a preview I only introduce some features as a first layer of understanding for a student. I like to see what a student can do independently in Book 2, with less parent involvement (the degree of autonomy is very variable). This often happens naturally, as a child will usually begin to take more responsibility for his assignments now. I hope a process of learning has been established which continues to develop through the weaning stage. By this point, self-reliance and confidence have been strengthened from learning by ear, and through nurturing instruction, developing skills and the sense of achievement as repertoire grows.

  In general, the criteria I use for selecting a new piece are the student's taste, that the technique and overall challenge be an appropriate next step for him, knowledge of a variety of periods, styles and composers, stimulation, inspiration, motivation, planning special repertoire for a coming event, previous pieces sufficiently mastered. We discuss many aspects of the piece, including the tonality which I assign as a workout key. (Schneiderman)

- *In the beginning, I assign listening to the pieces in the book and learning to hum or sing them. I encourage them to go as far ahead in this as they wish. After I see that their bodily approach to the piano is good and they are listening well, they may learn new pieces at home as fast as they wish, provided the parent judges that each one is done correctly before moving on. Learning new pieces is done at home, unless I see that the parent needs help in how to work with the child.*

  I usually do not preview unless there is some unusual feature that they have not yet been taught. Early on and throughout study, we learn how to begin a new piece, being aware of good body use and making musical sense, while carefully studying as many details as possible, usually hands separately. Learning how best to study a new piece is tremendously important. This is a big emphasis in the early years. At first, it is usually the parent who learns that process and supervises it at home. I like the students to know how to take responsibility for this as soon as possible.

  For more advanced students, I may point out characteristics of the period or composer to keep in mind in advance. It is usually at the first lesson after the student has begun the piece that a study plan is mapped out in detail. I have found that it makes more sense to do this once the student is somewhat familiar with playing the piece. (Koppelman)

- *With the Suzuki repertoire, I want the child to always be listening and finding the notes by ear before I listen to a new piece in the lesson. In Books 1 and 2, I work with the parent well in advance of the student, so that the parent can be helping the child, when ready, to put the fingering and other details in place accurately. When the child is into Book 2/3 and beyond, the student quite often begins to be ahead of the parent in reading skills, and I then want the child not only to approach a composition by ear but to be able to read the printed page so that they can check fingering, rhythm, phrases, dynamics, etc. as much as is possible on their own. At this time I will go over trills or tough spots so that the student can have good first encounters with the piece before he or she begins to work on it. I do not go over everything in a new piece because I believe that students need to think and apply as much information as is possible and begin to form some ideas of their own. Mistakes are not wrong, they are learning experiences and provide ways students can begin to take ownership of their music and become involved in feeling a sense of accomplishment. (Williams)*

- *The procedure often varies depending on lesson time available, how well the student reads and how capable the parent is of helping that student. Sometimes I will ask a Book 1 student to play a new piece at the lesson if I know they have had enough listening preparation. I think it is important for the teacher to be aware of how easy or difficult it is for a child to learn new material. I will do the same thing for a child who is reading a piece. After we have covered several phrases or a section, I may ask them to continue learning it at home. It is easier and more sensible to space out the learning of new material over the course of a week, rather than trying to cram it all into ten or fifteen minutes of lesson time. I also always check fingering and make any changes in the music before they begin working on it. I may circle or point out a particular difficulty in advance even if we have not been able to go over it at the lesson. Much of the new learning can and should take place at home. This frees the teacher to work on many other things at the lesson besides just note learning. (Liccardo)*

- *Thorough initial parent orientation is the key to establishing a clear understanding of responsibilities and a smooth working system. Once the parent has shown responsibility for the listening, fingering, review, and attention to the main points being taught, the teacher should not need to assign new pieces. The child and parent move on to new pieces as there is time. An astute teacher will always be aware if the parent and child are moving forward at the expense of main-point practice, polishing, reading, etc., because those signs will be apparent in the lesson. The teacher also needs to present previews of thorny spots well before a piece is learned, so the teacher must be aware of forward learning. Those previews can help a student sail through a new piece with a great can-do attitude.*

  Michiko Yurko devised a goal-oriented system called "Home Dot—Lesson Dot", which organizes responsibility very well. Once a child meets certain criteria for a home dot (basically learning correct notes, rhythm, fingering, a certain number of perfect repetitions, etc.) he may put a colored circle on a chart which lists children randomly as far as age and level are concerned. That means that the piece is now ready for lesson work. Another set of criteria leads to a lesson dot. The chart makes it clear to the teacher exactly where the child is in the repertoire.

  At every step of the way the teacher must be approachable so the parent can communicate any problems in learning pieces independently. At the beginning level, parents often feel inadequate to help their children learn by ear. A few short demonstrations by the teacher in 2 or 3 lessons should take care of that. However, the teacher should never fall into the trap of teaching notes in lessons. The exception is previews.

  Since practice (repetition) makes permanent, it is imperative that any technical point be repeated correctly by the student many times in the lesson. Repetitions could be inserted between other lesson activities for a maximum number. (Harrel)

- *What happens at the lesson when it's time for a new piece depends on the piece and whether or not it contains a new technical or musical element. After the middle of Book 1, I trust the parent and child to be able to do most RH work totally on their own, and I will preview anything new for the LH before they try it hands together. For example, Allegro is one of the ones we do first at the lesson, as is the middle of Christmas-Day Secrets. They do the first part of Musette and I show them how to practice the middle.*

  Before any piece is played, the child has no bad habits for that piece. If experience has taught you that certain traps always catch the innocent student, it makes sense to prevent the problem before it occurs by using lesson time for careful study of the trap and how to practice it. In the early years, I am very conservative—some might say too much so—about exactly what the students and parents may learn on their own; but as their practice skills and ability to recognize and solve technical problems increase with experience, I do less and less skill teaching at the lessons. More and more my work focuses primarily on musical details of interpretation and style after they have learned the pieces on their own, which is as it should be.

  The more advanced the students become (especially from Book 5 on into the full gamut of piano repertoire outside the Suzuki repertoire), the more they are the ones who decide the order and focus of the lesson. They tell me what they have worked on, what areas they want help with, and we proceed from there. Of course we have an overall plan for repertoire and certain dates that are deadlines for performances to guide us, but they are essentially in control, with the parent and teacher much more of a support system than the bosses we used to be. (Taggart)

- *Now and then I may suggest that a student begin work on a new piece, but usually the piece is already started. Sometimes a child will come in with a surprise—an entire new song. This is greeted with lots of smiles and usually a few corrections. This works because of how I set up the learning patterns in Book 1.*

  I feel the lesson time is not for learning new notes. This is really the easy way out for a teacher and not a good idea. By this I mean that learning notes is in the true sense of the word, a black and white task. One either learns the right notes, fingerings, rhythms and dynamics or the wrong ones. There is little gray area.

By contrast, subjective areas such as balance, tone, dynamics, phrase shaping, touch, technique and posture are more subtle and require a keen sense of musicality. These areas should be taught by the teacher who is a trained musician. There is only so much time in a weekly lesson. If it is used up with teaching notes, how is the student going to learn the other things?

Horrors, one may then think, won't students learn incorrectly? Isn't that worse?

This shouldn't happen if the parents are well trained. Since my families listen to their Suzuki CDs and tapes, they thoroughly know the sounds of the music. My parents all either know or learn how to read music. I have a notebook in my studio containing all seven Suzuki Piano School books. In pencil I have marked any details that might be overlooked. If there are alternate fingerings, those are suggested. Before a new piece is begun at home, the parent copies these notes into his or her own music, asking questions as necessary. With a good score and the CD they are ready to begin. If there are any new concepts, I go over them in the lesson. It works. (Yurko)

Home Assignments

Respondents all seem to agree on the need to be very specific about practice assignments. This can help parents to structure a practice session, and it helps in making sure the practice is done properly.

- I am as specific as I possibly can be. I note exactly what I would like done in the student's notebook, often writing in the various steps necessary in order to accomplish the task. I also verbally confirm the assignment with the student and the parent to make sure it is clearly understood. I try to impart to them the knowledge necessary to deal with a new problem that might arise during the week. Students and parents need to be flexible and creative in their practice sessions. (Liccardo)

- I am as specific as needed to achieve proper results. Many parents help their children instinctively to practice in this manner, but for most, precise practice instructions are necessary. (Adams)

- I am extremely specific in assigning the home practice. Whether it is in the area of technique, reading, or the Suzuki pieces, I am careful to tell the parent and child exactly how I want each piece done, various ways to practice it, metronome speeds to use (if needed), and how many times to do either the piece or parts of the piece. Years ago I was not as specific about saying how many repetitions I wanted done until one of my Suzuki parents stated quite frankly, "Mary Craig, why don't **you** tell him how many times you want him to repeat; he'll do it for you, and he won't for me." I realized that she was right, and since then I have been taking that responsibility. (Powell)

- I am very specific in terms of identifying measures and detailing points of improvement in written notebook assignments, on our lesson tape and sometimes, directly on the score. I also write general comments when appropriate, such as warmer tone, steadier pulse, or give written guidelines for using the metronome, sight-reading, preparing for performance, etc. Occasionally, I address the student or parent on the tape, directing their attention to certain sounds such as precise rhythm or articulation. (Schneiderman)

- I am specific on each particular assignment, but as students become more advanced, I leave amounts of time on each aspect up to them unless I think they are missing something. (Koppelman)

- I am very specific about the practice. The more specific I can be, the more helpful it is for the parents in structuring a practice session. Also, older, advanced students who work independently need specifics on how to construct a productive, disciplined practice session. (Fest)

- I am specific in assigning what and how things are to be done—the number of repetitions for a drill or section, fingering, technique, reading assignment, theory work or other facets of the lesson. Depending on the length of the lesson, sometimes it is not possible to hear or work on everything but my notes help me to be sure that, over two lessons, everything gets covered. (Williams)

Regarding the content of home assignments, some respondents answered with general comments emphasizing the individual needs of every student.

- *A weekly assignment depends totally on what is needed for each student. Some students do amazing amounts of work in a week and I leave them free to work ahead, but they know that I expect excellence in small amounts over sloppiness in larger amounts. If a student is lazy, I am very specific as to what I want done for the next lesson and hold them accountable. (Williams)*

- *I teach students according to their particular needs, spending time accordingly. I know what I want to achieve before moving on and this is my guide, rather than a particular plan. I focus on what I think is needed at that point and try whatever I know or can invent to teach that point until it is learned satisfactorily.*

  In general, Book I students begin with a body/ear warm-up and go on to cover points made in their lesson. Mindful repetition is asked for small parts where a change of some kind is needed. New pieces are learned a small section at a time, again with careful repetition of each new section. Previous pieces learned are to be played and refined each day.

  For later books, in addition to the kind of study described above, there is a reading assignment, new each week, and often some theory work. Review may be divided up throughout the week, depending on how often a particular student needs to review something to keep it comfortably. (Koppelman)

Other respondents were more specific and provided us with a detailed assignment plan.

- *A weekly assignment for a pre-Twinkler in my studio includes*
  1) *Posture Check—feet, back, shoulders, arms, hands, head (1 minute)*
  2) *Follow-the-leader game—eyes open, then closed (3 minutes)*
  3) *Tonalization (2 to 3 minutes)*
  4) *Right hand Twinkles (10 to 15 minutes)*
  5) *Other activities—learning note names and finger numbers (3 minutes)*

  Short practice sessions, preferably two or more a day, are encouraged at this level.

  A late Book I lesson assignment is longer in length and looks like this:
  1) *Posture Check (1 minute)*
  2) *Follow the Leader (3 minutes)*
  3) *Tonalization (3 minutes)*
  4) *Review (13 minutes)*
  5) *New working piece (10 minutes)*

  From Book 2 through Book 7, practice assignments are similar. They include
  1) *Technique (scales, arpeggios, etc.) (1/6 of the practice)*
  2) *Reading (1/3)*
  3) *Review (1/4)*
  4) *New working piece (1/4) (Powell)*

- *A weekly assignment in early Book I would include 1) beginning steps, each with a particular point of improvement (sometimes the same point for all steps, for example, "easy shoulders"); 2) review of all known pieces with one point in mind, using my 100 Days of Review Club chart (Variations may have more detailed instructions); 3) Sing and Play (for learning key names we sing the alphabet letters as we play three notes up and down from C—CDE, EDC, CBA, ABC—and similarly from F, making our own tunes when they are familiar; then name keys at random); 4) a listening game (high/low, etc); 5) correcting and polishing previous piece; 6) learning new song, right hand melody. The proportions can vary, but 3 and 4 are relatively brief, 1, 5 and 6 more substantial and 2 gradually grows longer as pieces accumulate.*

  In late Book I, the overall time grows, and review, including Variations, constitutes a larger segment. Reading (noteboard and theory books) replaces Sing and Play and the listening game. Correcting the most recent piece and polishing another are in about equal proportions. Learning a new song and new 5-note patterns rounds out the assignment.

In Books 2, 3, 4 and beyond, the proportions vary even more—with the season, individual needs, particular goals. Some students may be preparing intensively for Certificate of Merit exams, refining a piece for a festival or recital, focusing on a program for Guild Auditions. Usually, the largest segments would be 1) working on a new piece, learning the basics accurately, and 2) polishing another, working on corrections, interpretation, memorization, starting points. Technique (workout key, Hanon, etc) and review might be next in size, rotating review pieces when the list grows longer; sometimes retrieving a lapsed piece from deeper memory by reading the music with separate hands. Work on the circle of fifths, reading skills and theory completes the assignment. (Schneiderman)

The way assignments are recorded varies greatly from teacher to teacher. Some teachers keep detailed records of their students' assignments and progress, others do not. Some teachers write notes for their students to bring home, while others teach parents how to take notes at the lesson and use the parents' note book as a reference at the lesson. Others ask that lessons be recorded and give precise assignments on the tape.

- *I keep a record of everything I assign at each lesson in a notebook on my piano as I assign it and always check at the following lesson. (Koppelman)*

- *I keep weekly records of assignments given, especially in the area of technical work. (Williams)*

- *Students' assignment records are kept in spiral notebooks which the students bring to lessons (Adams)*

- *Lessons are recorded on tapes. Instructions on the recording must be very specific and the routine should have been negotiated between teacher and student in the lesson. (Harrel)*

- *In Book 1 (and for some Book 2 students), the parent writes notes during the lesson and I keep abbreviated records of weekly assignments for reference the following week. For an overview at a glance, I often highlight important issues to keep track of developments or problems that might persist. (Schneiderman)*

- *My record-keeping of assignments is done by the parents in each lesson. I provide a guide for taking notes and teach the parents how to take notes that are helpful to both of us. The parents take these notes with them to use during the week, then return them to me at the next lesson. This helps the parent to focus during the lesson and also leaves me free to teach. For students working independently, I make their lesson notes for them. (Fest)*

- *When I first began teaching, I would keep my own notes on each student's lesson. I usually could not do this until the end of the teaching day, so it was time consuming, but also very fruitful. It helped me better organize lessons and gave me a feeling of confidence before beginning the next lesson. I do not keep such detailed records any longer. However, I keep track of the repertoire my more advanced students have learned. (Liccardo)*

One respondent recommends not recording assignments.

- *One of the most important concepts I learned during my visit to study in Matsumoto in the fall of 1984 was that the parents do not take notes in the lesson. They are to listen and watch me and the child. If I am saying so much that they need to write it down so it won't be forgotten, then I am saying too much. I will mark corrections and suggestions in the music—I use colored pencils so the child has a different color to look for each week. (Yurko)*

This same teacher gave us a very detailed account of how she organizes the week assignments and how students keep track of their work. She finds this method a big help both for motivation and for making sure work is being done and done properly.

- *For many years I used a notebook for each student, writing the week's assignment on a page. Now I use a system of one 8½ " x 11" sheet which is used for the entire month. On one side is a calendar of sorts. There is also space for the important practice point each week, the repertoire list and a place for goals. The parent and student are to keep track of their daily practice routine. At the beginning of the lesson I can tell at a glance what has been done throughout the week and what may have been left out.*

  On the other side is the assignment sheet. This has space so I can write weekly assignments and notes. When appropriate, I am specific in my assignment — how many times to practice the scales each day (the child spins a wooden spinner on the piano to determine the number of repetitions for that week — if the number is too low, we add or multiply two numbers!), or what the metronome marking should be for practice, or what pieces to finish, or to listen and to be nice to Mom at home.

SUZUKI PIANO PRACTICE CALENDAR									
Name _____							June 1997		
Impt. dates	date	☺	T/Sc	New	Work	Rep	Read	Listen	One point focus - weekly
	S-1								1.
	M-2								2.
	T-3								3.
	W-4								4.
	T-5								5.
	F-6								
	S-7								
	S-8								Repertoire pieces:
	M-9								
	T-10								
	W-11								
	T-12								
	F-13								
	S-14								
	S-15								
	M-16								
	T-17								
	W-18								
	T-19								
	F-20								
	S-21								
	S-22								
	M-23								
	T-24								
	W-25								I want to learn:
	T-26								
	F-27								
	S-28								
	S-29								
	M-30								

☺ = Good work/No fussing   T/Sc = Twinkles or Scales   New = New Piece   Work = Working Piece   Rep = Repertoire   Read = Reading
Listen = 2 hrs. listening

☺ Assignments ☺

Date:	
Twinkle/Scale	
New Piece	
Working Piece	
Repertoire	
Reading	
Date:	
Twinkle/Scale	
New Piece	
Working Piece	
Repertoire	
Reading	
Date:	
Twinkle/Scale	
New Piece	
Working Piece	
Repertoire	
Reading	
Date:	
Twinkle/Scale	
New Piece	
Working Piece	
Repertoire	
Reading	
Date:	
Twinkle/Scale	
New Piece	
Working Piece	
Repertoire	
Reading	

(See full-size chart, Appendix 4 and 5.)

Home dots / lesson dots: I begin using 1'' dots at least fifteen years ago to help students learn when a piece is ready for performance. At the time I realized some students had learned many pieces but most of them weren't polished. So I created a system using this chart:

HOME DOT / LESSON DOT CHART

Book 1   Name _____

	Home	Lesson		Home	Lesson		Home	Lesson
Twinkle A			French Children's Song *Folk Song*			Chant Arabe *Anon.*		
Twinkle B			London Bridge *Folk Song*			Allegretto 1 *Czerny*		
Twinkle C			Mary Had a Little Lamb *Folk Song*			Good-bye to Winter *Folk Song*		
Twinkle D			Go Tell Aunt Rhody *Folk Song*			Allegretto 2 *Czerny*		
Lightly Row *Folk Song*			Claire de Lune *Lully*			Christmas Day Secrets *Dutton*		
Honeybee *Folk Song*			Long Long Ago *Bayly*			Allegro *Suzuki*		
Cuckoo *Folk Song*			Little Playmates *Chawtal*			Musette *Anon.*		

Home Dot: ¼ dot = melody with RH 19x correctly and LH 19x correctly (Twinkles-Claire). ½ dot = hands together 19x correctly   **Lesson Dot:** Polished Piece

(See full-size chart, Appendix 6.)

The child can put a dot in the space next to the title of each piece once the piece has been played nineteen times with the correct notes, rhythms, fingerings and phrasings. If the child stops to prepare a note, this is not considered a mistake. If the child is to learn the melody with the RH and LH, he or she may put one quarter of the dot in the space when each of these is played nineteen times. If the melody is to be learned with just the RH, then a half dot may be placed in the box when nineteen repetitions are played perfectly. The second half of the dot is for when the LH accompaniment is played nineteen times perfectly. Nineteen is my lucky number and magically it's the perfect number to use on this system.

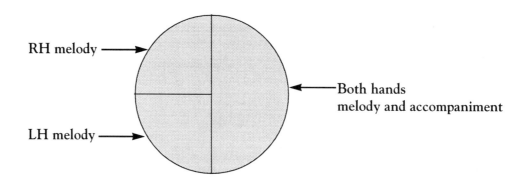

The lesson dot is achieved after the child has added all the polishing features which make the piece musical. It is the lesson-dot pieces that the child can choose to play in theory class, or school talent shows and recitals.

Dates are added next to the dot so we can keep track of progress. This system helps students polish and adds to the sense of accomplishment when home dots and lessons dots are earned. The children are very excited about this! (Yurko)

One teacher gave an account of her yearly parent/teacher conference where practice sessions and student progress are discussed.

- *The first week of the second semester I hold parent/teacher conferences in lieu of lessons so that I can give parents an update on progress, hear from parents what their long-and short- term goals are for their child, learn how practice sessions are progressing, and any feed back useful to me in working with their child, as well as other pertinent topics. If a child is not progressing, I set goals and tell both the parent and student what I expect to be accomplished over the next semester and that we will evaluate progress at the end of the semester. I have found that this puts the responsibility on the student and parent because they know what is expected up front and they then can determine what is best for their child. In almost every case I have discovered I have a better student and I also have learned that they respect me and my profession more. (Williams)*

Practicing Habits

All respondents feel that it is their responsibility to teach parent and student how to practice at home. Developing good practicing habits is one of the keys to successful piano playing. Portions of lesson time are often used to demonstrate how practice should be done so that good habits can be developed and progress will be made. Teachers also insist on the necessity of having regularity in the practice session.

- *Dr. Suzuki once wrote, "You can measure a teacher's abilities on how well he or she has taught his or her students to practice." I feel this issue is of paramount importance and I am always making inquiries as to how the child is practicing. (Yurko)*

- *It is important to teach students and parents how to practice and that must start at orientation and continue into the lessons.*

Students and parents must not only be taught how to practice but also how to make it fun and positive. Practice must be regular and preferably at a regular time of the day when the parent will be free from interruptions (put the telephone on the recorder). The parent and teacher need to learn how to give honest and sincere praise—the child needs to hear this daily. Being creative takes time, thought and dedication. Both parents and students constantly need to be encouraged and reinforced by the teacher. (Williams)

- *Because our aim is a student who is successfully independent, teacher and parent must constantly be working toward that goal. That means we must emphasize helping students to set their own goals, devise practice routines to achieve those goals, and constantly evaluate their own progress. Guiding students in this path involves asking a lot of questions to stimulate their independent thinking. (Harrel)*

- *I think teaching students and parents how to practice efficiently is of utmost importance. Good habits are developed through my checking and explaining at each lesson, if necessary. Most difficulties in music study are the result of faulty practice. In practice, students really teach themselves. Being alert and caring are essential. I try to help them be aware of the process and get them interested in devising their own strategies to help them learn particular points. (Koppelman)*

- *Most parents need guidance in how to structure practice sessions. Consistency is the primary factor in developing good practice habits. I emphasize the importance of daily practice and having a routine so that the parent and the student expect practice to happen at the same time(s) every day. I teach good practice by example in the lessons. A lesson is an opportunity to practice with the student. I reinforce the role of the parent as home teacher, so the child understands that what we are doing in the lesson will be done at home under the parent's supervision. (Fest)*

- *I feel it is one of the teacher's most important jobs to teach parent and child how to practice properly and efficiently. It is also one of our biggest challenges to teach people without musical experience how to effectively deal with the many difficulties of playing an instrument and learning an art form. From the beginning of their studies, I try to demonstrate at the lesson the best ways to analyze and break down a difficulty. I constantly ask the child and the parent for their evaluation as we are working on things. The first and most important skill that must be developed is the ability to listen to ourselves critically and objectively. There must also be an understanding from the beginning of study that daily practice is essential in order to make progress. I also give very specific assignments and set goals. I then give them the steps to reach those goals. I ask about practice each week at their lesson, and spend time showing the parents how to use games and activities to make practicing enjoyable and challenging. When the child is able, I ask the parent to assign them independent work. This work always contains specific goals which are to be checked by the parent after the child has worked on them. This begins the process of practicing independently, which is our ultimate goal. (Liccardo)*

Some teachers have concrete suggestions for helping with practice.

- *I definitely feel I have to teach my students and parents how to practice. Parents who are not accomplished musicians have no idea how much practice to do or how to do it, without our guidance; even parents who are fine musicians usually need to have their child hear assignments from their teacher to gain the child's cooperation during practice sessions. A parent who is confident because she understands exactly what to do at home is more likely to practice and to practice constructively, so it is well worth my time to help all I can. Here are some of the ways I help:*

  1) Preparing the parent and child for success through careful instruction at the beginning of each new piece.

  2) Breaking steps into smaller steps when needed

  3) Assigning a one-point focus for practice at times

  4) Marking the score for stop-prepare when needed

  5) Being specific in assignments

  6) Assigning exercises and repetitions for difficult parts of the music

  7) Following through with my assignments at the next lesson. (Powell)

- *Teaching students and parents how to practice is one of the teacher's biggest responsibilities. We instill from the beginning that playing-through the pieces is not really practicing.*

Specific assignments are necessary, especially in the early years, to teach students exactly how to practice. Several helpful techniques are to

1) *Isolate trouble spots by carefully marking measures in the music*

2) *Indicate the number of repetitions expected per day for the isolated passages*

3) *List several ways to practice this isolated passage:*
   a) *hands separately*
   b) *slowly with metronome (speed indicated)*
   c) *rhythmic practice (specific rhythmic patterns indicated)*
   d) *change in articulation (specifics indicated)*
   e) *isolate voices for melody versus accompaniment*
   f) *passage played backwards*
   g) *singing of melody*
   h) *exaggerate shape of phrases*
   i) *ghosting of voices*

4) *Assign the entire piece to be practiced in one of the aforementioned ways after isolated passages have been practiced. (Adams)*

One teacher gave a detailed account of her thoughts on practicing habits.

• *I do instruct student and parent in home practice methods. It is important to be systematic and consistent in how we go about learning music, to lay a strong foundation in the facts so that we can later express the emotions and moods inherent in the music. We need to instill a respect for the composer's score and an attention to detail, both in reading the symbols of notation and refining the skills necessary to re-create them beautifully. Because it is difficult to unlearn incorrect notes or inappropriate fingering, we aim to learn accurately the first time, establish comfortable fingering very early and digest any corrections soon after they are suggested.*

I initially discuss practice habits with parents, but that can only be an introduction. It is with actual daily and weekly experiences that the process becomes meaningful. We learn how important it is to analyze exactly what and where the problem is and solve it before repeating. In our lessons, I frequently demonstrate such practice techniques as finding, isolating, naming and repeating short bits of the music, encouraging students to listen carefully with an intended goal or improvement actively in mind—to plan, play, listen, enjoy, evaluate, re-plan and repeat. Mindless repetition is not productive and it can be deflating. Mindful listening with pleasure in one's progress is rewarding, even exciting and inspiring.

We try to instill this notion of active listening and present playful, challenging repetition games very early in a student's development (using an abacus, keeping score, calibrating a particular quality on a scale of 1 to 10, playing right way/wrong way game). Students learn to name the sections of their songs with numbers, letters or occasionally with the younger children, quite original titles. The point is for the student to clearly identify the unit as a finite entity with a beginning and an end, so he or she can work on it and improve it. Sometimes we focus on shorter problematic parts within a phrase, the particular knotty bit. Many playful approaches can be effective and motivating.

There are other valuable reasons for practicing in sections. Researchers have learned that repeating short bits of information at frequent intervals is the most efficient and effective way to learn. Also the process of determining where these units begin and end encourages listening for the story line, for punctuation. It develops clarity in perceiving musical ideas as they articulate the drama of a piece. Determining these units also prepares for our performance strategy, when we will rehearse picking up starting points if needed during practice performances.

Follow-up is extremely important in building good practice habits. Teachers need to work early on perceived gaps in the home system. If an assignment is not done, we need to find out why, then help, discuss and re-assign. We can involve the parent in our lesson demonstration, discuss process on the telephone, have parent-teacher conferences, ask occasionally for a tape of a home session or ask the parent and child to pretend they're at home and work on a project in the lesson. We can tape special instructions on the lesson tape, even leaving space for the student to imitate. Also helpful to parents are consulting with other parents and reading articles.

I continue to reinforce good study habits by defining and describing two general types of practice mode: 1) the sectional, repeating, crafting, trial-and-error, stop-and-fix kind, and 2) the continuous, through-performance style, where we go for flow, the story line, depth of emotion and a fully colored interpretation. We often work in lessons on the characteristics of both of these styles so they are clearly differentiated in the student's mind. (Schneiderman)

Group Lessons

The group lesson is seen by Suzuki teachers as a very good complement to the private lesson. First, they become an important social time for students, who create friendships with other music students learning piano just like them. Second, group classes give the opportunity for a more complete musical education, enriching the instrumental learning with a variety of activities in theory, music reading, ear training, keyboard harmony, transposition, improvisation, music history. Third, they provide regular group performance classes where students can benefit from informal performance opportunities, in contrast to the more formal recitals.

We see a big difference among the respondents in the frequency of group classes. It ranges from once a week to less than once a month.

Group classes	Once a week	Once every two weeks	Once a month	Less than once a month
Adams			•	
Fest			•	
Harrel	•			
Koppelman			•	
Liccardo	•			
Powell			•	
Taggart				•
Schneiderman		•		
Williams		•		
Yurko	•			

While the content of these classes may vary from teacher to teacher, all classes generally have some performance and a mixture of activities aimed at developing musicianship by broadening the students' musical abilities and knowledge.

Group class content	Performance	Theory	Pre-reading/reading/sight-reading	Ear training	Keyboard harmony	Transposition	Improvisation	Music history	Piano ensemble (duets)	Chamber music
Adams	•	•		•				•	•	•
Fest		•		•	•			•	•	
Harrel	•	•	•	•						
Koppelman	•	(•)		(•)						
Liccardo	•	•		•	•	•	•	•	•	•
Powell	•	•	•	•		•	•	•		
Taggart	•	•	•	•	•		•	•	•	
Schneiderman	•	•	•	•	•		•	•	•	
Williams	•	•	•	•				•	•	
Yurko	•	•	•	•					•	

Most respondents teach group classes themselves and seem to enjoy it very much.

- *I am so convinced of the importance of group lessons that I will not accept a student who cannot come twice a week, once for a private lesson and once for a group lesson. The cameraderie which develops when children share music together in a non-competitive environment binds them together into adulthood. From a practical standpoint, the group lesson is the most efficient use of the instructor's time. Group lessons can include almost anything except the child's very specific pianistic problems. Some activities include*

  1) Ear training at all levels

  2) Pre-reading (staff, clefs, rhythm, intervals, notes on staff)

  3) Note drills

  4) Rhythm drills

  5) Performance skills

  6) Theory

  A very good resource is Music Mind Games by Michiko Yurko. Emphasis is on non-competitive games, enjoyment, and theory. Teachers can set their own learning priorities and use the games that match them. Using the games becomes a jumping-off place to create one's own games. (Harrel)

- *I view the group lessons as of equal importance to the private lesson. The group lessons provide the social interaction so necessary for children and parents to want to continue music study. Hearing other children perform helps to inspire and motivate.*

  All of my students attend weekly performance and musicianship classes. Listening to their friends perform and performing for their friends in turn gives them the incentive to polish pieces and to maintain repertoire. The musicianship classes are an enormous supplement to their private lessons, helping to make learning at the piano much easier.

  I usually teach all of the performance classes in my Suzuki program. That enables me to hear all of the children on a weekly basis. We discuss performance etiquette and speak about handling various performance situations. We work on memory problems and techniques to help improve our performances. This includes discussions on practicing and how to best prepare for a performance. We also discuss musical terms and definitions, composers and go over some theory skills such as rhythm reading, key signatures, etc. (Liccardo)

- *To demonstrate how important I feel group lessons are, all my students participate in groups each week. As stated before, the Twinklers and Book I students are in groups. Once they move to a weekly half-hour lesson, they are grouped into a theory class that meets weekly for one hour. This continues throughout all the books, although I may make exceptions for my high-school students, since they are often just too busy to come to group class. With so many demands on their time at that age, I'm thrilled they are still able to make time for piano study.*

The theory class is attended by the participating Suzuki parent. In these sessions we play theory games as described in my book Music Mind Games *(1992, Warner Bros. Publications). There is time in each class for each child to perform a solo. We practice performance etiquette, often learn duets, and rehearse for recitals.*

These classes are scheduled throughout the week and most often the students have their lessons and class on the same day. They stay in the studio for an average of 2 hours taking a lesson, taking theory class and observing other's lessons. (Yurko)

- *I feel group lessons are a very important part of the process. They develop musical friendships, camaraderie and the social interaction so important to young people, and serve to counteract the solitude often experienced by pianists.*

  I try to have group lessons at least once every 4 to 6 weeks. I teach them myself and enjoy it very much, particularly the chance to hear them play one after the other (or together in ensemble). It serves as an overview and reality check for me on my own work.

  The group lesson is in two parts. First we have a concert in which each student plays a solo, either polished or work in progress, for the group, and then we move onto theory games and group theory activities. (Taggart)

- *I think group lessons are wonderful. It is a social time for the students and parents and their friendships seem to grow stronger each year. Since piano can be a lonely instrument, I am grateful that group lessons provide this opportunity. Preparing a piece to be played in this relaxed, non-pressured setting is enjoyable and motivates the students, and playing at every group lesson helps the students feel comfortable about playing for others. It also is fun to learn in the group setting.*

  My students participate in group lessons about once a month during the school year. I enjoy teaching my own groups and planning the activities for them. The length of our group lessons ranges from a half-hour for the pre-Twinklers to an hour for students in Book 3 and above. Activities for the Book 1 students include performance and pre-reading experiences. Activities for Book 2 and above students fall into three main categories: performance, theory, and music history. Everyone performs at group lessons, either playing a review piece or trying a new one. The theory includes ear training and work to strengthen what they are learning in their written theory books; I also add transposition skills and a little improvisation at times. Music history includes the study of periods of music and their composers. Much of the time the activities are game-oriented. We are serious about what we are learning, however. In fact, the parents take notes and I often hand out study sheets of information they are expected to know at group. The social aspect of it is strengthened by having about two parties a year—one at Christmas and later, a pizza party. (Powell)

- *I value the group format highly as an adjunct to individual lessons, for the feelings of communality generated, the mutual respect and appreciation among the children, the inspiration from exposure to others' knowledge and skills, the enhanced learning ease of a shared experience and the sociability which is another form of our nurturing environment. Group lessons allow the cultivation of friendship with others who love music and contact with older or more advanced role models. They can reinforce the content of the private lesson and offer instruction in certain topics facilitated by the group setting (theory, history), lending variety and enriching the overall program. Such gatherings permit attendance by the larger family and visiting friends who confirm the child's interest in music.*

  I offer two group lessons each month. One is a theory class in small groups geared to level, and the other is a multi-faceted, one-room-schoolhouse-style workshop for everyone up to high-school senior.

  In theory class, we work on the following: reading and sight-reading; rhythm, meter and tempo (clapping and drumming using metronome, visual aides, card games); alphabet games; musical symbols, terminology and vocabulary; singing as an integral part of ear training as well as reading; noteboard games including dictation and composing; duets; circle of fifths round-robins; Bea's Keys; Michiko Yurko's Musopoly; composer cards and other games; keyboard harmony; figured bass; two-piano improvisation; preparing for examinations.

  Our monthly workshop provides varied enrichment including regular performance opportunities and training in an informal environment, with support from other students encouraged and elicited. It is an important growth experience for the children, and parents enjoy it too. We listen for and offer appreciation for qualities in friends' performances. Each student shares a work-in-progress, a polishing or polished piece, a revisited review piece or even a bow and rest-position poem for a new beginner. We study music history one period a month, with listening; social background; discussion of styles; demonstrations; illustrations of instruments, art and architecture of the times; stories of composers' lives with pictures to take home and color; ending with a history memory game where a parent tallies points for the group as a whole as the students offer any information they remember. We also work on vocabulary, clap rhythms as a group, study theory charts, play ensemble games, Suzuki's take-a-chance game and celebrate individual book and Twinkle graduations.

We also gather regularly for special events: small workshops to prepare for theme festivals and recitals in the community, in institutions such as retirement or nursing homes. Recital parties, picnics and other occasional events offer the shared vitality of the group experience as well. We encourage overlapping lessons too for the stimulation, learning and friendship they provide. (Schneiderman)

* The students in our school have a group lesson every two weeks in addition to their weekly private lesson. All children play for each other in these sessions. Content includes a carefully coordinated curriculum from level to level, so that the student has the opportunity to reinforce some of the theory, singing and ear-training concepts taught in the private lesson. Orff and movement are used with young children, and intermediate students work with understanding basic chords and keys, periods of music and composers, rhythmic and melodic dictation. Advanced levels work in the piano lab with ensemble playing, sight-reading and improvisation.

At present I do not teach groups but have taught many over the years. Our school employs a group-class specialist. I place a very high priority on group classes, feeling that they go hand in hand with the private lesson. In our school, group-class attendance is better with younger students because of all the other commitments older students are involved with through school and other community activities. Our group classes meet every other week for 45–60 minutes in addition to the weekly private lessons and always include the students playing for each other. (Williams)

* Group lessons are necessary to reinforce work on theory and music history and to provide performance opportunities. We also use them to introduce additional classes, such as duets, chamber music, computer ear-training, Kindermusik, Orff, music appreciation, and advanced music theory. Group lessons in our program are held three times a semester. (Adams)

* I don't have group lessons. We gather once a month to play works in progress. At that time we may do some solfège, rhythm games, dictation or theory. There are three divisions—Books 1 to 2, Books 3 to 5 and Advanced. Students may stay as long as they wish. (Koppelman)

* I do not have regular group performance classes. I do have group theory classes once each month. During the year we also have three home concerts, which serve as informal performance opportunities. A family from my studio offers to host the home concert, we dress casually, there are no printed programs, and only students and their immediate families are invited. This is a type of performance class for the students. This contrasts with the more formal, dress-up recitals and festivals which we also do. (Fest)

CONCLUSION

The Suzuki® Method has been widely used for a number of years now. In the light of these years of experience, the respondents were asked if they feel any need for a revision of the method. Most of them see no need at all for a revision, but many had certain concerns about the repertoire.

- *I see no reason to revise the Suzuki® Method for piano. There is enough flexibility within the framework of basic Suzuki principles that teachers can adapt secondary teaching ideas to meet the needs of their students. The essential elements of the Suzuki® Method cannot be changed or one no longer has the Suzuki® Method.*

  The repertoire could certainly be revised, but it would be difficult to get a consensus on what the revisions should be. Some people would like an easier transition from Book 1 to Book 2. Others would like to see more Contemporany or Romantic music added. However, I do not see the repertoire choices as a problem; I simply supplement the repertoire or delete some works.

  I would like to see more accurate and readable books for the students and parents. Books 5, 6, and 7 are an embarassment. I refuse to use these new "revised" editions. The new Book 1 has errors; I refuse to buy it. The new Book 2 has changes in fingerings which I do not use; I edit all these revised books. Surely the publisher could take some pride in producing quality piano books that are actually usable as printed. (Fest)

- *I have been using the Suzuki® Method exclusively to teach piano for 24 years. That length of time has given me the opportunity to work with hundreds of students in my own program and as a clinician at workshops. I still find it to be complete and invigorating.*

  I feel the repertoire is very strong and know that all these years later that my students still enjoy the music and are happy to use the sequence of pieces.

  I have two ideas:

  1. *I would like to see a supplementary set of books compiled which would run parallel with our current books. These could be Romantic and popular music and could be learned when desired.*

  2. *A set of duet books at all seven levels would be very useful, too. I realize there are supplementary lists complied, but if series such as these were available they would be easy to use and also become common repertoire so that Suzuki students world-wide could use them. This would be exciting for workshops, institutes and conferences. (Yurko)*

- *The Suzuki® Method is based on logical, well-thought-out principles of learning. These principles of learning combined with the excellent repertoire source are the foundation of a preeminent learning method.*

  The Suzuki repertoire is an ideal source of literature when used with supplementary materials. (Adams)

- *I see no need for any major revisions of the Suzuki® Method as it is applied to piano teaching. Many Suzuki piano teachers, including myself, would be happy with a few minor revisions in the piano repertoire, although I have made it work as it is; I truly love and respect the beautiful body of literature it provides. (Powell)*

- *I have been in conversation at times with those who would like to change the order of pieces or add to the repertoire and usually our collective conclusion is that making those changes does not really enhance what we already have in place. We have the freedom now to add the Romantic and Contempory literature as we see fit, and we all do have our favorite teaching pieces. (Williams)*

- *I don't believe there is need for revision, but rather continuing study, clarification and improvement. The answer to the question: "What is Suzuki teaching?" and "Who is a Suzuki student?" are far from resolved. We should continue to explore these questions and share our different and changing responses.*

  The Suzuki piano repertoire is not, in my view, exclusive. It is a suggested core of study. The beginning books are the most significant. With the huge world of piano music available, I think it would be foolish to try to prescribe advanced literature. A teacher who is equipped to teach at that level already knows what material is available. In the other instruments, where students play the same repertoire together, (and have a much smaller repertoire to draw from), there is more incentive to have a prescribed repertoire in the upper books. But that is not so for us. The philosophy and methodology are what is significant, the repertoire much less so. We could use completely different repertoire.

There are many advantages in the early books to having a common repertoire, whatever it may contain. The commonality is what is important, giving students a sense of shared experience and levels of achievement. (Koppelman)

- *As I've indicated elsewhere in this study, I do feel there is a definite need for revision of the Suzuki piano repertoire from the end of Book 3 onward. Until this occurs, I would have to say that the Suzuki piano method is incomplete.*

  Also, as I stated before, even though the Twinkles *have value for the piano, I feel they are not as complete a vehicle for first piano studies as they are for the other Suzuki instruments. Because* Twinkles *are treated so reverentially, out of custom and sentiment, there has been an overemphasis on the staccato skills needed to play them on the piano in Book 1A and 1B teacher-training courses and consequently, a neglect of many other skills absolutely essential to the foundation for excellent piano playing in teacher training. I base this observation on the teacher-training courses I myself have attended and observed, and the playing I have heard of hundreds of students of other Suzuki teachers. (Taggart)*

- *I believe the Suzuki® Method for piano has been and is still an outstanding approach to teaching young children the piano. I feel it is the most natural and musical approach that I have witnessed. It seems to be most successful when used with children (beginners) between the ages of three to six. Although it would cause controversy and disapproval from many Suzuki teachers, I believe that there is a need for revision of the repertoire, especially from Book 4 up. I would be very careful about touching the first three books. I think they are put together in a very logical way from the standpoint of musical and technical development. I also feel that many teachers are very comfortable teaching most of materials in these books. However, at the Book 4 level, a major revision could be very useful. Many teachers already do a great deal of supplementing and rearranging at this level already. There are many good pieces that could still be used, but the order could be rearranged. For instance, in my opinion, the Beethoven Sonatina in F makes more sense coming before the Sonata, the Bach Little Prelude before the Prelude in C and all of these pieces, including Invention #1 before the Partita movements. Adding several other inventions would also better prepare a student for the Partita. We have nothing substantial in the way of Romantic literature and very little to even begin to prepare a student for a Chopin waltz, for instance. We would need pieces to first develop some sensibilities for this literature and also to develop the pedal technique necessary to perform more mature Romantic works. We also have no exposure to Contemporary music or Impressionism. Even the classical literature is disproportionately stacked towards Mozart, with two sophisticated and difficult sonatas (K. 311 and K. 330) and only one mediocre Haydn sonata. Who would make these types of revisions would of course be the biggest obstacle towards meeting these goals. I think the later books would serve a much better purpose if they were more rounded with more exposure to different styles, similar to the Celebration Series published by Harris, for instance. (Liccardo)*

- *I do not believe there is a need for a revision of the Suzuki piano method but I would like to see an expansion. This book's pursuit of such topics as history, musicality, keyboard harmony, improvisation and theory in general suggests their inclusion in our programs, and I heartily agree. The world of music is an enormous, rich realm. I believe a more eclectic, inclusive approach could add depth and subtlety to our already outstanding system of learning.*

  I don't feel there is need for revision of the repertoire. It can be a function of the independence accorded a well-trained teacher that he or she select and supplement as needed for each student. The freshness and uniqueness of this variety are welcomed by both teacher and child, and other students will thus be exposed to a wider range of literature in group sessions.

  The particular pieces themselves are less important than the principles of teaching and learning we use. However, the commonality of the repertoire for both students and teachers is one of its virtues. The pieces known by all can be shared in many settings. The fact that they have been digested and assimilated over time by teacher-trainers and teachers permits more depth, efficiency and ready access to musical elements and teaching ideas. In this sense, a large change of repertoire could become an interruption in our growth rather than an enhancement. (Schneiderman)

Three respondents shared their concerns regarding the teacher-training programs and suggested that this is an area that strongly needs revision.

- *I think the Suzuki piano movement continues to be an isolated movement. I would love to see it move more into the mainstream of piano teaching as the string methods have. In order for this to happen and for us to gain respect and attention from the music world, we need to develop guidelines that raise the standard of Suzuki teaching, a kind of quality control including required courses that would instruct teachers not only on teaching the Suzuki literature, but require that the teachers can play the materials themselves before teaching them. We could also use courses that would instruct teachers how to teach reading since Suzuki teachers are in a rather unique position on this point and could use some additional information. It might also be useful to have technique classes that survey the history of piano technique and outline useful sources to develop this aspect of a student's ability. I think we also need to reach out to more professionally trained pianists at the college or conservatory level, and offer more opportunities for college credit for Suzuki pedagogy, more degree opportunities in this field and more scholarships to recruit these professionals. Finally, we need a more open dialogue about different approaches to playing the piano, and greater access for our teachers to the accomplished artists and artist/teachers for their points of view. More master classes and lectures from a greater diversity of sources can only help to strengthen our movement. (Liccardo)*

- *For the future I have only one suggestion and that is to raise the standards for teachers who teach the Suzuki® Method. Recently I was fortunate to be a clinician at the Pan-Pacific Suzuki Convention in Brisbane, Australia. There were many fine teachers and families participating. After the convention, I spent a few hours visiting Sydney before catching my long flight home. It was then that I learned that each year the grand Sydney Opera House is filled to capacity with Suzuki graduation recitals. Not only is the method popular there, it is also respected. It is my belief it is respected because the teachers are of a high caliber. In order to begin Suzuki training, a potential Suzuki teacher must play the Bach Italian Concerto. In North America, teachers need only play at the level of a Clementi sonatina.*

    No man or woman is allowed to enter any respected profession on desire alone. Much schooling and study is necessary. It is up to each of us to hold the Suzuki® Method in high esteem and be the best teachers and musicians. But our group needs guidance and standards. In all honesty I do not feel the Suzuki® Method has as much respect as it deserves. If some inadequately trained teachers are producing poor students, this reflects on all of us. We can not hope to change this totally, but neither should we sanction it.

    I believe that the Suzuki® Method will continue to thrive. (Yurko)

- *I feel there is a real need for revision in the piano teacher-training course work, particularly that of Book 1. The training needs to pay much more attention to the details of the co-ordination of hands-together playing, and the complexities of instant switches from staccato playing to legato when using both hands simultaneously. Until this happens officially, many of the Suzuki piano trainees, who themselves are not excellent pianists, will continue to be inadequate teachers, even though they do not want to be inadequate.*

    My sympathies are with the teachers, who usually know something is not quite right with either their own playing or that of their students. They come full of hope to the teacher-training courses, eager to learn how to do better. All too often, they go home from an institute not much better off than when they came.

    I know many fine institute teacher-trainers are also frustrated at the amount of material (philosophy, pre-Twinkle, Twinkles and then all the other basics) they are expected to teach in one to two weeks, to classes which may contain people whose skills range from concert pianist level to just barely able to play. Sometimes it must seem like an almost impossible task, and it probably is, given the present situation.

    The SAA has recognized that there are problems with teacher training, and as we all know, some changes are in the wind. It remains to be seen what will happen.

    I am very hopeful that, working together in the Suzuki spirit, we will be able to make significant improvements in the teacher-training area, especially for piano. We all care a great deal about what we do, and care about the students and their families with whom we share this wonderful process Dr. Suzuki has brought into being. As he is fond of saying, we must always be doing research, always looking for better ways to teach, and then share what we have found. (Taggart)

When asked if the Suzuki® Method is a complete or an incomplete method, most agree that it is incomplete in the sense that teachers have to supplement certain elements. But most respondents feel that all methods are incomplete and it is always up to the teacher to provide the elements they feel are necessary.

- *The Suzuki® Method, like any method, does not include everything a teacher would want to include. There is no one Suzuki technique. We develop our own Suzuki approach to reading. We organize whatever standard technique we want to incorporate. We add "reading the composer's mind", theory, history and other subjects important to a comprehension of what music is about. We plan the way to teach use of the pedal. We add repertoire. We bring ourselves, with all our individual interests, skills and personalities. As Dr. Suzuki has said many times, "Only I teach the Suzuki® Method." I teach the Suzuki-Koppelman method. (Koppelman)*

- *The Suzuki® Method is incomplete relative to the Suzuki Piano School volumes available. To insure its completeness, the teacher must have a thorough understanding of piano pedagogy, and supplement the method with Romantic and Contemporary literature, scales and exercises, basic theory and music history materials, and a systematic approach to the learning of reading. (Adams)*

- *I do not believe there can be a "complete" method as the study of music and the piano is a life's work. I think that the Suzuki® Method is a good one because it brings the student to a high level of musicianship and gives a good technical foundation. However, there are many holes that need to be filled in to create a more complete musician and pianist. Independent technique work is needed at some stage, and of course we must go outside this method in order to teach reading. The repertoire itself has weaknesses as detailed in the previous sections. (Liccardo)*

- *The Suzuki® Method requires that the individual teacher supply the reading, music theory and technical skills to the student. In that sense, the method is not complete and it becomes the responsibility of the teacher to make it so. I do not know any method, however, that is complete. (Powell)*

- *No method is complete in and of itself. There is no Suzuki reading method, there are no supplementary books, and there are no theory books. Any teaching method is only as good as the teacher using the method. The method is a tool chosen by the teacher, and there is no perfect method. (Fest)*

- *I taught traditionally styled piano for many years before I became a Suzuki teacher and I know that there is no one method that can be the be-all-and-end-all for all teachers. Art is subjective and I consider piano teaching an art form. The teacher must know who they are, what their strengths and weaknesses are, and work very hard and dedicatedly to find the how, what, where, when, and why of their successful version of teaching. No one method can provide that for a teacher. In my opinion, the Suzuki® Method can be as complete or as incomplete as you want it to be, depending on your background and philosophy of teaching. The beauty of Suzuki is the wonderful way to start a student by ear before he begins to read the printed page. It is building one step at a time without mixing up many concepts all at once, reinforcing each step by adding to the language of music, strengthening the listening, and involving the parent each step of the way. That is hard to improve upon. Personally speaking, the Suzuki way has made teaching rewarding, exciting, challenging and fulfilling for me. The longer I teach, the more I am convinced that the Suzuki philosophy is in fact the Suzuki® Method. It is not a series of graded piano books with multiple books at each level. If taught well the Suzuki approach can make a big difference in children's lives. (Williams)*

In conclusion, respondents were also asked to share their thoughts on the future of the Suzuki® Method. These teachers have great respect for this method, and after experimenting with it for many years, they feel more than ever the value and the special contribution of this method to music learning.

Many of the respondents shared their personal hopes and concerns about the actual state of the Suzuki movement. All of them hope that the method will continue to grow and contribute to the musical education of children.

- *The Suzuki® Method has made an impact on the way piano is taught. At traditional pedagogy seminars, workshops and conferences over the last twenty years, you hear about group class lessons, the use of recordings, parent involvement, the use of seat and foot boosters and more ear training. Whether it would be admitted that Suzuki has brought that about is perhaps doubtful, but the fact remains that it has happened since Suzuki has been in North America. We also see many music publications with accompanying recordings.*

  I believe that Suzuki will remain a strong influence if current and future teachers are dedicated to the highest standards of teaching excellence. If we do not, Suzuki will become just one more method on the market and not a very good one, because there is so much more to the Suzuki® Method than appears on the pages of those seven books. The philosophy is the method. The difficulty is that anyone can pick up a Suzuki book and claim to be a Suzuki teacher. Do other teachers label themselves as a Bastien teacher or a Faber and Faber teacher? The answer is no. We therefore have a mandate to do the best job we can at training teachers who come for short- or long-term training, and to be careful not to give candidates with weak pianistic skills a certificate bearing the right to teach until they have qualified adequately. A good Suzuki teacher must be loving, patient, motivating, nurturing and musically prepared as well.

I am pleased that the Suzuki movement has moved to involve many people in the greater musical world and I hope that will go on. We must continue to forge paths in quality education for our youth, contribute and help with the early childhood research, train teachers well, and to work on Dr. Suzuki's dream of developing beautiful people through love and music to make a big contribution to a better world for all peoples. *(Williams)*

- The Suzuki philosophy and pedagogical principles are innovative and visionary. They show a profound understanding of how we human beings learn and what we need to develop musically, emotionally and cognitively—as research on early music education continues to verify. Thus our system provides a solid foundation for developing fine musicianship and if carried farther, eminent artistry. Suzuki's brilliant theory that music is analogous to language and could be taught by adapting the principles of language-learning has been realized with distinguished results. Many fine artists and devoted music-lovers have emerged from these beginnings.

  I believe the concept of environmentally based instruction has been shown to work. What is required for its continuing success and maturity are nurturing teachers well-versed in the art, history and theory of music, broadly educated, classically trained on their instruments, and steeped in the Suzuki philosophy and pedagogy. We also need families deeply educated in the method and, along with the children, well-prepared for their roles. The well-trained teacher should then be permitted a high degree of individual freedom and flexibility. The growth of the Suzuki movement depends on the continued, enriching contributions of such people. Creativity in teaching, as well as in the art of interpreting and performing, results from personal self-confidence and self-esteem. Teachers need to be confirmed as much as do our students.

  I would therefore support an inclusive attitude rather than an exclusive one. In training teachers, launch well but let the journey be unique. Respect and draw upon the wide resources of information, ideas and talent from the greater world of music; from such fields as psychology, pedagogy, medical arts; from individual Suzuki teachers' educational backgrounds and originality. Already we see Suzuki influences upon traditional methods—the creation of listening tapes of repertoire and advocacy of parent involvement for example. The sharing can flow in both directions and enrich the lives of children—which is the goal we all desire.

  Encouragement and formal recognition can be given for current Suzuki teachers' continuing education. Teacher training can embrace more breadth and depth—very possible in small groups in trainers' studios where the long term, personal setting allows detailed exploration of the literature as well as intense individual attention and growth. Suzuki training for undergraduate music majors, either simultaneously or as an advanced degree, can be further developed.

  I can imagine the Suzuki movement growing in numbers and re-vitalizing itself continually in North America and throughout the world. Suzuki's philosophy leads us in the direction of personal validation and fulfillment. If his ideas are extended to teachers, teacher-trainers and movement leaders, all will be liberated to do our best thinking, to foresee logical consequences, to plan our future with imagination, and the process Dr. Suzuki initiated will keep evolving and re-inspiring itself. *(Schneiderman)*

- I would like to see the Suzuki movement share ideas on an international scale much more than is done at present. There are interesting and innovative things going on everywhere. I would like to see a broad and open outlook, with mutual respect by and for all who are working to find the best ways to help children express themselves with music and become better people. Trying to establish the one correct way or the one correct person is the greatest danger we face.

  The Suzuki movement is becoming more mature and experienced in many places around the world. We are in a good position to help people who are just starting out. We need to expand our outreach to these people wherever they are. We have made a lot of progress, thanks to the effort of many people around the world. Our current efforts to find ways to help upgrade our teaching are commendable, and should continue. We can view ourselves as Suzuki teachers with self-respect. We can be proud to be part of the Suzuki movement. *(Koppelman)*

- I would like to see the Suzuki movement become more unified. The many accomplished Suzuki piano teachers already involved can inspire and motivate young musicians and music majors to become associated with and trained in the Suzuki philosophy and methodology. We must strive to preserve all great teaching methodologies in order to survive the decreasing value of the arts in general, and the declining numbers of teachers and students of classical music.

The future of the Suzuki® Method can and should be a growth in involvement in the learning of music. We must continue in our efforts to provide the best training possible, because the future of the art of music is in the hands of today's beginning students. (Adams)

- *I am distressed that Suzuki lessons, as with most music lessons, are elitist. One must have money for an instrument, tapes, and books, money for lessons, free time to practice with a child, and time to take a child to lessons, group classes, and recitals. Many families cannot afford to take time off from work and spend the money necessary to participate in lessons or have the luxury of a summer institute. I believe that the Suzuki® Method is for every child, and the benefits are felt far beyond the piano studio. I would like to see the Suzuki movement in the inner city providing instruments, books, tapes, and lessons for children who will otherwise never have the opportunity to study music.*

  So much time has been wasted by Suzuki piano teachers in building fences around isolated groups and their gurus. I would like to see the fences removed and an acknowledgment of our common purpose. So much progress could be made by building bridges instead of fences and fostering mutual respect rather than divisiveness and back-biting. Music will never bring peace to the world, as Pablo Casals hoped, if we can not find peace within the circle of Suzuki teachers.

  I expect that the Suzuki® Method will continue to grow in North America. There never seem to be enough teachers to meet the requests for Suzuki piano. I hope that in this growth, quality is not sacrificed for quantity. I would like to draw in teachers who are skilled pianists, solid musicians, justifiably confident in their abilities as performers and teachers. With qualified teachers, the Suzuki® Method will be seen as respectable and legitimate by the music world. When less qualified people try to teach, it is unfortunately not the teacher who is criticized; it is the Suzuki® Method itself. (Fest)

- *My dream and hope for the Suzuki movement in the future is to see it recognized and accepted more fully throughout the world for the fantastic method that it is; I want everyone to realize its ability to reach each child's fullest potential. I want its future to be glorious! However, its future, as I see it, is in the hands of its teachers, for no method is any finer than the teacher behind it. It is my hope that all of its teachers will continue to grow and produce more and more of the quality students that can be developed through this beautiful method and philosophy. (Powell)*

BIOGRAPHICAL NOTES

Adams

I began piano lessons at the age of six years and knew immediately that I wanted to be a piano teacher when I grew up. My early lessons were under the guidance of a local piano teacher and my mother. My mother always played an important part in my early lessons. Although she was not allowed to attend my lessons, she was my "home teacher" and encouraged and guided me through my early years of instruction. I loved to practice piano, and since I was an only child, piano helped me fill many lonely hours. My first solo recital was given when I was eight years old, and it was the result of at least two hours of practice each day.

I received a Bachelor of Music degree in Piano Performance from the New England Conservatory of Music, and a Master of Music degree in Piano Performance from the University of Tennessee. I have been a member of the University of Tennessee Music Faculty for 24 years and presently hold the rank of associate professor. My duties include being coordinator of the Keyboard Area, the Accompanying coordinator, a teacher of piano and piano pedagogy (undergraduate and graduate), and the accompanist for faculty recitals. I am also the President and Director of Suzuki Piano of Knoxville which originated under the direction of Connie and William Starr as a precollege program at the University of Tennessee.

I have a large private studio of piano students and am an active participant in all local music organizations, including the Knoxville Music Teachers Association. I was chosen Tennessee Teacher of the Year for 1996. I have had numerous students major in music at prestigious music schools, and I have students teaching piano throughout the southeast and accompanying throughout the United States.

I became acquainted with the Suzuki® Method shortly after I arrived in Knoxville, Tennessee. My roommate was a Suzuki violin teacher who had studied in Japan, and I was quickly recruited to accompany for the violin program. I enrolled in a Suzuki pedagogy course taught by Connie Starr and I was "hooked". I loved the positive approach and the response from the students. Connie and Bill Starr moved to Colorado, and I inherited the piano program and Connie's fine students. I have continued to study the Suzuki philosophy and literature with teachers throughout the country.

There are many characteristics of the Suzuki® Method which I have always found helpful. One aspect that my style of teaching and my personality particularly have in common with the Suzuki® Method is the positive approach to improving one's ability. I believe that a great deal may be accomplished by use of a positive attitude and a caring approach to each student. I hope to always be able to exhibit these characteristics and to pass these ideals on to my own pedagogy students.

For the past eighteen years, I have shared my enthusiasm for teaching, and for the Suzuki® Method, with students at workshops throughout the country. I enjoy working with students who have been trained by teachers of various teaching philosophies and attitudes. I was invited to be the facilitator of a group discussion on parent education at the 1990 National Suzuki Conference, and Suzuki Piano of Knoxville gave a presentation entitled "Variations on a Familiar Theme: Group Lessons" at the 1996 National Suzuki Conference. I have had students selected to perform at various workshops and master classes throughout the country.

I feel fortunate to be a part of this method of teaching, and I hope that through my involvement the tradition and excellence of the Suzuki® Method may be carried on for many years. I appreciate the effort of many fine teachers throughout the United States who have dedicated their lives to the enrichment of children through the Suzuki® Method.

Fest

I received a B.M.E. from Morningside College in Sioux City, Iowa. I received a M.Mus.Ed. with an emphasis in piano from the University of Colorado. I taught piano at Morningside College. Also, I taught piano pedagogy at the University of Colorado.

I first learned of the Suzuki® Method when I was an undergraduate student. There was a professor who taught Suzuki violin. I would watch him teach because I was fascinated by this new method. He noted my interest and gave me what little literature was available so that I could learn more.

At this time I was teaching piano in a traditional fashion. One day I happened to see a brochure about the American Suzuki Institute in Stevens Point, Wisconsin. It told that this year (1972), Suzuki piano would be offered for the first time. I was intrigued, but also skeptical. How could this possibly work for piano? That summer I traveled to Stevens Point to learn what I could. Constance Starr was there sharing her experience of studying Suzuki piano in Japan. She had films of the young Japanese children playing, and I truly could not believe my eyes and ears. Surely there must be a trick to this!

With my 2 ½ days of training, I returned home and used two five-year-olds as my guinea pigs, offering a refund to the parents if this did not work. It did work! Each week I was thrilled to see the progress and the enthusiasm the children were showing in their playing.

In the following summer of 1973, I returned to Stevens Point with a notebook full of questions. I observed Constance Starr and Haruko Kataoka. I also went to Knoxville, Tennessee to observe Mrs. Starr. This seemed to be such a logical way for children to learn music. I felt very comfortable with the Suzuki® Method and knew that it was the method for me.

I continued to go to Stevens Point each summer for several years before there were organized SAA teacher-training courses. I would simply go, observe, ask questions, and soak up all that I could. I observed excellent violin teachers in addition to piano. I had the honor and pleasure of watching Dr. Suzuki teach many times. In 1982, I went to Japan to watch Dr. Suzuki and to observe and play for Mrs. Kataoka.

I am still teaching the Suzuki® Method because I cannot conceive of teaching piano any other way. This method makes sense, it works, and I see wonderful results.

My teaching style is low key. I have a calm approach to the children, the parents, and the music. This calmness does not imply low standards. I have very high standards for students and parents, and insist on the discipline necessary to reach and maintain those standards.

I have been teaching Suzuki piano since 1972. I have served on the Board of Directors for the SAA, served as secretary to the SAA board, and worked on numerous SAA committees. Currently I am the piano coordinator for the 1998 Teachers Conference. I have written *Suzuki Pianist's List of Supplementary Materials* and have contributed many articles to the *American Suzuki Journal*. I have also served on the Board of Directors and as president of Suzuki Association of Colorado. I am a teacher-trainer and have taught at workshops and institutes throughout the United States, in Canada, South America, and Australia.

I live in Boulder, Colorado with my husband, younger daughter, and two dogs. In addition to my Suzuki work, I am a Diaconal Minister in the United Methodist Church, serve in a church, and work as a hospital chaplain. In my free time I love to exercise, hike, read, play tennis, and watch the Rockies play baseball.

Harrel

Dr. Doris Leland Harrel is a graduate of the Juilliard School of Music (B.S. and M.S.) and of the University of Texas at Austin, where she earned the Doctor of Musical Arts degree in piano. Her long career as a pianist-teacher has included appointments to the faculties of several colleges and universities, including the Universities of Texas at Austin, San Antonio, and Tyler, as well as Southwest Texas State University in San Marcos.

Following extensive training in Suzuki pedagogy, she taught a large class of students ranging in age from three and one-half to eighteen in her private studio in San Marcos. Many of those students became consistent winners in piano competitions throughout Texas.

As a Suzuki teacher-trainer, she has served in that capacity at workshops and institutes in Arizona, Florida, Utah, Idaho, Colorado, Illinois, Kansas, Missouri, Nebraska, California, Washington, Minnesota, Louisiana, Arkansas, Oklahoma, and several locations in Texas. At present she is conducting long-term teacher-training programs in Houston and in Central Texas— Austin, San Antonio, San Marcos region. In January of 1993 she served as teacher-trainer for the Santiago, Chile, and Lima, Peru, Suzuki Teachers.

Dr. Harrel is the author of "A Plan for Better Sight Reading", published in the spring 1978 issue of *Piano Quarterly*. The article described experiments in reading improvement with the use of a tachistoscope.

She has been active in professional organizations in addition to the Suzuki Association of the Americas. She has served as President of the San Antonio Music Teachers' Association, and in 1988 was named "Teacher of the Year" by the Austin Area Music Teachers' Association.

Dr. Harrel was Chairperson for the Piano Sector of the 1994 Teachers' Conference of the Suzuki Association of the Americas. At the 1996 Conference, she was Master Teacher for students in Books III through VII.

In May 1995, the Austin District Music Teachers' Association nominated Doris Harrel for the Outstanding Pre-College Teaching Achievement Award of the Texas Music Teachers' Association.

Koppelman

My early piano study was with Dorothea Anderson La Follette, where fellow students included Wiliam Kapell and Byron Janis. I received my B.A. from the City University of New York and studied composition with Vittorio Giannini, analysis with Ernst Oster and piano with Vivian Rifkin and Eugene Mancini. I was a licensed pianist for the New York City Board of Education, and I taught traditionally for 25 years.

I discovered the Suzuki® Method when my oldest son began violin lessons with a Suzuki teacher, shortly after the family moved to San Diego. I was enthusiastic about the philosophy and approach. There was no information about the piano method, and no repertoire books were available. I experimented with some repertoire I thought would work, and since I was starting in a new place with new students, I began with my interpretation of the method, in 1968. A few years later, a Suzuki summer institute for teachers and students was held in San Diego with Haruko Kataoka, the piano teacher who taught with Dr. Suzuki in Matsumoto. I studied with her when she came to the U.S. and also for a short time in Matsumoto. I have observed many fine Suzuki teachers of all instruments, all over the world, who have expanded my understanding of the method. My body-work studies over the past nine years have contributed greatly to the way I now teach. I hope to continue to learn and be open to change. One of the most attractive aspects of my career as a Suzuki teacher is the opportunity it affords for interacting with other people in the field and the freedom to experiment and change in the quest for more knowledge and better skills.

I have been active in the Suzuki piano movement for over 25 years. I am the author of *Introducing Suzuki Piano* (available from Dichter Press, 8565 Hudson Drive, San Diego, Ca 92119) and co-author of *Natural Piano* (insights from the Alexander method applied to piano technique), as well as being a teacher-trainer. I have received the SAA Distinguished Service Award and been selected as an Honorary Life Member by the International Suzuki Association (ISA). I am a past member of the SAA Executive Board, the Board of Directors, Piano Committee, the Teacher-trainer Review Committee and piano editor of the *American Suzuki Journal*. I was Piano Coordinator of the first National Suzuki Conference, and the 1981 International Conference. I have given Suzuki demonstrations to the Music Teachers Association of California, the Music Educators National Conference, and the National Council on Piano Pedagogy. My teaching has included workshops throughout the United States, Europe, Asia, Canada and South America, and at the last five international Suzuki conferences. I maintain an active teaching and teacher-training program in San Diego. As well, I am the director of "Making Music Together", an outreach program involving chamber music by and for children.

Liccardo

I began my piano studies at the age of 4½ with a local piano teacher. The teacher thought I was too young to begin, but my father convinced her to teach me for a trial period. With the help of my parents, I prepared my lessons and was able to continue. At the age of 10, I began studying with the very fine teacher, May L. Etts. Miss Etts was the editor of a series of piano books called *Beginning to Play (Beethoven, Bach, Mozart, Haydn and Schumann)*, which contain many of the pieces found in the Suzuki repertoire. She was a very dedicated teacher who gave generously of her time and energy, often giving extra lessons free of charge. Miss Etts also held workshops in New York City each summer, where I performed recitals and helped demonstrate some of her teaching techniques. It was here that I met composers such as Lynn Freeman Olson, David Glover, Mark Nevin and others, as they presented their newest teaching materials.

Between the ages of 10 to 18, I performed in many recitals, auditions and radio broadcasts. I was accepted to the High School of Performing Arts, a well known school for the arts. In this small school of just 600 students, I was immersed in an environment that greatly stimulated my musical interest and growth. Besides our academic training, we received training in sight-singing, theory and music history. We also had many opportunities to perform. I was fortunate to perform concertos on four occasions, two of which took place at Lincoln Center with professional orchestra.

I received my college education at the Aaron Copland School of Music at Queens College. I did my undergraduate studies with Nadia Reisenberg, who was a magnificent pianist and had studied with the great Josef Hoffman. She was also a kind and generous person who greatly inspired me with her own playing at my lessons. It was under her tutelage that I earned my Bachelor of Music degree in piano performance. Unfortunately, Madame Reisenberg became ill in my senior year and passed away shortly thereafter. I went on to earn my master's degree in performance studying with Morey Ritt, another fine pianist and former student of Madame Reisenberg.

It was while I was a college student that I was first exposed to the Suzuki® Method. I took a job as an accompanist in a very successful violin program. I have never had any doubt or cynicism about the Suzuki® Method because I personally witnessed the magic of this method from my very first day as an accompanist. My earliest recollection of this experience is the look of great joy on the faces of three-year-olds as their parents applauded them for their efforts in group class. I continued accompanying Suzuki students for six years and was able to observe many fine teachers at work.

After teaching transfer students for some time and struggling to correct their bad habits, I decided to work with beginners, and the Suzuki® Method was the natural choice. I enrolled in a two-year teacher-training program at the School for Strings in NYC where I worked with Sheila Keats. I twice received scholarships from the SAA to attend summer institutes for further training with Mary Craig Powell.

I began my Suzuki piano program at the Center for Preparatory Studies in Music at Queens College in 1986. The program was designed to provide a comprehensive musical education for beginning children between the ages of 3 to 6. Each student attends a private lesson as well as weekly classes in musicianship and performance. Many of the students in this program have gone on to win prizes in local, state and national competitions and to perform in many recitals, festivals, auditions and master classes. I am always proud to send them to these events with their Suzuki editions. I think it is important for other teachers and judges to know that these students were trained using this method.

I am sure other Suzuki teachers experience the same pleasure, joy, excitement and anticipation when beginning a new, four-year-old student. For me this thrill never ends! To watch them grow and develop as people and also as musicians is truly a privilege. I have also derived pleasure from teaching at institutes and workshops throughout the country. It is very satisfying to meet children, parents and teachers who share similar ideals. I am happy to share my thoughts with them and to listen and learn from them as well. It is one of the greatest strengths of the Suzuki movement that teachers are always willing to share the ideas and the techniques that have proven successful. My life has been enriched by meeting these people.

I continue to perform solo recitals and chamber music as well. I was recently delighted to perform a concerto with the orchestra from the preparatory division in the school in which I teach. I have also just completed five years as president of the Associated Music Teachers League, an organization of independent music teachers. This organization provides performance opportunities for students, auditions, scholarship awards, and lectures and workshops for teachers. I learned a great deal working with teachers of all instruments from all different backgrounds and many different perspectives on teaching.

I currently live in New Hyde Park, New York, with my wife, Pamela, who is a Suzuki piano and flute teacher, and my two musical children, Joseph and Katherine. Joseph has developed into a fine pianist and Katherine is studying both violin and piano.

Powell

Mary Craig Powell received her baccalaureate degree magna cum laude from East Carolina University, Greenville, North Carolina. Her Master of Music in Piano Performance is from Wichita State University in Kansas.

She has taught piano at colleges in North and South Carolina and Illinois. Currently, she offers Suzuki teacher-training and student lessons through both the Community Music School and the Conservatory of Music faculty at Capital University in Columbus, Ohio.

Her interest in Suzuki piano pedagogy began while her sons were studying Suzuki violin in the early 1970s; the results she saw and heard made her feel that she must learn to apply the method to the piano. Training followed with Haruko Kataoka, Carole Bigler and Valerie Lloyd-Watts. Already known as a fine teacher, her reputation grew to international proportions when she based her instruction on the Suzuki philosophy. Her young students are consistent winners in auditions and competitions. She communicates high standards, a deep love and respect for children, and common sense in her approach to students, parents, and teachers.

She has served the Suzuki movement through numerous elective offices in the Suzuki Association of the Americas and the Suzuki Association of Ohio. As a teacher-trainer, she travels internationally. She was the piano editor of *Suzuki World* Magazine and is the author of *Focus on Suzuki Piano*. In recognition of her achievements, she has received the Distinguished Alumni Award from the School of Music at East Carolina University and in May, 1996, the Suzuki Association of the Americas awarded her the Outstanding Teacher Award for her contributions to the field of Suzuki piano.

Schneiderman

Barbara Schneiderman, pianist, teacher-trainer and author of *Confident Music Performance: The Art of Preparing*, has taught, lectured and performed throughout North America. Having made her piano debut on radio at the age of ten, she studied with Sidney Foster, Walter Piston, Horazio Frugoni, Aube Tzerko and Edith Oppens. Barbara has degrees in music from Harvard University, the Royal Academy of Music, England, and the University of California, San Diego with further study at Eastman School of Music and the Aspen Festival. She has been a registered Suzuki teacher-trainer since 1983 and has taught pedagogy, master classes, theory, improvisation, repertoire and parent classes at institutes for over two decades.

Ms Schneiderman has spoken at national conferences, both Suzuki and traditional, served on the SAA Piano Committee and written articles for the *American Suzuki Journal*, where she currently contributes as piano columnist and special adviser. Her earliest topic was *The Role of the Wrist and Arm in Shaping Phrases*, appearing in 1978 and 1979.

Her lectures have covered diverse topics such as *You, Your Child and Music; Working with Adolescents; Application of Variation Techniques Throughout the Repertoire; Evolving as a Suzuki Teacher; You can Improvise; Interpretation and Analysis of Beethoven Sonatas, Inner and Outer Curve* (the relationship between the emotional experience of music and its architecture). For SAA National Conferences: *The Review Process, Supplementary Repertoire, Nurturing Musicality in our Students* and *Confident Music Performance, The Art of Preparing*. For SAA National Teacher-trainer Conference: *Replenishing Your Reservoirs*. For California State Music Teachers' Convention: *The Confluence of Suzuki and Traditional Methods*. For The Biology of Music-Making international conference on *Music, Growth and Aging: Become the Music*.

Barbara is devoting increasing time to writing and lecturing. She is often invited to teach courses and seminars in confident music performance, most recently at the University of California, San Diego and the University of Northern Iowa, where as visiting Artist she also spoke on principles of life performance derived from music. She shares with students of all ages her program of performance preparation, a system that honors and integrates all our human faculties. Barbara was invited to write an article on this topic, *Standing in the Wings*, for the *California Music Teacher*, the journal of the *Music Teachers' Association of California*. She frequently adjudicates at music festivals and auditions.

Barbara resides in Del Mar, California where her studio instruction includes long-term and apprentice teacher-training as well as student lessons. Her students have performed at the SAA National Conference, at numerous festivals and at the State MTAC Convention.

Taggart

Marilyn Taggart began piano studies at age five with her pianist mother, which was followed by study with Esther Howe, then undergraduate work as a piano performance major both at Oberlin Conservatory and Converse College School of Music, where she transferred to study with pianist Ozan Marsh at his express invitation.

Following graduation from Converse College in 1966 with a Distinction in Performance award for recital work, she performed and taught privately for twelve years, then entered graduate school at the Catholic University School of Music for the express purpose of finding better solutions for certain technical problems common to most students, no matter which one of the many traditional technical regimens were used in their studies.

In addition to her own independent research and subsequent experimentation with students, she was guided by Dr. Thomas Mastroianni at Catholic University, noted for his expertise in the area of the mind/body relationship to piano playing; and by Dr. Robert Mumper at the State University of New York during two years of intense work on the application of the Dorothy Taubman approach to piano technique.

A Suzuki piano teacher since 1978, Mrs. Taggart presented a well-received lecture series on technique at the American Suzuki Institute in 1983, is the author of two *American Suzuki Journal* articles concerning technique (Fall, 1983; Spring, 1984) and was a featured speaker at Suzuki National Teachers Conferences in 1984, 1990, and 1996. A frequent master class and workshop presenter, she also has recently been appointed one of seven pianists on the Committee on Technique, Movement and Wellness of the *National Piano Pedagogy Conference*.

Well-known in her home state of New York for her professional expertise, and the award winning performances of her students, Mrs. Taggart has served as Secretary, Vice President for Conventions, Vice-President for Auditions, and Chairman of State Competitions for the New York State Music Teachers Association. She is certified at the professional level both by NYSMTA and the affiliated Music Teachers National Association, and was given a special Distinguished Service Award by NYSMTA in 1992. She is listed in *International Who's Who in Music* (1986), *Who's Who in American Music* (Classical) (1986), and *American Keyboard Artists* (1989).

Marilyn Taggart continues:

From 1966 to 1973, I was a Yamaha Music School teacher in addition to my work as a piano teacher, so I was both aware of and a firm believer in music education for children as young as four, even before encountering the Suzuki® Method.

In 1973, my oldest daughter—now an aspiring opera singer—and I began Suzuki violin together, when she was five years old. As I learned with her, and observed the others in the violin studio, it became obvious to me that something really amazing was going on here, and I had to become even more a part of it. By 1977, I made two decisions which changed my life. First of all, I would become a Suzuki piano teacher exclusively. Secondly, I would discard all my old training in piano technique, which years of teaching had shown me was largely ineffective with all but a few, and do everything I could to study all the existing theories of piano technical training to find out what really works and why it works.

Both decisions led to enormous growth and discovery for myself, my family and my students. I have never regretted taking those steps, and twenty years later, I can't imagine a more fulfilling life work.

My initial Suzuki training in 1978 was a wonderful introduction and grounding in the philosophy and how to use it with the children and their families, but the technical approach to the instrument taught by the trainer was a disappointment—just more of the same cramped hand positions I knew were ineffective. It wasn't until the International Conference in 1981 at Amherst, MA, that I had a chance to see teachers like Doris Koppleman who used and understood a much more fluid, natural approach. Then I realized that some Suzuki piano teachers, but not all, were still stuck in the failed theories of the past, and that there needed to be some work done within the Suzuki piano movement in this regard.

I worked with Mrs. Kataoka in London, Ontario, and observed her many times after that. I particularly enjoyed the International Conference in Edmonton, Alberta in 1984, where I watched Dr. Suzuki a great deal, and had a chance to meet and talk with him.

In some ways, the violin teachers (particularly John Kendall and Ronda Cole) have had at least as great an influence on my teaching as the pianists. They represent the epitome of great teaching: meticulous attention to detail; an ability to explain again and again in ways the children can comprehend; a wonderful sense of humor and play even though the work is hard; and a profound commitment to musical communication as an end product. I hope that these characteristics which I admire so much in them are also present in my own teaching, particularly the humor and sense of joy.

The Suzuki movement has been very generous to me and my particular interest in technique, and I've been honored by numerous invitations to speak at conferences, etc. I also hold private workshops for Suzuki piano teachers—one group in Minnesota has met with me every summer for six years. I've been too busy with teaching, my family, MTNA business and workshops to finish revising the book about piano technique I started in 1981, but that will happen someday. Also I hope to become more involved with the workings of the SAA, when time permits.

Williams

I grew up in a musical family and started piano at the age of five. Throughout my young years, I competed and won many awards in solo piano throughout Pennsylvania. I graduated cum laude from John Brown University with a B.Mus. in piano performance, and did additional work at Westminster Choir College in organ performance, and as well at the University of Wisconsin. My late husband, a baritone soloist and choral conductor, and I gave concerts and eventually spent thirty years together in the field of church music, developing fully graded vocal and bell choir programs in Royal Oak, Michigan and in Wheaton, Illinois. Our church high-school choir was invited to tour in Europe two different years, as well as giving many other concerts in the United States and Canada.

In 1976, I became interested in the Suzuki® Method, took training and was invited to start teaching with the Wheaton College Suzuki Program. In 1986, I became its director and in 1989, was asked to become the director of the pre-college program at Wheaton College, which now has in addition to the Suzuki program an early childhood program, a preparatory program and an outreach program for bilingual early childhood students. Our student enrollment is over 1000 with a faculty and staff of 33.

I was fascinated with the Suzuki students' ability to play so beautifully using such advanced repertoire at a very young age and decided that I must know and learn about this approach to music education. I went to Stevens Point, Wisconsin, for my first exposure to this wonderful method. It has made all the difference in my teaching, and I have continued to attend classes, institutes and workshops, learning, sharing and teaching. I know that through the Suzuki philosophy and method I have received many musical rewards from teaching, and in turn, I trust, have been able to bring a higher standard and enjoyment of music to my many students over the years. I would hope that my "signature" has been passed on to my students through love and dedication not only for an art form but for music and humanity.

Since 1976 I have been involved with the Suzuki movement in a variety of ways through teaching at institutes, acting as the SAA piano chairman for four years, writing articles, and working on committees.

I am the mother of three grown children all of whom currently enjoy music making in some way, and the grandmother of six, three of whom are Suzuki students.

Yurko

I am a native of Arizona, spending early years in Sedona and school years in Mesa. I have played piano since I was a toddler, violin since fourth grade and sang in church and school choirs. In 1969, I won the Phœnix Symphony Young Musicians Concerto Competition. I received my undergraduate music degree, with scholarship awards, from Ohio University in Piano Performance where I studied with George Katz (Julliard). I also did graduate work in music theory at Ohio University, beginning work on my original theory ideas.

Since 1973, I have enjoyed a succesful, private Suzuki piano studio and am a registered teacher-trainer with the Suzuki Association of the Americas. I enjoy Suzuki activities! I have served on the SAA Board of Directors twice, helped to establish the piano committee, served on it and served as piano editor for the SAA Journal. Meeting Suzuki families and teachers is a wonderfully enriching pleasure. I have traveled to teach at over 150 music workshops in nearly all fifty United States as well as Canada (including Newfoundland), Australia, Puerto Rico, New Zealand, England and Sweden.

In 1979, my book, *No H in Snake: Music Theory for Children* (Alfred) was published. I formed the company Music 19 at that time to distribute these game products. This was sold to CPP Belwin in 1990, which was acquired by Warner Bros. in 1994. They publish *Music Mind Games* (1992), *Musopoly, Incredible!* and other publications.

In 1985-86, I was National Chairperson for the SAA Children-to-Children African Relief Project. Students nationwide raised over $85,000 during a two-week Practice-a-Thon.

In 1997, I and my 4-year-old student were featured on the ABC World News Tonight in a study of how piano lessons affect logic development in preschool children.

Making my home in Maryland, I have three wonderful children. I am on the faculty of the Levine School of Music (Washington D.C.) as co-ordinator of the Suzuki Piano Program.

Comeau (Editor)

After completing an associate's degree in piano with the Royal Conservatory of Music of Toronto, Gilles Comeau did a double major in music and philosophy at the University of Ottawa. He holds a master's degree from the same institution, his thesis being a comparative analysis of three methods of music education, Dalcroze, Orff and Kodály. As a part of his program, Mr. Comeau studied Dalcroze Eurhythmics at the Manhattan School of Music, New York, with Bob Abramson, and at the Longy School of Music, Cambridge, with Lisa Parker, Anne Farber, and Elizabeth Vanderspar. He also studied Orff methodology at the Université du Québec à Montréal, with Anne-Marie Grosser, Director of the Orff Institute in Paris and Jos Wuytack of Belgium. He received his Ph.D. in 1995 from the Université de Montréal, studying aspects of creativity and suggesting some fundamental principles for teaching composition in music education programs for children, especially for young piano students.

Mr. Comeau has been teaching piano for 20 years, with students ranging from age 4 to adult. Many of his young students have won prizes in various competitions, particularly in contemporary music performance and composition. He has taught in both the Faculty of Music and the Faculty of Education at the University of Ottawa, and in the education departments at the National Arts Centre and the National Gallery of Canada in Ottawa.

Several of Mr. Comeau's articles have appeared in academic journals such as the McGill Journal of Education, The Canadian Journal of Education and the Journal of Educational Thought. His master's thesis, *Comparing Dalcroze, Orff and Kodály: Choosing Your Approach to Teaching Music*, was published in both English and French. He has also published an impressive list of teaching materials for children, including *The Arts in Harmony*, an interdisciplinary program incorporating music, dance, dramatic and visual arts, *À la découverte de la musique*, a program for teaching music to four- to eight-year-olds used in many French schools in Ontario, *Poésie, poésie*, a program for teaching poetry to children from 8 to 12, *La Ronde des comptines*, a kit containing a series of activities that exploit the child's familiarity with nursery rhymes in order to encourage exploration of music and movement, and *La musique à quatre pattes*, a teaching kit for parents and teachers designed to encourage early awareness of music and movement in infants (0 to 24 months).

Mr. Comeau's interest in the Suzuki® Method began when he was studying different methods of music education for his master's program. He has completed long-term teacher-training and taught Suzuki piano over the 10 years since then. His commitment to the Suzuki® Method encouraged him to found the Institut Studea Musica in 1996. The institute, located in Quebec's Eastern Townships, offers both teacher-training programs and student programs in piano, violin, cello, and chamber music. His wish that he could gather together a group of Suzuki teachers renowned for their excellence and ask them how they work and experiment with the method was the motivation for this book.

Things to Do

Pre-Twinkle Check-off

Every activity must be preceded by "Ready-Go." No "Ready-Go" means no go!

Cards

1 set of finger cards, 1-5
1 set of things to do cards
1 set of number of repetitions

Some activities need only one card. Some may use all three.

Remember: left hand or hands together, and hands slap knee between repetitions

1. Bow
2. Finger grab, finger on head, nose, floor, ear, etc.
3. Thumb stand freeze, count age
4. Feet freeze, fingers walk, 1-2-3-4-5-4-3-2-1
5. Tin man: lift and drop shoulder, elbow, wrist. Feet still. Check posture.
6. Finger feelers: 5 soft things. Pumpkin pie rhythm
7. Octopus with tissue
8. Octopus with lift-off and stroke back of hand
9. Open – shut 1-2, 1-3, 1-4, 1-5, 1-4
10. Walking fingers Stand on each
11. Bunny sniffing at piano
12. Black key twins, triplets. Do high-low, up-down. Finger 2-3 or 2-3-4
13. Fingers and letters. Find all Cs. Add other letters
14. Singing 3 songs
15. Horses'hooves (stand on thumb)

157

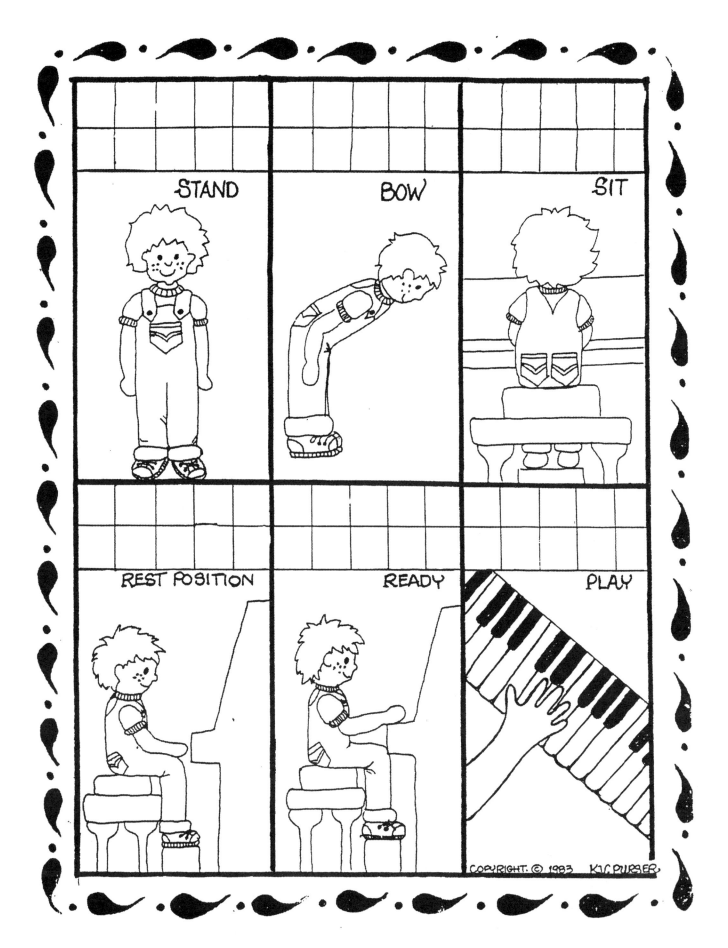

SUZUKI PIANO PRACTICE CALENDAR

Name _____   June 1997

Impt. dates	date	☺	T/Sc	New	Work	Rep	Read	Listen		One point focus - weekly
	S-1									1.
	M-2									2.
	T-3									3.
	W-4									4.
	T-5									5.
	F-6									
	S-7									
	S-8									Repertoire pieces:
	M-9									
	T-10									
	W-11									
	T-12									
	F-13									
	S-14									
	S-15									
	M-16									
	T-17									
	W-18									
	T-19									
	F-20									
	S-21									
	S-22									
	M-23									
	T-24									
	W-25									I want to learn:
	T-26									
	F-27									
	S-28									
	S-29									
	M-30									

☺ = Good work/No fussing T/Sc = Twinkles or Scales New = New Piece Work = Working Piece Rep = Repertoire Read = Reading
Listen = 2 hrs. listening

Assignments

Date:

Twinkle/Scale	
New Piece	
Working Piece	
Repertoire	
Reading	

Date:

Twinkle/Scale	
New Piece	
Working Piece	
Repertoire	
Reading	

Date:

Twinkle/Scale	
New Piece	
Working Piece	
Repertoire	
Reading	

Date:

Twinkle/Scale	
New Piece	
Working Piece	
Repertoire	
Reading	

Date:

Twinkle/Scale	
New Piece	
Working Piece	
Repertoire	
Reading	

HOME DOT / LESSON DOT CHART

Name _____

Book 1

	Home	Lesson				Home	Lesson				Home	Lesson
Twinkle A				**French Children's Song** Folk Song					**Chant Arabe** Anon.			
Twinkle B				**London Bridge** Folk Song					**Allegretto 1** Czerny			
Twinkle C				**Mary Had a Little Lamb** Folk Song					**Good-bye to Winter** Folk Song			
Twinkle D				**Go Tell Aunt Rhody** Folk Song					**Allegretto 2** Czerny			
Lightly Row Folk Song				**Claire de Lune** Lully					**Christmas Day Secrets** Dutton			
Honeybee Folk Song				**Long Long Ago** Bayly					**Allegro** Suzuki			
Cuckoo Folk Song				**Little Playmates** Chawtal					**Musette** Anon.			

Home Dot: ¼ dot = melody with RH 19x correctly and LH 19x correctly (Twinkles-Claire). ½ dot = hands together 19x correctly **Lesson Dot:** Polished Piece

Printed in May 1998, CFORP